D1617452

After the Peace

After the Peace
Resistance and Reconciliation

edited by
Robert L. Rothstein

LYNNE
RIENNER
PUBLISHERS

BOULDER
LONDON

Published in the United States of America in 1999 by
Lynne Rienner Publishers, Inc.
1800 30th Street, Boulder, Colorado 80301

and in the United Kingdom by
Lynne Rienner Publishers, Inc.
3 Henrietta Street, Covent Garden, London WC2E 8LU

Library of Congress Cataloging-in-Publication Data
After the peace : resistance and reconciliation / edited by Robert L.
  Rothstein.
    p.   cm.
  Includes bibliographical references and index.
  ISBN 1-55587-828-8 (hc : alk. paper)
  1. Peace. 2. International relations. 3. Reconciliation.
I. Rothstein, Robert L.
JZ5538.A33   1999
327.1'72—dc21   98-47374
                                                              CIP

British Cataloguing in Publication Data
A Cataloguing in Publication record for this book
is available from the British Library.

Printed and bound in the United States of America

The paper used in this publication meets the requirements
of the American National Standard for Permanence of
Paper for Printed Library Materials Z39.48-1984.

5 4 3 2 1

Contents

Part 2 Strengthening a Fragile Peace

Preface

The weak and fragile peace agreements of the post–Cold War years that have sought to resolve a number of protracted conflicts fall well short of being genuine peace settlements. While these agreements are inherently unstable and may indeed in the worst of circumstances become "bad" agreements that ultimately exacerbate already bitter conflicts, they also offer new opportunities for conflict amelioration and perhaps even— should the opportunities be grasped—conflict resolution and transformation. One hardly needs to add that undue optimism is clearly unjustified and that premature ceremonies of success (on the White House lawn and elsewhere) may be misleading and counterproductive. By the same token, however, cynicism about the possibilities for progress is also misplaced and potentially destructive. There are, after all, powerful pressures within each of the parties to most protracted conflicts, between the parties, and in the external environment that open new possibilities for movement and for breaking the stalemate between ancient enemies and ending the cycle of violence and retribution—the "politics of the last atrocity."

The chapters in this volume share a common goal. All of the authors seek not merely to analyze the process of reaching a fragile peace agreement, but also (and especially) to analyze an equally important but much less discussed topic: how to strengthen and deepen such agreements and how to think about and perhaps even conceptualize the period after a tentative peace has been negotiated. This period obviously has many continuities with the period before peace and is also heavily affected by how peace was negotiated and what was included in or excluded from the agreement itself. Nevertheless, the postpeace period also has unique qualities of its own that require analysis and interpretation. It should be noted,

of course, that the chapters in this collection vary in the extent to which
the primary emphasis is on reaching an agreement or strengthening it after
it has been negotiated, largely because of differences in degree of progress
in individual cases.

In the first chapter, I attempt to set the stage for the chapters that follow by discussing a series of structural and procedural conditions that
seem to characterize most protracted conflicts, despite the manifest differences between each conflict. These conditions are consequential because
they create the deep context within which peace agreements must be negotiated and because the agreements themselves tend to focus on the
agenda of the moment and not on the need to deal with the underlying conditions that have sustained and exacerbated the conflict. The latter failure
thus illuminates not only why peace agreements in these circumstances are
inherently fragile, but also what needs to be done to strengthen them.

First we turn to the Middle East. Khalil Shikaki, a Palestinian social
scientist, notes some of the dangers of a staged peace agreement that
"breeds ambiguity, conditionality, and reversibility," that leads each side
to create its own (inflated) expectations, and that generates divergent dynamics, one leading toward peace and the other toward legitimizing
some dimensions of continued occupation and violence. Besides providing us with some striking and important results of his polling efforts,
Shikaki also analyzes the state-building efforts of the Palestinian National Authority and the conflict between this agenda and the agenda of
democratization. As the latter loses to the former, and as democratic free-
doms are sacrificed, accountability is ignored, corruption grows, and disappointment with the peace process escalates—and would do so even if
Benjamin Netanyahu's government were generous and wise, which it is
not.

Moshe Ma'oz, a well-known Israeli historian and director of the Truman Institute at Hebrew University, traces the history of the Arab-Israeli
relationship in a balanced and evenhanded fashion, arguing in effect that
the current conflict cannot be understood without studying its origins and
development. Ma'oz also illustrates how the Oslo Agreements have been
undermined by extremists on both sides. He outlines a framework for
agreement but one that is unacceptable to the extremists. Internal disunity
on both sides makes widening the constituency for peace extremely difficult, as the naysayers are either beyond rational persuasion or ask too
much for their support. As Ma'oz suggests, this implies the need for strong
external pressure to provide various kinds of support for weak and risk-
averse leaders.

The next two chapters examine the conflict in Northern Ireland. Paul
Arthur, a member of the Catholic community, discusses a number of the
issues that are of concern in this book: the "huge capacity for mythmak-

ing," how difficult it is "to forgive politically," the "political economy of helplessness" that develops over time, and the difficulties of peacemaking in a society "without a sense of empathy." He also illustrates the negative effects of factionalism within each side, a factor that grows in importance as (or if) peace nears. Finally, he provides a more hopeful perspective when he discusses changes in attitudes that may facilitate negotiations and even a willingness on the part of some in the loyalist community to apologize for crimes of the past. He also comments on the May 1998 breakthrough to peace and the likelihood that it will survive.

Duncan Morrow, a member of the Protestant community, warns of a peace strategy that is a disguised means of seeking victory (as with Netanyahu in the Israeli-Palestinian conflict) and notes that the peace process in Ireland has not yet generated "consistency in trustworthiness" or a willingness to take the large risk of definitively breaking away from the cycle of violence. As he notes, getting people (or leaders) to act with generosity before they feel secure is like asking turkeys to vote for Thanksgiving. He also makes some useful comments about democracy and its ambiguities in the context of peacemaking. He concludes rather grimly that the current cease-fire is still perceived as a zero-sum game because of high levels of mistrust and that "reconciliation" is frequently seen as what the other side must do to reconcile itself to its defeat. He too offers some tentative judgments about the current breakthrough but within the context of his previous analysis of obstacles to peacemaking.

Bosnia and the Dayton peace process are the focus of the next two chapters. Susan Woodward, a noted expert on the conflict in Bosnia, argues that each of the parties to Dayton acted as if the "accords were only a new stage in the war over political control." The agreement stopped the war before any of the parties had achieved its goals, and, as she notes, the parties thus used the truce to continue the war by (more or less) peaceful means. She also notes that all of the strategies that were to be used to transform Dayton into a sustainable peace were aimed at providing a quick retreat for the international community. Since the strategies would take years to implement, and since some were contradictory, success was limited—although hardly inconsequential—and the role of outsiders in maintaining a very fragile peace was still decisive; but for how long? One might also note that Woodward emphasizes the conflict between the economists' demands for stabilization and reform and the citizens' demands for jobs and the protection of property, a conflict that appears elsewhere also.

Dusko Doder, a journalist with both personal and professional experience of the Bosnian crisis, tells us that the people of Srebrenica were "betrayed by everybody," perhaps a fitting metaphor for the whole conflict. Leadership is a critical component of the peace process, but here the leaders were "provincial warlords . . . narrow-minded men filled with hate . . . who think 'through their blood, not through their brains.'" Not surprisingly, the people became cynical about politics, seeing it as nothing more than a means of getting rich. The harmony supposedly reflected in Marshal Tito's Yugoslavia was based not on tolerance and respect but, rather, on defense against foreign enemies. Each group continues to deny its own crimes, to be paranoid about the evil others, and to wait only for an opportunity for revenge. This does not suggest much optimism about the prospects for the Dayton Accords, which Doder describes as a "schizophrenic treaty that seems tailor-made for dodging responsibility."

The last three chapters move away from the details of particular cases to discuss more general aspects of peacemaking and peace building. Herbert Kelman, an eminent social psychologist, discusses interactive problem solving and the contribution it might make to the peace process. He points out the need in intense conflicts to address underlying grievances and existential fears because both sides must come to understand and accept the need to live together. Meeting psychological needs (e.g., identity, security) may be relatively easier because they are not inherently zero sum, which may be the case for many material needs, although both sets of needs may require accommodation for stable peace to be achieved. Kelman goes on to discuss in illuminating detail the four elements of "positive peace": mutual acceptance and reconciliation, a sense of security and dignity for both sides, a pattern of cooperative interaction, and the institutionalization of a dynamic process of problem solving.

Donald Shriver, a renowned theologian, discusses the importance of, indeed the necessity of, collective acts of forgiveness to break the cycle of violence and vengeance. Shriver analyzes four interacting elements of collective forgiveness: moral judgment, forswearing revenge, empathy for the (former) enemy, and the intent to construct a civic relationship. He also discusses with great subtlety the vexing but crucial issue of accountability for the past, or what is sometimes called in another context "transitional justice." In contrast to the hard-nosed pragmatists who favor forgiving but not forgetting, Shriver argues that promises of impunity and blanket amnesties are ultimately destructive of peace in that the desire for vengeance continues to simmer and that a civic relationship between ancient enemies remains a hopeless quest.

In the final chapter, rather than summarizing the preceding chapters, I have attempted to set out some of the ways in which the postpeace period is different from the prepeace period and to discuss the practical implications of this argument in regard to several crucial areas of concern: the new political axis, the need for physical and psychological security (confidence-building measures and containing the terrorist threat); the political economy of sustaining a weak peace (which differs from neoclassical orthodoxy); a morally and practically sustainable approach to the issues of justice, fair-ness, and political survival; and the limits and possibilities of external support. A carefully constructed postpeace strategy may thus transform a fragile peace into a stepping-stone toward peaceful coexistence and, ulti-mately, the reconciliation of ancient enemies. But this will begin to happen only if leaders and their followers genuinely want peace and not merely a peace process that they can manipulate to gain resources and time, to maintain the myth of ultimate victory, and to stay in power. Realists will bet heavily on the manipulators, and there is much to sustain their pes-simism. But the tentative and fragile peace agreements that have been ne-gotiated or are in the process of being negotiated in a number of conflicts that were once seen as "insoluble" do suggest—even if some agreements fall apart—that the forces propelling toward peace may be gaining ground and that even some "true believers" may finally be willing to think about the unthinkable: compromise, mutual recognition and respect, and peace-ful coexistence.

—Robert L. Rothstein

Acknowledgments

This book grew out of a conference held at Colgate University in 1997. The conference could not have been held without the financial support provided by Jane Pinchin, dean and provost of Colgate University; I am grateful to Dean Pinchin not only for this support, but also for her attendance at the conference.

I am also grateful to my colleague Nigel Young, the director of the Peace Studies Program at Colgate, for additional financial help and for some very helpful suggestions for participants in this project who could address the Northern Ireland conflict effectively. I would also like to thank my research assistant, Leigha Wilbur, for substantial help in compiling the index.

—*R. L. R.*

1

In Fear of Peace:
Getting Past Maybe

Robert L. Rothstein

The peace agreements and the postpeace periods that are studied in this volume, as well as those to which reference is made only indirectly (as in South Africa, the Sudan, Sri Lanka, and Central America), are widely different on a variety of dimensions. For example, patterns of causality, levels of development, political ideologies and political goals, and the degrees of external involvement are hardly identical, and each case contains unique elements that make comparison difficult, if not potentially misleading. Indeed, I have often been struck in discussing one or another of these conflicts with agreement participants that they respond in a similar fashion to efforts to compare across cases: yes, interesting, but we are different, sui generis.

Nevertheless, the impetus for this collection is completely different from those who see only the factors that make, or seem to make, each case unique. The differences among cases are obviously crucial, and it would be foolhardy to ignore them. But I think a strong case can be made for the existence of a similar set of structural and procedural conditions in virtually all of these cases, conditions that make comparison not only possible but also potentially of great value. Moreover, as I shall argue later, the disjunction between these conditions and the terms of most of the weak peace agreements that have been negotiated in a number of cases help to explain why the postagreement period is so filled with risk and so frequently disappointing to both sides—thus generating the possibility of a "bad" peace, a peace that ultimately worsens a conflict by increasing distrust and bitterness.

I should emphasize that one focus of this collection is on the period after a weak peace agreement has been signed. It is my assumption that this period, which contains powerful continuities with the earlier stages of the conflict, also contains enough new elements to treat it as a distinct and discrete stage of its own. I hasten to add that this hardly means that we can ignore the structural and procedural conditions of these conflicts or that the process of reaching agreement and the substance—or lack of it—of the agreement itself are of no concern. The point, rather, is that we shall look at these factors from the perspective of the postagreement period and that we shall seek to use them, in part, to help generate insights about how weak peace agreements might be strengthened and might help to begin the long and painful process of reconciliation.

We assume that peace is the highest good and that peaceful settlement is the only acceptable means of resolving conflicts of interest. After all, we give Nobel Prizes to our peacemakers and not to our great warmakers. These principles were also deeply embedded in the Covenant of the League of Nations and the Charter of the United Nations, even if honored more in the breach than in the observance. We need to keep in mind that the mind-set of many of the participants in these great conflicts is very different. It is not that the men of violence, the "hard men," do not value peace—how many times have they justified their own violence as a necessary means to end violence against themselves and to achieve a "just" peace?—but, rather, that they value other things more. The achievement of the other goals of the conflict, whatever they may be, is clearly of importance, but so is or may be the survival of the leadership and a continuing role for the men and women whose status has rested on the willingness to use violence and to resist compromise.[1]

Getting to Maybe

There are, as we shall see, many obstacles to reaching a genuine peace agreement; peace building takes much time and immense effort (whereas the destruction of peace need not take much of either), and the mutually bearable stalemate that emerges in many conflicts (neither winning, neither losing, acceptable levels of pain that reinforce divisions) is frequently more agreeable or easier to live with than the risks of an unstable peace. Why, then, have the post–Cold War years seen several unanticipated breakthroughs, near breakthroughs or serious but failed breakthroughs to peace?

There are obviously no simple answers to this question, nor is the mix of factors driving toward peace or increasing the incentives to break the stalemate likely to be identical in all cases. Nevertheless, there do seem to be some common elements present in most of these cases—and absent or not sufficiently strong in the failures—to generate a "ripe moment" to probe for peace. These elements constitute a kind of syndrome linking together changes in the international political and economic systems, changes within one or both sides of the conflict, and changes at the individual level.

The effects of the end of the Cold War have been contradictory, in some places unleashing previously contained conflicts yet in others increasing pressures for peace because external patrons have been weakened and/or have altered political orientations, the acquisition of arms has become more costly, and external funding has disappeared or been sharply curtailed. The latter pressures clearly affect dissident groups more than constituted governments and may in fact begin to change calculations about whether time is or is not on one's side. It is, after all, tactically wise to proclaim a willingness to fight to eternity, but some near-term gains may be necessary to maintain support and morale. These changes are reinforced, in this case for both sides, by changes in the international economy that make the continuation of an apparently insoluble conflict seem a costly distraction: globalization of the world economy and the rapid shift to knowledge-based production raise fears about marginalization (or declining prosperity for the richer side) through badly trained workforces, distorted patterns of trade, insufficient foreign investment, and excessive spending on domestic arms industries or imported arms. If the richer side has also enjoyed a measure of prosperity in the recent past and has some confidence that that prosperity could be maintained or accelerated in a more stable political environment, risk aversion—which requires having something one does not want to lose—may rise and the willingness to compromise may grow.[2]

The power and status of rebel leaders come from the conflict, and both may be threatened by a peace agreement that inevitably compromises hallowed goals. In such circumstances, even external pressures to move toward peace may not be persuasive or may only evoke a willingness to talk—but not to compromise—with the enemy. One thing that might be capable of generating some willingness to "think about the unthinkable" is a shift in the internal balance of power, especially in the rebel group. The leaders may live abroad and enjoy a reasonably good life as the symbol of resistance, but the people left behind usually pay a high price for the strategies adopted by the leadership (especially terrorism) and for the resulting repression and socioeconomic deprivation. What sometimes happens in these circumstances, particularly if the external leadership has produced few tangible benefits for its constituency, is the emergence of an internal leadership and/or a more activist internal response. For example, in Northern Ireland there was a gradual shift in power within the Irish Republican Army (IRA) toward leaders living in the six counties; and in the Middle East, there was some increase in influence for leaders in the West Bank and the Gaza Strip (a development accelerated by the intifada, which at least initially was not implemented or controlled by the Palestine Liberation

Organization [PLO]). This implies only a relative shift in the internal balance of power because the external leadership is still crucial (symbolically,
economically, strategically). But the shift may also indicate more willingness to compromise or to accept pragmatic gains short of victory, if largely
because many of those gains will go to the locals who need them most and
perhaps also because the locals know their enemies better and can see
some hope of living with them in (relatively) peaceful coexistence. (I shall
return to this issue below.)

There are other factors that may also be consequential, if not in "giving
peace a chance" then at least in increasing joint willingness to probe and
explore new ground. One such factor is simply "battle fatigue," the debili-
tating consequences of living in fear of endless tit-for-tat atrocities in a conflict that has no obvious solution and that prevents the enjoyment of nor-
mality—and hence the desire for "normalization" as part of any peace
process. Battle fatigue may not have much effect on the fanatics, who
march to their own drum, but it does or may emerge in the large and moderate center of both communities, a point that might be symbolized by the
increased willingness of Catholics in Northern Ireland to inform on planned
IRA terrorist actions or by the efforts in Israel to work out the terms of a
mutually acceptable peace agreement between moderates in both the Labor
Party and Likud.[3] Perhaps, just perhaps, the conflict becomes most ripe for
resolution when the silent majority begins to raise questions and to withdraw support. This may change the central questions of the conflict—in
Northern Ireland, for example, not how to get Great Britain out, but how
to persuade the Protestant community to let Great Britain go—so that it is
no longer a zero-sum or an either/or situation but a (partially) positive-sum
or "more or less" one. Finally, the "demonstration effect" may exert some
effect—if them, why not us?—especially with dreams of peace prizes, ap-
pearances on CNN, and ceremonies on the White House lawn.

Perhaps other factors (e.g., changes in leadership, apparent changes in
the power balance between the two sides) might also be important in particular cases, but the foregoing considerations at least give some sense of
why even hardened participants are asking tentatively and provisionally
whether the intractable is or may be tractable. We can infer the precarious nature of the peace agreements that result from these pressures from some very
salient limitations in their scope and breadth. The peace negotiations and the
peace agreements that may or may not eventuate are not driven by a change
in judgments about the enemy, who is still hated and still evil, or necessarily
by a sudden willingness to compromise central goals. Rather, while the exact
balance between internal and external factors pressing for peace varies
greatly in different cases and different time periods, and while it is probably
true that a successful peace process requires some convergence between
internal and external pressures, the peace processes that have emerged in

recent years tend to be relatively more driven by external pressures (outside/in) and by elite calculations (top/down) about who is winning or losing, whose weight in the balance looks likely to grow.

The more or less silent majority may have suffered most from the conflict and may feel battle fatigue deeply, but they (and the extremists) are still dominated by old stereotypes, still educated in the old canon, and still largely ignorant of the implications of external political and economic changes. Since the masses must be dragged along and the extremists contained or controlled, and since the leaders themselves are ambivalent about taking the risks of dangerous peace, what is usually offered is not only very limited—an armed truce to explore new territory with the not so latent threat of a quick return to business as usual—but is also presented to the majority not as an end to the (lost) war, but as a means of getting more now through politics. Thus the dissident side usually insists that the agreement is merely a stage that does not exclude pressing for more later. But this tactic, understandable but dangerous, may undermine the agreement itself because it exacerbates fears on the other side that it is being asked to give up something tangible only to be asked to give up even more later after the initial slice of the salami has been digested. Ambivalence meets ambivalence and frequently generates a peace process that is always at risk and agreements that resolve little of substance and are masterpieces of ambiguity. In short, the fragile peace agreements that have been negotiated or may be negotiated in some protracted conflicts do not mean that the conflict has been resolved; rather, there is a momentary agreement to suspend violence and to seek new means or new rules to manage a hostile and potentially unstable stalemate.

Still, short of a decisive war that ends in unconditional surrender, we rarely get an ideal peace process, one in which both sides are willing to compromise sacred goals and to contemplate living side by side with equanimity. Peace is a form of cooperation, and, as with the supply of international public goods, the supply regularly falls short of the demand. We need to be aware of the deficiencies of these peace processes, but we also need to understand that they create or may create a small window of opportunity to put peace on the agenda and to stop using the quest for peace as a tool in the propaganda wars. Moreover, we should remember that cooperative outcomes are possible even between sworn enemies (as in the Cold War) and that cooperation can benefit from common or compatible goals but does not always require them.[4] As Ralph Bryant notes, there are means available to increase the possibility that the self-interested mutual adjustment of behavior will increase cooperation or, in the cases at hand, increase the possibility that a weak peace agreement can be strengthened.[5]

What we have been discussing thus far is a different take on I. William Zartman's notion of a "ripe moment" for peace that emerges when both sides, suffering from a "mutually hurting stalemate," sensing a potentially negative turn in the military balance, and fearing that the conflict will get much worse if the stalemate is not broken, begin to explore possible compromises that achieve at least some important goals for both of them.[6] However, the failure to define critical terms more precisely risks turning Zartman's argument into a tautology: in effect, we have negotiations by definition when a "ripe moment" and a "mutually hurting stalemate" are present, and we do not have negotiations when they are not present. There are so many factors that can affect the emergence of a ripe moment, and there is so much uncertainty about its timing, that we may know only after the fact whether it did or did not actually exist.[7] In the same sense, a mutually hurting stalemate may exist for a long time before it generates movement toward peace, and the critical questions are left unanswered: How much does it have to hurt, who does it have to hurt, and how can present pain be transformed into a willingness to take the risks of a peace process that cannot guarantee lesser pain in the future?[8] In any case, because of these ambiguities, I have avoided using ripe moments or mutually hurting stalemates as descriptive metaphors for agreement decisions, tentative and reluctant as they may be, to start down the road toward peace negotiations.

Structure and Process in Protracted Conflicts

In a very general way, most protracted conflicts are very similar. A powerful group, usually in control of a particular territory, resists the demands (at least initially) of a much weaker side for a greater share of the available material benefits, a greater recognition of its distinct identity (culturally, linguistically, religiously, etc.), and a greater degree of political power (from power sharing through federalism to separation into different entities). This initial asymmetry in power also tends to affect strategic choices: the stronger side—the legitimate authority—tries to repress "illegitimate" dissent (perhaps joined to cosmetic efforts to improve the quality of life for the dissident group), and the weaker side uses the only weapons it has (guerrilla war, terrorism, a deep level of conviction) to fight back. Over time, however, such conflicts also begin to be characterized by certain structural (i.e., long-lasting) conditions—a syndrome of conflict—that define the nature of the conflict and set limits on what we can and cannot expect from any peace process.

My discussion of these structural conditions is abbreviated, given the limitations of time and space, but I hope sufficiently indicative.[9] I want to emphasize strongly that each of these conditions has been widely discussed in the literature on conflict resolution (although less so for the first two), but I have outlined them here for three reasons. First, treating them as elements of a linked syndrome is a useful way to begin thinking about protracted conflict. Second, the syndrome provides a framework and context for the chapters that follow. And third, the syndrome also generates important procedural and substantive consequences that have a profound effect on the period after a peace agreement has been negotiated, consequences that are frequently ignored or forgotten in the euphoria attendant on (apparent) peace.

In the first place, all of these conflicts are dominated by high levels of mistrust and by the fear that trusting the other side can entail great risks. The persistence of the grievances that generated the conflict, the hatreds generated by the inevitable atrocities attendant on the strategies of terrorism and repression, and the lack of knowledge about each other's intentions or about whether apparently benign intentions can or will be transformed into benign actions create elements of the fabled Prisoners' Dilemma.[10] Both sides get trapped into making suboptimal choices because they lack information, trust, and a sufficiently long-run perspective. Cooperation, where attempted, is tentative, superficial, and always at risk. Assuming that the worst might happen—the other side will cheat—virtually guarantees that it will happen.

The standard tactics to diminish the effects of a structural relationship based on distrust and fear are not always very helpful. Thus, encouraging a focus on long-run consequences of short-run actions, generating patterns of reciprocity through tit-for-tat strategies, or relying on the effects of a joint learning process may take too long to alter behavioral patterns that are constantly exacerbating mistrust and misperception.[11] Increasing the payoffs to both sides for compromising might help, but resources to do so may be insufficient and each side might fear the consequences of internal disunity over the terms of a compromise more than they expect to benefit from increased payoffs. Moreover, if new knowledge and new attitudes were to be generated by repeated interactions with the other side, that new knowledge will not only take time to develop, but will also affect primarily the elite and the educated classes. That implies a top-down peace process with the masses dragged reluctantly along—a formula that guarantees large problems in the postagreement period. Moreover, the learning process is likely to be inhibited by the misuse of history by both sides and the tendency to isolate both communities in separate educational and socialization systems, each imposing a one-sided vision of the conflict. I shall return to these points momentarily.

I do not want to leave the impression that these problems are insuperable. Some things can be done, especially in the short run, to diminish risks and to increase the likelihood of careful steps toward mutually beneficial cooperation. With fear and distrust necessarily being taken as givens, each side needs some guarantees about the other side's behavior, guarantees that involve more than pious rhetoric about mutual interests in cooperation and that insure that the risks that the other side will cheat will not be too great. For example, actions that each takes to protect itself against defection and cheating by the other side may also increase suspicions and induce reactions that create even worse fears and insecurity. Third-party guarantees and/or the presence of peacekeeping or observation forces may help here. So too will a very careful concern with compliance mechanisms (e.g., implementation of agreements in carefully controlled stages) and confidence-building measures. In addition, efforts to provide each side—but especially the poorer side—with enough material resources to give supporters some evidence that standards of living will gradually improve and that leaders have the will and the means to help the public at large may begin to broaden and deepen the constituency for peace. Prosperity alone cannot resolve these conflicts, but continued poverty and a loss of faith that conditions will improve guarantee that the conflict will not be resolved.

A second structural condition, which also becomes a procedural condition, concerns the internal or domestic constraints on the leadership of both sides. The peace process in most cases really constitutes a three-level bargaining game: the aggrieved parties with their external patrons and/or audience; the parties confronting each other face-to-face; and the leadership of each party with its own domestic supporters and opposition.[12] Any move at one level must be considered not only on its own terms, but also in terms of its potential impact on the other levels. There is therefore a game of complex positioning, with some moves at each level done largely for their effects elsewhere, yet other moves made to reinforce or undermine initiatives started elsewhere, and yet others made with indifference to, or ignorance about, effects elsewhere. Multiple chessboards with shifting players make the games difficult to follow and the results uncertain.

There are also other problems associated with multilevel bargaining games: increased doubts about the willingness to implement agreements because of uncertainties about real intentions; the difficulties of estimating support at each level for actions taken on another level; and a tendency to assume that all offers or actions should be discounted as efforts to garner support at another level. In short, the process is frequently indeterminate and opaque, which may be one reason an external mediator can perform a useful role in increasing the probability that a serious offer will be taken seriously. In any case, the simple point is that the structure of the peace process is always more complex than the public and private exchanges at the formal peace negotiations.

All three levels are clearly important, but the domestic level is *primus inter pares*: very little is likely to work at the other levels or across levels if the leader cannot bring his or her troops along and contain or control the extremists. The crucial structural condition in this context concerns the relative strength of the leader not only vis-à-vis his or her own supporters—whether he or she is powerful, respected, and assured of support even for unpopular policies by a strong majority—but also vis-à-vis the leadership of the other side. Presumably, chances for stable peace are greater if strongly supported leaders who favor compromise are in power on both sides and if external patrons also support compromise, are willing to commit resources to the settlement, and are not intent on using the game itself for their own positioning purposes, domestically or internationally. Unfortunately, the very nature of protracted conflict makes it unlikely that all of these conditions will hold, and in some cases, none of them do. Consequently, we need to explore other permutations in these relationships not only at any particular time, but also as they change over time, or as a structural condition becomes a procedural condition.

If both sides have strong leadership willing to compromise and to risk getting out in front of mass views, as happened between France and Germany in the 1950s and between Nelson Mandela and F. W. de Klerk in the recent past, a peace agreement will obviously be easier to achieve and more likely to survive.[13] However, if this agreement cannot be reached quickly, which is likely because the views of both the masses and the extremists tend to lag elite views on the need for compromise, the result is usually a protracted stalemate, punctuated by terrorism.[14] Moreover, even if the leaders arrive at a settlement, it may be inherently unstable because one or both leaders may have to oversell what has been achieved, promise that ultimate goals have not been sacrificed, and read too much between the lines, thus guaranteeing disappointed expectations and escalating frustrations—especially if external promises of aid do not materialize or are badly used, as has happened in the West Bank and Gaza after the Oslo Agreements.

If both leaders are weak and unsure of staying in power, the prognosis is bleak. Such "leaders" tend to shift with mass moods, be unable or unwilling to confront extremists, fear large concessions, and try to shift the risks of agreement to the other side by asking for quick tangible gains for themselves in exchange for long-term promises of reciprocity; they survive largely by suggesting that their successors will be even worse—or by eliminating possible successors. As the stalemate continues, and as the prospect for a bearable compromise grows even dimmer, dissent within each side (but especially the rebel side) is likely to become more intense and fractious, moderates are easily undercut by the violence and the radical rhetoric of the extremists, and the voices that assert that there is no solution to the conflict (except more violence and a "long war" strategy) become more strident.[15]

In such circumstances, each side becomes more comfortable with a bad but bearable status quo than with the risks of a weak compromise because the possibility of a mutually beneficial compromise seems small and because the risks of a compromise that produces too few benefits for what has to be given away are particularly great for the elites themselves. The stalemate is particularly hard to break precisely because it is *not* unbearable. The violence is embittering and polarizing, but it does not usually impinge heavily on daily life and adaptations have been made to the inevitable economic costs, the security fears, and the psychological traumas. As John Whyte has said of Northern Ireland:

> the current situation is unsatisfactory to all the contending parties, but it is not the worst conceivable. [The parties] hold on to what advantages they have, lest in the course of bargaining they lose even more than they already have.[16]

In effect, for the status quo party, it is possible to manage the conflict at a relatively acceptable level, but neither to crush resistance definitively nor to offer more than cosmetic concessions. Conversely, the weaker party can continue to inflict pain indefinitely, but it cannot offer significant concessions to the other side without fracturing its own unity, and it cannot force concessions from the other side and may indeed make them less likely by the very nature of the tactics that it (seemingly) must adopt. Put differently, in this set of circumstances, everyone supports the peace *process* because it seems to represent movement, it generates widespread praise, and nothing yet has had to be given away; but they do not necessarily support a peace *agreement* that is usually essentially procedural—an agreement to talk—but could require significant concessions down the road. This scenario of weak leaders confronting weak leaders is something of a paradigm for protracted conflict, and breaking out of its constraints may be a necessary (but not sufficient) prerequisite for peace.

Finally, one can imagine a situation in which one leader is relatively strong and the other relatively weak. One might hope here that the stronger would be farsighted and courageous, perhaps as was General Charles de Gaulle during the Algerian crisis. But that hope may be forlorn because the dynamics of asymmetric power relationships are not encouraging. Progress is likely to be stymied because the weak side will be reluctant to negotiate from weakness (unless convinced things are about to get much worse, a judgment that might have influenced the PLO in the Oslo negotiations) and the strong may not feel a pressing need to be generous. Israel's policies after the 1967 war may be illustrative. One might try to make the power balance more symmetrical, although it is not always clear how this can be accomplished, and it might even generate more violence as the stronger feels the need to strike before symmetry is established and the weaker may try to strike before the stronger can reassert supremacy. Mediation by a powerful outsider may be the only real hope of progress in this context.

I have spent a good deal of time discussing the first two structural conditions because it seems to me that they set the baseline from which analysis needs to proceed. Above all, they help us to understand why it is so difficult to transform all the factors pushing for peace into much more than a tentative truce without any clear agreement on the nature of a final settlement. The second condition, in particular, helps us to understand why, even if a majority on one or even both sides genuinely wants peace, the negotiating process is so convoluted and frustrating: peacemakers need a partner who can deliver, a partner in control of his own constituency. By contrast, what we usually see are reluctant and mistrustful partners more comfortable with the familiar rituals of the status quo than the unfamiliar risks of peace.

A third factor that seems to characterize most protracted conflicts and that has profound implications for the policy process after a peace agreement concerns the presence of extreme patterns of socioeconomic segregation, fragmentation, and inequality.[17] Israelis and Palestinians in the Middle East, Catholics and Protestants in Northern Ireland, blacks and whites in South Africa, and Buddhists and Hindus in Sri Lanka are severely segregated: people have different religions (or races), different residential areas, different schools, different jobs, sometimes different languages, and so on. One result is that the crosscutting and overlapping ties that have done so much to reduce the significance of ethnic and other divisions in many democratic societies simply do not exist. Encounters with the "other" are thus largely formal, distant, and tense, with little opportunity to develop shared interests or a common identity. Moreover, the persistence of school segregation makes it much easier for negative stereotypes to remain unchallenged, for biased history to be taken on faith, and for ignorance about the culture and beliefs of the other side to grow. In short, these are enemies who do not communicate with each other very well, who do not understand each other very well, and are prone to see only the worst in each other.[18]

The problems attendant on segregated communities may be compounded by the fact that each community may also be internally fragmented or divided, which complicates the problem of arriving at and maintaining an internal consensus. Of course, a consensus can be difficult to sustain even in a homogeneous society. Disagreements about strategy and tactics are inevitable: whether to use violence or to adopt a political strategy, or whether to accept a particular compromise or to fight on in the hope of achieving more. Nevertheless, internal fragmentation compounds

the problem of developing a majority consensus and endangers its continuation because of differing degrees of commitment to its terms.[19] Initially,
before compromise looms on the horizon, the rebel side may be relatively
more unified because of a shared goal and a shared belief in the imperative
of unity, and the dominant side may be sharply divided on the need for, or
the content of, compromise. But this asymmetry is likely to disappear as
the moment of choice nears, and internal fragmentation will only deepen
the problems of reaching agreement.

In all of the conflicts that are examined in this volume, there is a large
and frequently escalating economic gap between the dominant community
and its opponents. This gap constitutes a fourth structural condition of protracted conflict. Whether this gap is a direct result of biased economic
policies by the dominant party or whether it is a result of different levels
of productivity—or both—can be judged only on a case-by-case basis, but
it is clear that the existence of so evident a gap makes segregation even
more troublesome. This is especially so if the gap seems to be deliberately
generated or exacerbated by government policies. In Sri Lanka, for example, the dominant Sinhalese created a generous (too generous, given the
level of income) welfare state that benefited the Buddhist community but
systematically discriminated against the Tamils. When an economic crisis
hit Sri Lanka in the 1980s, inequalities increased sharply, many of the poor
Sinhalese blamed their plight on the Tamils and thus constituted fertile
ground for Buddhist extremists, and a relatively stable ethnic conflict de-
generated into a bitter, no-holds-barred war.[20] Patterns of discrimination
were equally obvious—or seemed so—in regard to the blacks in South
Africa, the Catholics in Northern Ireland, and the Palestinians in Israel, the
West Bank, and Gaza.[21]

What to do about this is obviously a crucial question for the postagreement period, one that has both a short- and a long-run dimension. I
would note here only that if the dominant party is merely intent on protecting an inherited economic structure that is biased in its favor and is
typically characterized by substantial inefficiencies and misallocations of
resources, and if the aggrieved minority, with expectations rising and
knowledge of economic policies rudimentary, demands a greater share of
existing benefits and rapid restructuring to compensate for past discrimination, then the outlook is grim.[22]

The combination of segregation, economic deprivation, and repression
may also generate another characteristic of protracted conflicts, if one usually confined to the weaker side.[23] The absence of prosperity, the exile of
many of the most educated and skilled individuals, and the repression of,
or suspicion about, the activities of various professional and social groups
suggest that the development of the kind of civic society that supports and
nurtures democracy will be sharply limited. A culture of democracy is

unlikely to develop in such circumstances; the beliefs and attitudes that sustain democracy have no place to grow and are (frequently) easily overwhelmed by the patrimonial values of many traditional groups and by the conspiratorial, antidemocratic practices of the organization leading the revolt.[24] In addition, the entrepreneurial attitudes that facilitate conversion to a market economy may not have developed or may have been transferred elsewhere in the diaspora. The negative implications of this for the post-peace agreement period are potentially quite severe. The point is not merely that the long-term benefits of the development of a democratic society and a market economy may be lost, but also that what is likely to replace them might be dangerously inappropriate. Hence, both the masses and the elite may favor statist, governmental solutions for societal problems, they may be prone to rely on a single, authoritarian leader for guidance, and they may be quick to blame the new regime—if one is established—for disappointed expectations.[25] The dangers of instability are likely to escalate if the new governing authority acts arbitrarily, engenders obvious patterns of corruption among the leader's closest associates, and inhibits—just as its predecessor did—the free flow of ideas.

Patterns of segregation and fragmentation may be especially disabling if they are reinforced by religious conflicts. Virtually all of the conflicts that are discussed herein obviously have a very powerful religious dimension. But to say that they have a religious dimension is not to say that they are religious conflicts. In many cases, the religious dimension was transformed into a religious conflict only over time as socioeconomic inequalities festered and grew, as group conflict intensified, and as unscrupulous leaders began to use or misuse an extreme interpretation of religious dogma to mobilize the masses into hatred, to provide a warrant for intolerance, and to offer justification for acts of cruelty and barbarity. As this happens, and as the other side is forced (or chooses) to reply in the same currency, and as moderates in one's own community are marginalized, violence becomes a legitimate, routinized means to settle disputes with nonbelievers or different believers. Adding religion to an essentially secular conflict can thus help to generate the "invention of enmity" and the polarization of uncompromising belief systems.[26]

These points seem to imply that the major contribution of religion to a conflict is to intensify it. And there is a good deal of evidence to sustain this view. In the Middle East, Northern Ireland, Bosnia, Sri Lanka, and Cyprus, the church, or church leaders, or believers in fundamentalist doctrines have sometimes led or exacerbated the conflict and/or resisted pragmatic compromises.[27] Indeed, the conflict between the secular community and the more extreme parts of the religious community has become so intense and divisive in Israel that there are questions being raised about whether a secular democracy and a fundamentalist theocracy can coexist:

there are, at the extremes, almost no common meeting grounds.[28] In any event, religious groups that feel threatened by modernization are predisposed toward intensifying their religious identities and appropriating extreme, almost mystical forms of nationalism as part of the religious canon. Marginalizing or containing these views, which are usually only minority views, is difficult when the religious are willing to use terrorism not only against external enemies, but also against internal opponents.

It would of course be misleading to leave the impression that religion can have only negative effects on protracted conflicts. If conditions are right (politically, economically, psychologically), and if both sides are serious about the peace process, individual religious leaders or religious groups can play a crucial facilitating role: they have a reputation for speaking the truth, they may provide or be able to acquire financial resources, they may elicit trust more readily than ancient enemies, and it may be easier to make concessions to a presumably higher spiritual force, among other things.[29] One notes, however, that the religious individuals and groups who contribute to the escalation of conflict are rarely, if ever, the individuals and groups who help to mediate and resolve conflicts. It is difficult, for example, to imagine the Greek Orthodox Church being a credible mediator in the Cyprus conflict or the Serbian Orthodox Church playing a useful peacemaking role in either Serbia or Bosnia. The major points are that "religion" is an inadequate term to describe a complex set of relationships, that there is no single or consistent positive or negative effect of religion on conflict, that we have to make many distinctions about the interacting effects of religion and conflict, and that the conversion of the religious role from instigator of conflict to facilitator of compromise is likely to be possible only in a few cases and only after other developments in the secular realm make religious intervention sensible.[30]

There is another aspect of the religious issue that is of some importance. This relates not so much to the conflict between different religions but, rather, to the implications of a particular set of religious views. Donald Akenson has argued that Israel, South Africa, and Northern Ireland have in common that most or many citizens feel themselves to be people of the Covenant—that is, people for whom an ancient Covenant with God still constitutes a serious commitment. Such societies, according to Akenson, are harsh and unforgiving to enemies, strongly attached to the (holy) land, and more concerned with unity among the chosen than agreement with the enemy. As Akenson argues, "These societies will not be given to easy compromises, committed to religious or racial pluralism, or overly concerned about keeping the good opinion of the outside world."[31]

Two points are worth noting about this argument. In the first place, while compromise with "true believers" of any kind is extraordinarily difficult, clearly only a relatively small number of people in any of these societies are really genuine "Covenanters"; many more are moderates, and perhaps even more are simply indifferent to mystical attachments to "the land." Still, the other side to this argument is that it does not take many fanatics willing to use violence to bring a society or a peace process to a grinding halt. In the second place, as Akenson indicates, what may be even more interesting is that in Northern Ireland and South Africa, the dominance of the Covenanter outlook has been broken, more secular views are on the ascendant, and, consequently, previously unacceptable compromises have suddenly become "thinkable."[32] By contrast, the case in the Middle East is much less clear and much less promising. Islamic fundamentalists are growing in power (in direct response to the failures of local governments, not least the Palestinian National Authority) and willing to use any means (including democratic elections) to achieve their ends, and some Jewish fundamentalist groups have threatened to do the same if too much is offered or given to the Palestinians. Nevertheless, in Northern Ireland and South Africa, there are some straws in the wind that suggest the "civil war" threatened by the Covenanters is more rhetoric than reality and that the silent majority opposing them may be greater than anticipated. Note such things as the increased willingness of the Catholic community to inform on the IRA; the willingness of the Protestant loyalists to maintain the recent truce, even after the IRA resumed its violence; and the muted right-wing reaction to the empowerment of the Mandela government and the acceptance of the "one man, one vote" formula. The situation is more clouded in the Middle East. In Israel, religious extremists have the support of "security hawks" on the peace issue, either group could bring down the Netanyahu government by defecting on a crucial Knesset vote, and Netanyahu may be "committed" to the peace process only as a tactic to disguise settlement policies that make peace impossible. By the same token, some Islamic fundamentalist groups reject compromise and remain committed to maximalist, all-or-nothing goals.

Another crucial structural condition concerns not merely the misuse of history by each side but the particular ways in which history is misused. In effect, each side constructs a kind of mythical history mingling elements of truth with dangerous fantasies about a "golden age" destroyed by alien intruders of inferior quality.[33] These are "imprisoning historical perspectives" because they are inculcated virtually from birth, reinforced by reciprocal violence, reemphasized with a patina of scholarship during school years, and defended against "traitors" (i.e., revisionists or other challengers of the conventional wisdom).[34] Critical here is that this version of history, while clearly not held by all members of a community (especially the educated elites), tends to provide a continuing justification for violence, a continuing supply of recruits (especially susceptible because of discontent with other aspects of their lives), and a continuing rationale for the rejection of pragmatic compromises. What can be gotten from peace always seems less valuable than what must be given up for peace, particularly when tentative and (initially) marginal and uncertain gains are measured against the presumed benefits of a reconstruction of the golden age—or the final destruction of the nemesis. This "rejectionist front" (or state of mind) may be dangerously reinforced if the historical golden age has a religious component: what is granted by God's will cannot be compromised away; the theological history may justify waiting decades, indeed centuries, for revenge; and faith in ultimate triumph may be sustained not only by belief in God's will, but also by the more practical belief that time is on one's side—that God will be just, someday. In any case, time and again in virtually all peace negotiations, one or the other side will refer with great bitterness to its version of ancient history, as if it were only yesterday and true beyond doubt.[35] Stable peace, then, may require a concerted effort to revise the historical canon, to begin teaching a new version of history, to apologize for genuine misdeeds, and to marginalize and contain the extremists who reject this effort.[36]

Peace is obviously easier to establish if the dominant party begins to see a net benefit in compromising and if it does not seek to use its power advantage either to reinforce the status quo or to seek further gains. This simple point brings us to another structural factor that seems to characterize many protracted conflicts: however outside observers see the distribution of power in any conflict, both sides perceive themselves as embattled minorities surrounded by enemies intent on their destruction.[37] The illogic is not as profound as it might appear: the Israelis, the Protestants in Northern Ireland, the whites in South Africa, and the Sinhalese in Sri Lanka were all clearly dominant in the direct conflict with their antagonists, but they were also minorities in the wider region. There are important consequences of this state of affairs. For one thing, if both sides display the insecurities, the anxieties, and the sensitivities of a threatened minority, the fears of giving away too much in a compromise will be great (the fear of negotiating from weakness); the willingness to take risks for peace will be limited; and reciprocal fears about security, about the future, and about the intentions of the other will dominate negotiations. This is another case in which third-party interventions and guarantees may be crucial, especially in the short run when the fears and insecurities will still make the risks of peace too high.[38]

Connected to the last point, and indeed to a number of earlier structural conditions, is the increased likelihood that the (initial) hope of a quick victory is gradually replaced by the realization that victory—in the sense of achieving most central goals—is not imminent, that the terror tactics of the weak intensify and harden the will to resist of the other side, and that the only hope is a "long war" strategy. The promise of ultimate victory diminishes the significance of short-run losses, sustains the morale of enough partisans, and justifies a major shift in tactics. The ultimate goal remains the same, as does the refusal to accept compromises that sacrifice some sacred goals, but there is a new emphasis on a war of attrition that raises the costs for the other side, that seeks to make the area of conflict ungovernable, and that attacks and terrorizes its *own* compromisers and doubters to intimidate and maintain control.[39] The diffusion of targets and the lack of any direct connection to changes in short-term policies by the enemy make the adoption of a long war strategy, which is probably the inevitable result of short-run failures by "true believers," particularly difficult to contain or to end by the normal process of negotiated compromise.

Finally, there is one structural condition that cuts across and influences all the others. Anyone who analyzes protracted conflicts quickly comes to understand that they are not merely conflicts about land, or resources, or sovereignty—that is, conflicts of interest. What is missing from interest-based analysis is the emotional depth of the conflict, the intensity of hatred, mistrust, and contempt that has developed and deepened over time. In some cases, the depth of these feelings may be so profound that some or many of the participants in the conflict may prefer to inflict pain on the other side than to gain something for themselves.[40] Thus these are conflicts that have gone beyond incompatible interests and the bargaining strategies appropriate for completely "rational egoists." Amos Oz has recently argued,

> Fortunately, this conflict is essentially nothing but a dispute over property: whose house? Who is going to get how much out of it? Such conflicts can be resolved through compromise.[41]

This view seems to me profoundly mistaken, even dangerously so. If the Arab-Israeli conflict, or any other protracted conflict, was about only the distribution or redistribution of assets, compromise solutions would have been much easier and much quicker. But such conflicts are about much more than that, and failing to recognize the psychological and emotional depths involved here may only make these conflicts more difficult to resolve—and more likely to resume after a compromise peace fails to meet expectations.

Changing the negative stereotypes of the other and ending the process of demonization and psychological distancing cannot be done quickly.[42] These perceptions and attitudes have deep roots and may serve some useful purposes—as well as hostile ones—in strengthening group identity and maintaining group unity. Insights from psychocultural conflict theory and social identity theory may help to explain why these feelings develop, persist, and intensify, and they may also help us to understand how projections of aggression by the other may be used to justify one's own aggression.[43] But in the short run, one can only hope that incremental changes and new information about the other will facilitate, at least among the elites, a degree of "working trust" that focuses on the common interests that exist amid continuing differences in perceptions and attitudes.[44]

Marc Howard Ross has argued that the problem in attempting to resolve a conflict is not merely to seek "a formula on which the parties can agree but also to first find a way to alter the hostile perceptions and mutual fears that lock the parties into a zero-sum view of any proposals."[45] I would disagree only with Ross's assertion that it is necessary "first" to find a way to alter perceptions and fears. It is profoundly important to think about ways of doing this, but this is a long-term effort that must be joined to short-term efforts to resolve conflicts of interest. After all, the psychological elements of the conflict have usually developed only after prolonged efforts to resolve the clash of interests have failed. Put differently, neither psychological nor interest-based theories of conflict by themselves provide a fully adequate interpretation of any conflict, but ignoring either may also generate dangerously simplistic versions of conflict resolution.

From Structure to Process

All of the structural conditions discussed above create a syndrome of protracted conflict that sets the framework within which efforts at conflict resolution must proceed. But they also have procedural effects on how the conflict is carried on and on what options for compromise and resolution will be considered.

In many such conflicts, the leadership group and a strongly committed group of followers carry on the bulk of the conflict from the outside in: they seek support abroad, they train abroad, they launch attacks from abroad, and their efforts become the very symbol of the struggle. Those who stay behind provide "a sea to swim in," but they tend to have very minimal impact on the strategy and tactics pursued. Over time, however, as the conflict settles into immobility and as the outside leaders fail to produce much—if any—progress toward shared goals, there is usually a relative increase in power for the internal supporters, in the development of internal leadership, and perhaps some shift toward moderation; those who bear the greatest cost of the conflict, who are most deprived, and who are most familiar with the enemy from daily contact may begin to demand a voice in the process.[46] This is not to argue that the internal leadership entirely displaces the external leadership. Rather, there is a shift from hierarchial dominance to mutual dependence: each still needs the other. This may also imply that, if and when a peace agreement is negotiated, conflicts between the two leadership groups may grow and may complicate the process of reaching agreement and implementing its provisions.[47]

Signing a weak peace agreement rarely alters the conflict fundamentally—that is, it does not greatly affect the structural syndrome—but it may offer some new opportunities for exploration. It may also change the political dynamics in another way. Taking any risks for peace will be difficult for weak political leaders and is likely to be done only when the risks of not acting seem greater, when an unstable equilibrium seems to be tilting against one or both sides. Once risked, however, the leaders on both sides have comparable needs to widen the coalition for compromise, to produce some tangible and symbolic benefits quickly, to control and isolate extremists, and to see the other side act to do the same. This partnership of risk rests on the possibility that the agreement will fail, that it will internally divide each side and threaten the legitimacy and power of the leaders, and that failed peace will generate a resumption of more bitter and futile conflict. Thus the hated other may suddenly become the necessary, if reluctant and tacit, ally against extremism. Since more compromises and more back-channel negotiations will be necessary to keep the peace process going, the relationship between the old warriors must change quickly from total hostility and total distrust to a quasi partnership. As the adage goes, they must hang together or hang separately. A dialectic of reluctant salvation and mutual dependence may need to emerge, as obviously difficult as it may be. There was some evidence of this occurring in South Africa, only episodic and erratic evidence in the Middle East and in Northern Ireland, and little or no evidence of such movement in Bosnia and Sri Lanka.

The end of the Cold War and the reconsideration of external interests by the major powers may also have created another procedural condition. The external patron or patrons may, as their own interests change and as they want to refocus on domestic problems, be increasingly unwilling or unable to expend resources on a futile and costly conflict and consequently put increasing pressure on the local parties to find a livable compromise. The problem is that this shift in perspective at one level of the conflict compels the local parties to take large risks while weak domestically, short of resources, in need of time to persuade followers of the necessity of compromise, and doubtful about the intentions of the enemy. The parties to the conflict may be able to negotiate a flawed and limited peace agreement without much external support (as in the Oslo Agreements), but they are unlikely to be able to deepen and extend the peace process without substantial external support. This implies that the local parties will be exceptionally dependent on external support just as external supporters are losing patience and losing the incentive to invest heavily in the resolution of a conflict that seems to belong to another era. The need for support may be especially great because each side is likely to oversell what has actually been achieved in the peace negotiations—to convince the masses and contain the extremists—and to indulge in wish fulfillment about how much the other side has conceded and how much in terms of resources the external world will provide. In short, there may be an unfortunate dialectic at work: external patrons pressing for settlements because they are losing interest and want to reallocate spending elsewhere, with local parties taking the risks of compromise only if they receive a range of support that is increasingly improbable.[48]

Conclusion

The combination of structural and procedural conditions that we have been discussing, which creates a syndrome of conflict, significantly affects how weak and flawed peace agreements will be negotiated, perceived, interpreted, and implemented. The syndrome is complex because it mixes together short-run and long-run factors, tangible and intangible issues, and conflicts of interest and conflicts of vision and value. They cannot all be dealt with at once, some may not be able to be dealt with at all, and others may be diminished in force only as other aspects of the conflict are dealt with and as (one hopes) progress in solidifying a weak peace generates new perspectives.

This syndrome helps to explain why apparently sensible compromise agreements on a variety of discrete issues—for instance, autonomy or power sharing, compensation for violations from the past, security issues—may be rejected or fail to be implemented because they are perceived as part of a larger mosaic that is still dominated by suspicion, risk aversion, a desire for a decisive victory over bitter enemies, a willingness to wait out the enemy, and an unwillingness to relinquish maximalist goals. In these circumstances, the euphoria that one or both sides may feel after the signing of an agreement is rarely justified, and public celebrations of triumph are decidedly premature and may even generate dangerously inflated expectations. The euphoria may indeed create a kind of moral hazard, and both sides may forget or undervalue the need to work on the amelioration of the syndrome that has sustained the conflict—a necessity that will not have been diminished by a weak, tentative peace agreement. The grand hope of "normalization" may thus easily fade away into an increasingly fragile and embittered "cold peace," or worse.

Conventional bargaining strategies also may not work very well in this context. The offers that leaders are able to make and the offers that they are likely to be given are minimalist—and not irrationally so, given the limits of what has been accomplished and the difficulties of what still needs to be resolved. Each fears dissent within his own community and noncompliance, not to say deceit, from the other side, which helps us to understand why presumably reasonable suggestions by outsiders to be more generous in initial proposals are unlikely to be accepted. Every agreement is therefore signed with mental reservations, with doubts about its true worth; as a result, very little cumulates, and the prudential strategy of building peace brick by brick, resolving the easy issues first and leaving the hard issues for the endgame, does not usually work well because the bricks seem insecurely grounded and momentum is not easily generated by cosmetic concessions or agreements to talk about talking. One should not, of course, totally dismiss such agreements because they may be preferable to a deteriorating status quo and they may offer some windows of opportunity, but one must also be aware of their limitations, of how much more needs to be done, and of the possibility that a bad peace may be worse than no peace at all if it generates unfulfillable expectations and increased hostility.

There is another point about the conflict syndrome that needs emphasis. If the structural and procedural conditions set the context for the peace process, it is also true that the evolution of these conditions may create the opportunities for progress or the obstacles to progress in that process. They are not written in stone, and some of them may be amenable to movements toward peace, especially if they intersect with external developments that seem to be pushing in the same direction. Put differently, awareness of the elements of the syndrome of conflict and of how little they have been affected by the negotiation of a weak peace agreement should at least alert analysts and practitioners to what remains to be done, and how difficult it will be to do it, in the postpeace period. The great practical question, of course (borrowing from V. I. Lenin), is: What is to be done? I shall suggest some very tentative answers to that question in the concluding chapter of this volume.

Notes

1. The existence of a "third culture" of violence—men and women committed to violence and terror whose status comes from the gun and the bomb and who have few peacetime skills—is a persisting problem in most protracted conflicts. These terrorists are usually committed to extremist solutions, and compromise peace agreements always give them something about which to protest and with which to rationalize the continuation of terror. Obviously, containing and marginalizing these individuals are prime tasks in the postpeace period.

2. The rise in prosperity, as in Europe after 1955 and in Israel after the mid-1980s or so, may illustrate the point.

3. On Northern Island, see James F. Clarity, "As More Catholics Turn Against I.R.A. the Number of Police Informers Rises," *New York Times*, January 14, 1997, p. 7; on Israel, my information comes from a participant in the talks.

4. See Ralph Bryant, *International Coordination of National Stabilization Policies* (Washington, D.C.: Brookings Institution, 1992), pp. 38–39.

5. Ibid., pp. 43–44.

6. See I. William Zartman, "Dynamics and Constraints in Negotiations in Internal Conflicts," in I. William Zartman, ed., *Elusive Peace: Negotiating an End to Civil Wars* (Washington, D.C.: Brookings Institution, 1995), pp. 3–29. Note that the elements of a compromise agreement have frequently been on or near the table for some time. What changes is perceptions of how bearable the terms of this agreement are likely to be.

7. On the timing issue, see especially Jeffrey Z. Rubin, "The Timing of the Ripeness and the Ripeness of Timing," in Louis Kriesberg and Stuart J. Thorson, eds., *Timing the De-Escalation of International Conflicts* (Syracuse, N.Y.: Syracuse University Press, 1991), pp. 237–246. Other chapters in this collection are also useful on the timing issue.

8. Stephen John Stedman, *Peacemaking in Civil War: International Mediation in Zimbabwe, 1974–1980* (Boulder, Colo.: Lynne Rienner, 1991), pp. 235–242, offers some other useful "refinements" or criticisms of Zartman's arguments. I should note that others have also criticized the passivity of waiting for a ripe moment and suggested trying to equalize the power position of the two sides or trying to get both sides to "revision" the conflict by altering cognitive dynamics. But neither of these approaches seems realistic in any near-term time frame, and the first might indeed generate more—not less—violence, should it occur.

9. See also Robert L. Rothstein, "After the Peace: The Political Economy of Reconciliation," Inaugural Rebecca Meyerhoff Memorial Lecture (Jerusalem: Harry S. Truman Institute, Hebrew University, 1996). I make a distinction throughout this chapter between the underlying conditions of conflict and the issues that are on the negotiating table—how they are linked but different. A somewhat similar distinction is made by David Bloomfield in *Peacemaking Strategies in Northern Ireland* (New York: St. Martin's, 1997).

10. There are elements of a classic Prisoners' Dilemma game present, but complexities arise because the power balance (at least initially) is usually asymmetric, each side is likely to be internally divided, and each or both may act largely to garner external support. Thus an isolated game—or even iterated games—may obscure more than they reveal.

11. Another standard strategy, collusion, is not likely to work in the context of pervasive mistrust, but this may change (or should change) if a peace agreement is negotiated. In the latter case, tacit and overt collusion between previously hostile elites may be both possible and necessary. This is or may be a procedural condition of such conflicts and will be discussed later.

12. Note that the fact that each side is likely to be internally divided may also mean that each subgroup appeals to a different external constituency—and perhaps even to a different constituency on the enemy's side.

13. One key dimension here is whether the leader controls a unified movement or party or has a dominant majority or, conversely, whether he or she must manage a coalition—which implies frequent splits, high degrees of leverage for minority groups, delays, and lowest-common-denominator offers. The Camp David Agreement could thus work because Anwar Sadat was strong enough to make a big offer and take big risks and Menachem Begin (like de Klerk in South Africa) was strong enough to hold his own constituency and to gain significant Labor Party support. Sadat and Begin were also confident that they could contain the extremist threat. The contrast with weak leaders like Yasir Arafat and Benjamin Netanyahu should be apparent.

14. The lag effect, which seems to recur frequently enough to be considered a structural condition, will also appear below in a short-run context as a procedural condition of protracted conflict.

15. In effect, weak leaders need to use the peace process as much to bolster their own standing vis-à-vis internal competition as to reach agreement with the enemy. Mixed motives in seeking peace are of course par for the course, but the relative weights of different motives vary with circumstances—here, the relative strength or weakness of the leadership.

16. John Whyte, "Dynamics of Social and Political Change in Northern Ireland," in Dermot Keogh and Michael H. Haltzel, eds., *Northern Ireland and the Politics of Reconciliation* (Cambridge: Cambridge University Press, 1993), p. 116. This is not to say that the "domestication" of protracted conflict—learning to live with its traumas—is without costs. The cumulative effects include deepening hatreds and a tacit willingness to ignore or devalue democratic norms and rules, a kind of coarsening of civic virtue.

17. See, for example, John Whyte, *Interpreting Northern Ireland* (Oxford: Clarendon, 1990), pp. 52–60; and Martin J. Murray, *Revolution Deferred: The Painful Birth of Post-Apartheid South Africa* (London: Verso, 1994), pp. 3–4, 15–18. The degree of segregation and inequality varies, needless to say, with a variety of circumstances.

18. This is one reason that unpublicized, back-channel negotiations and other private efforts to bring individuals from both sides together over a period of time may be more important than they seem. See, for example, Allister Sparks, *Tomorrow Is Another Country: The Inside Story of South Africa's Road to Change* (New York: Hill and Wang, 1995); David Makovsky, *Making Peace with the PLO: The Rabin Government's Road to the Oslo Accord* (Boulder, Colo.: Westview, 1996); and Chapter 8 by Herbert Kelman in this volume. Also interesting is Patti Waldmeir, *Anatomy of a Miracle: The End of Apartheid and the Birth of the New South Africa* (New York: W. W. Norton and Co., 1997).

19. It is especially bad if one of the internal groups fears losing on all dimensions (political, economic, religious, etc.) because the fear of marginalization or loss of status in peace may rationalize a resort to violence, the quest for internal scapegoats, and, at best, ambivalent support for implementation of agreements.

20. See S. J. Tambiah, *Sri Lanka: Ethnic Fratricide and the Dismantling of Democracy* (Chicago: University of Chicago Press, 1986), pp. 35–53.

21. On the latter case, see Hisham Awartani, "Palestinian-Israeli Economic Relations: Is Cooperation Possible?" in Stanley Fischer, Dani Rodrik, and Elias Tuma, eds., *The Economics of Middle East Peace: Views from the Region* (Cambridge, Mass.: MIT Press, 1994), pp. 281–304. More generally, see Nicole Ball, with Tammy Halevy, *Making Peace Work: The Role of the International Development Community* (Washington, D.C.: Overseas Development Council, 1996).

22. There may be a brief honeymoon period when political and symbolic gains can substitute for material gains, but this is not likely to last indefinitely. In addition, while peace will inevitably generate rising expectations, such expectations are not likely to be revolutionary and are likely to be focused on improvements in such things as job prospects, housing, and education. Thus radical redistribution and/or aggressive populist demands are usually not on the immediate agenda—and they will not appear if the government begins to meet some demands, seems to have benign intentions toward the masses, and does not descend into corruption and repression, as has unfortunately happened with the Arafat regime in the West Bank and Gaza. On the general point here, see R. W. Johnson and Lawrence Schlemmer, "Into the Brave New World: Post-Election South Africa," in R. W. Johnson and

Lawrence Schlemmer, eds., *Launching Democracy in South Africa* (New Haven, Conn.: Yale University Press, 1996), pp. 353–375.

23. This point will probably be true for both sides if the stronger party is not democratic.

24. There is a good discussion of this in the South African context in Johnson and Schlemmer, "Into the Brave New World," pp. 365ff. However, the point obviously has wider relevance not only in the Third World, but also in various post-communist or socialist countries.

25. For an illustration of this in the South African context, see ibid., p. 365. A bias toward statist policies is obviously especially problematic in current circumstances where aid agencies and private investors strongly favor market orientations.

26. On the general point, see Tambiah, *Sri Lanka,* pp. 55–64. The quoted phrase is from David Little, *Sri Lanka: The Invention of Enmity* (Washington, D.C.: United States Institute of Peace Press, 1994). This situation can also undermine, if not destroy, the other political and economic policies that might be used to diminish conflict.

27. On the complicity in terror of some Serbian religious leaders, see, for example, *New York Times*, February 3, 1997, p. A3. Similar behavior has occurred in the Middle East, Cyprus, and Northern Ireland.

28. One should be careful to emphasize here that religious groups are themselves frequently internally divided and that many within the religious camp may be willing to compromise in exchange for concessions on matters of concern.

29. For evidence in this regard, see the essays in Douglas Johnston and Cynthia Sampsom, eds., *Religion: The Missing Dimension of Statecraft* (New York: Oxford University Press, 1994). For the important role of one private Catholic group in another protracted conflict, see Cameron Hume, *Ending Mozambique's War: The Role of Mediation and Good Offices* (Washington, D.C.: United States Institute of Peace Press, 1994).

30. One might argue that, other things being equal, the worst effects of religion are likely to occur early in a conflict—polarizing, intensifying, rationalizing—and the best effects are likely to occur late in the conflict, when battle fatigue has set in and both sides are seeking a way out.

31. Donald Harman Akenson, *God's Peoples: Covenant and Land in South Africa, Israel, and Northern Ireland* (Ithaca, N.Y.: Cornell University Press, 1992), p. 17.

32. See ibid., pp. 273–285, for Northern Ireland and pp. 297–302 for South Africa.

33. See especially Roy Foster, "Anglo-Irish Relations and Northern Ireland: Historical Perspectives," in Keogh and Haltzel, eds., *Northern Ireland and the Politics of Reconciliation*, pp. 31–32; see also Tambiah, *Sri Lanka*, pp. 87–113, and Akenson, *God's Peoples*, pp. 335ff.

34. The quoted phrase is from Foster, "Anglo-Irish Relations," p. 32.

35. On this effect in Bosnia, see Roger Cohen, "History vs. History: Foes in Bosnia Invoke the Past," *New York Times*, December 15, 1995, p. A7.

36. Note that I am not arguing that the misuse or invention of history causes the conflict. The misuse may indeed be an effect of a prolonged failure to resolve conflicts of interest. Over time, however, cause and effect become entangled, and the biased use of history can become an impediment to resolution of the clash of interests.

37. For one illustration of this phenomenon, see Whyte, *Interpreting Northern Ireland*, pp. 181–182.

38. Trying to rectify this situation by fiddling with the power balance by providing arms and aid may only generate an arms race and even greater tensions.

39. For an interesting discussion of this development in Northern Ireland, see Brendan O'Brien, *The Long War: The IRA and Sinn Fein, 1985 to Today* (Syracuse, N.Y.: Syracuse University Press, 1995), pp. 21ff.

40. This may help to explain a community's support for terrorism, even when the community knows that it will pay more quickly and deeply for the terror (through retaliation) than the terrorists. And perhaps it offers a little insight into support for, if not idolization of, a terrorist like Baruch Goldstein by parts of the religious right in Israel. On the lack of empathy for suffering by the other side and the approval of atrocities committed by one's own side, see Vamik D. Volkan, *The Need to Have Enemies and Allies: From Clinical Practice to International Relations* (Northvale, N.J.: Jason Aronson, 1988), pp. 86ff.

41. Amos Oz, *Under This Blazing Light: Essays* (Cambridge: Cambridge University Press, 1995), p. 7.

42. Perhaps the Israelis failed to realize how slowly the process of reconciliation would go after the Camp David Agreement and thus have been unnecessarily disappointed in the "cold peace."

43. See especially Marc Howard Ross, *The Culture of Conflict: Interpretations and Interests in Comparative Perspective* (New Haven, Conn.: Yale University Press, 1993).

44. For the quoted phrase, see Herbert C. Kelman, "Interactive Problem-Solving," in Vamik D. Volkan, Demetrios A. Julius, and Joseph V. Montville, eds., *The Psychodynamics of International Relationships*, vol. 1: *Concepts and Theories* (Lexington, Mass.: Lexington Books, 1990), pp. 145–160.

45. Ross, *The Culture of Conflict*, p. 160. This argument also suggests why merely agreeing on a formula or on the elements of a mutually agreeable long-term settlement may not suffice.

46. For a clear illustration in regard to Northern Ireland, see O'Brien, *The Long War*, pp. 103ff.

47. This conflict may be especially severe if, during the "long war," a kind of Gresham's law of conflict led to the destruction and silencing of voices of moderation in the external camp. The conflict may also grow if the external leadership returns, begins repressing its own population, and acts corruptly—as has happened in the West Bank and Gaza (see Chapter 2 by Khalil Shikaki herein). The point is that this behavior diminishes support for peace because expectations of improved standards of living are thwarted and because this generates fertile ground for extremists and opponents of compromise.

48. The tensions between external patron and one or another party to the conflict are apparent in the relations between Bill Clinton's administration and Netanyahu's government: both are constrained by the obvious influence of the Jewish community in the United States (whose support for Israeli policy is no longer monolithic) and by uncertainty about whether the Arafat regime either can or will fulfill its commitments.

Part 1
Case Studies

2

The Internal Consequences of Unstable Peace: Psychological and Political Responses of the Palestinians

Khalil Shikaki

Time after time, violence has demonstrated the fragility of the Palestinian-Israeli peace process. The nature of the agreement, the disparity in power relationships and political status, the language of the agreement, and the fact that it is an agreement between a state and a nonstate actor all combine to make it possible for violence to threaten the process. The transitional and open-ended nature of this agreement creates conflicting tendencies: one toward peace and the end of conflict, and another toward continued resistance and use of force. The great power disparities allow the strong to dictate terms and implementation processes at will. Its vague language and implicit conditionality allow each side to interpret the agreement differently. A change in the balance of power allows the weak to reinterpret the agreement in its favor and to violate it.

Open-ended transitionalism breeds ambiguity, conditionality, and reversibility. In the Israeli-Palestinian case, it also postponed for up to six years the resolution of the vital issues of the conflict. The logic of transitionalism and open-endedness is simple: it is expected to transform the political and psychological environment, making possible the resolution of very difficult problems. Conflict resolution in stages, however, carries risks. Each side in the conflict creates its own expectations; if unfulfilled, the disillusionment may block further progress and may take the process backward. The case in point is the Israeli expectation that an interim agreement must by necessity put an end to all acts of violence and the Palestinian expectation that it must put an end to occupation. The Israelis see that they are getting what they did not expect; the Palestinians fear that they are not getting what they did expect.

The September 1993 Israeli-Palestinian Declaration of Principles (DOP; also called "Oslo I") generated two dynamics: the first, by starting the process of ending occupation, is pushing for peace and reconciliation; the second, by "legitimating" some dimensions of occupation, is pulling toward conflict and violence. Since the major vital objectives of one or both sides may not be achieved during the transitional phase, neither side may be willing to completely give up its negotiating assets, including the ability to inflict violence, pain, and suffering.

Public opinion surveys among Palestinians reflect people's confusion: many support the process but also continue to support violence at times. Gradually, and as the peace process makes headway, people tend to abandon support for violence and increase support for the peace process. Support for the peace process is real and can be seen in advocacy of the negotiations, opposition to armed attacks against Israelis, approval for Yasir Arafat and for factions that embraced the peace process, defense of specific agreements, and backing for amending the charter, among other things.

Support for violence is discriminatory and not all out. For example, there is little support for attacks on civilians who are seen as innocents (as is the case in suicide attacks). There is more support, however, for attacks on soldiers and settlers who represent the symbols of continued presence of occupation.

The surveys indicate that the young, the students, and the educated tend to be more militant than the old, the women, the laborers, and the less educated. The young have fewer responsibilities, tend to be idealistic, and do not accept compromise. The more educated tend to be better informed and more critical of the conditional, tentative, and uncertain nature of the peace process. Students—because they are young, educated, and more politicized—tend to be hawkish, while housewives and laborers tend to be more dovish because they are generally less educated, older, and also have fewer responsibilities.[1]

* * *

The Israeli-Palestinian agreements—Oslo I and Oslo II—gave rise to three interconnected and interrelated processes within the Palestinian psychological and political environment: the peace process, the process of national reconstruction, and the process of transition to democracy. The first process provides the political context for the latter two. With the signing of the September 1993 DOP, the West Bank and the Gaza Strip have witnessed the acceleration of the development and interaction of all three processes.

The peace process affected Palestinian public attitudes regarding peace with Israel. It led to a transformation in the Palestinian psychological environment, causing more and more Palestinians to support negotiations and oppose violence. However, as the peace process stalled during 1996–1998, a significant number of Palestinians came to simultaneously support violence and the peace process. The young and educated in particular showed reluctance to embrace the process.

The peace process caused a change in the domestic Palestinian balance of power. It put an end to the continued rise of Islamists, diminished the appeal of the leftist nationalist forces, increased the support of the centrist nationalist forces, and shifted the overall balance in favor of the pro-peace camp. It also had an impact on the structure and composition of the ruling elite, with the national bourgeoisie emerging as the most powerful, the commercial class being rehabilitated and in control of the economy in the West Bank, and the popular leadership of Fatah (the largest maninstream nationalist movement) in control of the security services. The peace process put an end to the debate about a Jordanian role in the West Bank. As the Palestinian National Authority (PNA) expanded its effective control to the West Bank, the Jordan option was buried. However, it also raised questions about the legitimacy of the Palestinian political order.

The peace process also provided an opportunity for greater public participation in the political process. As the Israelis began a process of disengagement, a power vacuum was created, encouraging the emergence of many popular organizations and nongovernmental organizations (NGOs) and thus strengthening the role of civil society. The process also allowed general political elections to take place for the first time in modern Palestinian history. The peace process helped in consolidating a new legitimacy for a new Palestinian political order replacing a collapsing and aging one. At the same time, however, the process of transition to democracy has not been an easy one.

Lack of legitimacy of the Palestinian political order in its early stage affected the level of violence. The political group Hamas continued to see in violence a legitimate means of resistance since it did not recognize the legitimacy of the new political order.

The Israeli response to violence (the policy of closure, the threat of cantonization, the suspension of the peace talks, and the infliction of collective pain and suffering on the Palestinians in the West Bank and Gaza) led to a rise in support for violence among Palestinians (especially among students) after months of steady decline.

Measures taken by the PNA in response to Hamas violence have heightened concern among Palestinians about possible internal conflict. The optimism generated by the January 1996 elections has been fading away. These measures threatened the Palestinian process of transition to democracy.

The Peace Process

The Palestinian-Israeli peace process has been the most effective of the three processes affecting Palestinian politics and society. Above all, it has directly affected the two processes of national reconstruction and transition to democracy. The DOP provided a basis for ending decades of conflict and hostility between the two peoples. It allowed the mutual recognition of the legitimate and political rights of the two sides and began a long process of ending the Israeli occupation of the West Bank and the Gaza Strip. The Cairo Agreement (also known as the Gaza-Jericho Agreement) of May 1994 ended the Israeli occupation of most of Gaza and a small part of the West Bank. The Taba agreement (or Oslo II) of late September 1995 called for the Israeli redeployment from about 31 percent of the West Bank in a first stage to be followed by three further redeployments that would take the Israelis out of most of the West Bank by the end of 1997. In December 1995, Israeli forces were deployed outside all Palestinian cities and towns (except Hebron and Jerusalem) and other populated areas. In May 1996, Israelis and Palestinians opened the first session of permanent status negotiations. Despite continued violence from both sides—but especially from the Islamic Resistance Movement, Hamas, and Islamic Jihad—attacks on Israelis by the Fatah have completely ceased. The Palestinian authority has been gradually able to maintain security in areas under its jurisdiction and, in recent months, to take effective measures to prevent armed attacks on Israelis.

Citizens' attitudes toward the peace process, measured by several survey questions, mostly indicate a general high level of support for its continuation. This support is tempered by reservations about its future and some aspects of its outcome. For example, there are serious doubts among Palestinians that final status negotiations will result in an acceptable solution to both the Israelis and the Palestinians. There is also a sense of disappointment in the national reconstruction and transition to democracy efforts on the domestic level. For a majority of the supporters of the peace process, trust in the new Palestinian government remains high, and the perception that freedom of expression is better under the PNA prevails. The views of those in the opposition, those who do not support the continuation of the peace process or identify with the "peace camp," tend to be pessimistic on domestic issues.

Palestinian public opinion has been very supportive of the peace process and of factions that embrace it, and it has gradually shifted from supporting to opposing armed attacks against Israelis. Data from regular polls conducted by the Center for Palestine Research and Studies (CPRS) in Nablus has shown consistent support for the continued Palestinian-Israeli negotiations. Figure 2.1 reveals that a majority of 51 percent supported such negotiations in January 1994, despite widespread disappointment at the time due to the Israeli failure to show respect for deadlines indicated in the DOP. Support increased to over 65 percent in March and May of 1995, when progress in the negotiations created a measured degree of optimism on the street.

Figure 2.1 Support for Israeli-Palestinian Negotiations Among the General Public

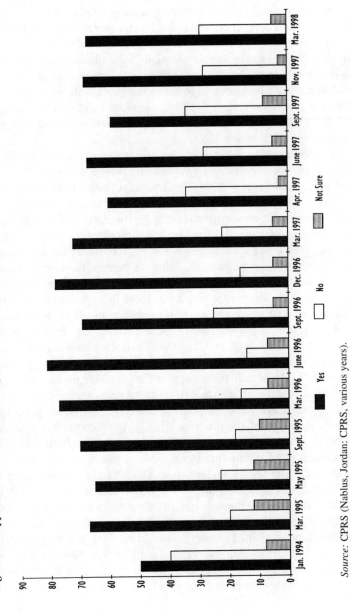

Source: CPRS (Nablus, Jordan: CPRS, various years).

In a September 1995 poll, in the wake of leaks of an impending agreement, support for the continuation of the peace process reached 71 percent. It continued to rise despite Israeli harsh measures and suspension of peace talks in the aftermath of the suicide attacks of February 1996, reaching 78 percent in March 1996, with a further rise to its highest level in June 1996, 81 percent, despite the election of Benjamin Netanyahu as Israel's prime minister in May. Yet support dropped eleven points by September 1996, to 70 percent, after the Israeli government's opening of Jerusalem's Wailing Wall tunnel that month. It increased to 79 percent in December 1996 as Israelis and Palestinians were putting the final touches on the Hebron Agreement, only to drop again to 60 percent in April 1997 as Israel announced its intention to build the Har Homa settlement in the Abu Ghnaim mountain area of Arab East Jerusalem. The ensuing deadlock in the peace process kept the level of support below 70 percent for the next twelve months, up to March 1998.

Even among students, the most hard-line group in the Palestinian community, support for negotiations gradually increased, as Figure 2.2 shows, from 44 percent in January 1994, to 62 percent in September 1995. However, a special CPRS poll conducted in May 1996 among students at three mainstream national universities (al-Najah, Bir Zeit, and Bethlehem) revealed a much more radical attitude among university students. The May student poll indicated that support for the continuation of the peace process did not exceed 42 percent, while 38 percent thought it should be stopped. In June 1996, after the Israeli elections, support among all students also began to drop, reaching 55 percent in September 1996. In the same month, opposition to the peace process among all students rose significantly to reach 39 percent, the highest since March 1995. Student opposition continued in April 1997, in the aftermath of the dispute over the Har Homa settlement, reaching 53 percent but dropping to 47 percent by September 1997. In March 1998, support for the peace process among students stood at 49 percent and opposition at 47 percent.

Palestinians have shown support not only for the peace process, but also for the outcome of the process—that is, for the specific agreements signed by the two parties. Support for the agreements, though, has been less stable and more fluctuating in response to major events and the pace of negotiations. The Oslo I agreement received 65 percent support in September 1993, but that support dropped to 40 percent in February 1994 due to continued deadlock in the negotiations after the two sides failed to reach an agreement on its implementation. As Figure 2.3 shows, however, support for agreements gained momentum in May 1994, reaching 57 percent after the signing of the Cairo Agreement. In October 1995, Oslo II, or the Taba Agreement, received 72 percent support, the highest level of support for the Oslo process ever registered. In a CPRS exit poll conducted during

Figure 2.2 Support for Israeli-Palestinian Negotiations Among Students

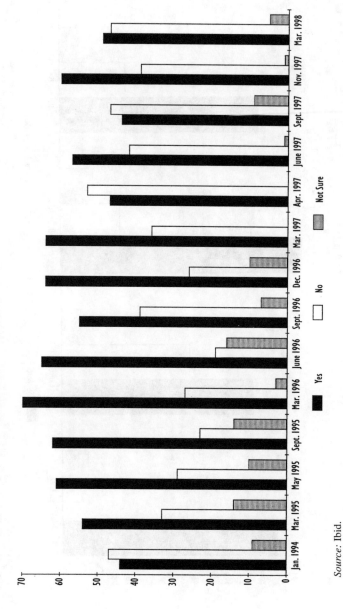

Source: Ibid.

Figure 2.3 Support for Specific Israeli-Palestinian Agreement Among the General Public

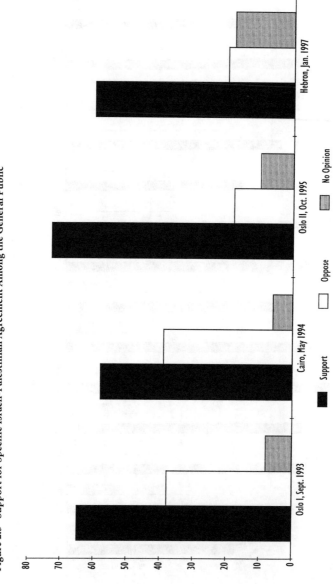

Source: Ibid.

the first Palestinian national elections in January 1996, only 17 percent of the voters expressed opposition to the Oslo Agreements, 50 percent were supportive, and 33 percent were between support and opposition. In March 1997, support for the Hebron Agreement reached 61 percent. In September 1993, about 57 percent were willing to amend the Palestinian National Charter in order to gain Israeli recognition of the Palestine Liberation Organization (PLO). In October 1995, 50 percent supported the amendment of the charter as required by Oslo II. In the same exit poll mentioned above, 40 percent said that they supported the amendment of the charter while 38 percent said they opposed it; the rest were undecided.

The success of the peace process can also be seen in the level of support and political sympathy received by the factions that embraced that process. Today there are three main political forces in the West Bank and Gaza: the "peace" or support camp, consisting of Fatah, Feda (the Democratic Front for the Liberation of Palestine [DFLP] split faction headed by Yasir Abd Rabbo), and Hizb al-Sha'b (the Palestinian People's Party); the national opposition camp, consisting of the Syrian-based Popular Front for the Liberation of Palestine (PFLP) and DFLP; and the Islamic opposition camp, consisting of Hamas, Islamic Jihad, other Islamist parties, and independent Islamists. Among the young and educated, especially students, support for the opposition is much higher than among the general public. Until early 1995, students divided their support almost equally between the peace and the opposition camps.

Figure 2.4 shows an increase in the general public support for the peace camp, from 39 percent in January 1994, to over 50 percent one year later, and to 58 percent in December 1995 during the Israeli redeployment from the West Bank cities. In June and September 1996, that support began to retreat to earlier levels. During 1997, support for the peace camp dropped somewhat, 40–42 percent, but increased to 47 percent in early 1998. Figure 2.5 shows that among students too, support for the opposition dropped from 41 percent in January 1994, to 34 percent and 33 percent in July and December 1995, respectively. A further decline in support for the opposition took place among students during 1996, dropping close to 20 percent from June to the end of that year. Support for the peace camp among students is noticeable for its fluctuation in 1997–1998, falling to 28 percent in the second half of 1997 and increasing to 39 percent in early 1998.

Support for the peace camp can also be seen in the level of support given to Yasir Arafat and his rivals. Figure 2.6 shows the rise in the level of support for Arafat from 44 percent in November 1994, in the midst of a poor performance by the Palestinian authority, to 58 percent in October 1995, after the signing of the Taba Agreement. One month before the January 1996 elections, support for Arafat stood at 69 percent. During the

Figure 2.4 Political Sympathy Among the General Public (by three political camps)

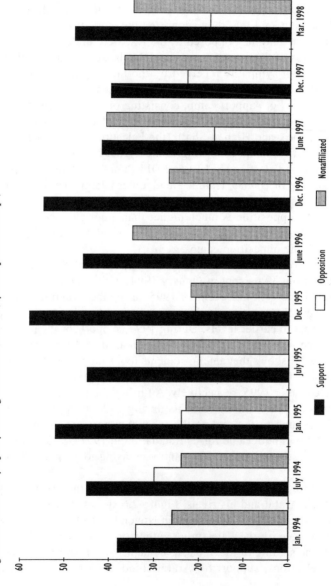

Source: Ibid.

Figure 2.5 Political Sympathy Among Students (by three political camps)

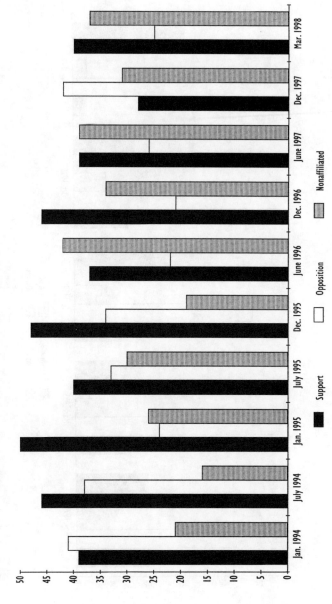

Source: Ibid.

Figure 2.6 Support Among the General Public for a PNA Future President

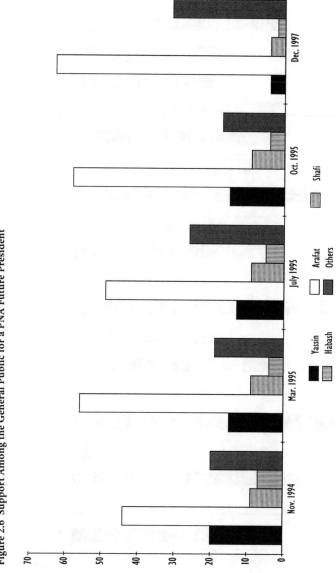

Source: Ibid.

period between November 1994 and October 1995, support for Ahmad Yassin, the leader of Hamas, dropped from 20 percent to 14 percent and support for George Habash, the head of the PFLP, dropped from 7 percent to 3 percent. A November 1997 survey showed support for reelection of Arafat as president at 62 percent, while Yassin and Haidar Abdul Shafi received 3 percent each, and Habash received less than 1 percent.

As the peace process made progress, Palestinian support for armed attacks against Israeli targets declined. Figure 2.7 shows that support for armed attacks against Israelis has dropped from 57 percent in November 1994, to 46 percent in February 1995, to 33 percent a month later, and to 21 percent in March 1996. These polls were conducted in the aftermath of major suicide attacks carried out by members of Hamas or Islamic Jihad. A significant rise in support for violence occurred for the first time since the beginning of the peace process in April 1997, in what might be seen as a public response to the Israeli decision to build the Har Homa settlement in Arab East Jerusalem. In September 1997, that level of support for violence had dropped by five percentage points to 35 percent.

In September 1995, Palestinians were asked specifically whether they supported attacks on Israeli civilian targets. Only 18 percent supported such attacks; but approximately 70 percent indicated support for attacks against settlers and military targets. The high level of support for armed attacks against soldiers and settlers should be interpreted as Palestinian insistence that the peace process must put an end to Israeli occupation and the presence of settlers, not as opposition to the peace process.

Even among students, the drop in support for suicide and civilian attacks has been remarkable. Figure 2.8 shows a decline in support from 72 percent in November 1994 to about 30 percent in September 1995 and March 1996, and a similar dramatic rise in opposition to such attacks from 23 percent in November 1994 to 58 percent in September 1995 and 62 percent in March 1996. Support for violence among students increased, however, during 1997, reaching 45 percent and 38 percent in April and September, respectively, while opposition to such attacks remained at about 46 percent during the same period. These figures, though, do not show the extent of support for violence among *university* students, as revealed by the May 1996 special poll mentioned earlier. That poll indicates that a majority (58 percent) of university students support armed attacks against Israeli targets, while only 25 percent oppose them. Moreover, 70 percent of university students believe that armed resistance is a realistic option for Palestinians if the current negotiations fail.

Support for peace, however, does not mean that an overwhelming majority of Palestinians expect the current process to lead to a Palestinian state or to a lasting peace between Israelis and Palestinians. As shown in Figure 2.9, in September 1993, only 45 percent believed the Oslo I agreement

Figure 2.7 Support for Armed Attacks Against Israeli Civilian Targets Among the General Public

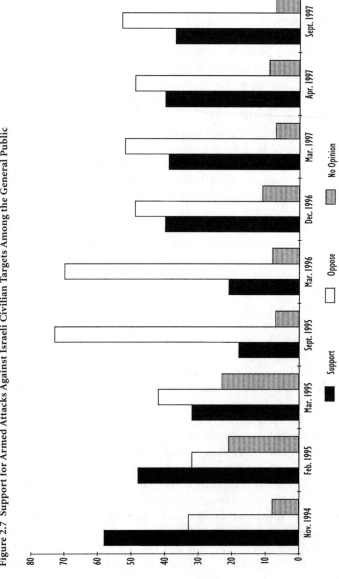

Source: Ibid.

Figure 2.8 Support for Armed Attacks Against Israeli Civilian Targets Among Students

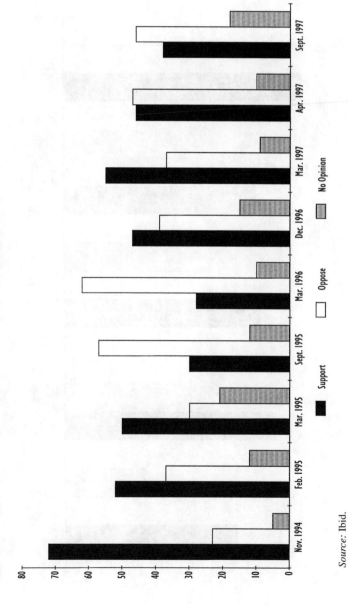

Source: Ibid.

Figure 2.9 Expectations Regarding the Establishment of a Palestinian State

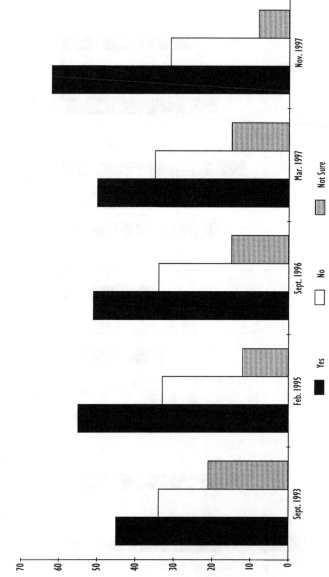

Source: Ibid.

would lead to the establishment of a Palestinian state. Some 30 percent expressed the belief that the agreement will not lead to such an outcome. In February 1995, 55 percent believed that the peace process would indeed lead to a Palestinian state but 33 percent still believed that it will not. In September 1996, during the violent confrontations between Palestinians and Israelis in the aftermath of the Israeli decision to open a Jerusalem tunnel, only 51 percent expected to see a state emerging from the peace process. However, in November 1997, almost two years after the extension of the Palestinian authority to about 30 percent of the West Bank, a strong majority of 62 percent expected to see a Palestinian state emerging in the next several years.

Nonetheless, in September 1995, almost 60 percent did not expect a lasting peace between the two peoples. Moreover, the better educated had more doubts about the potential for a Palestinian state or for a lasting peace. For example, in February 1994, only 49 percent of those with a university degree expected the establishment of a Palestinian state, and in August 1995, almost 69 percent of those believed the peace process would not lead to lasting peace. Part of the explanation for the lack of confidence in the future lies in the fact that most Palestinians do not trust Israeli intentions; when asked whether they trust Israeli intentions toward the peace process with the Palestinians, only 7 percent said yes while 81 percent said no. The lack of trust in the Israeli government intensified after the election of Netanyahu and the Israeli decision to build the Har Homa settlement, rising to 91 percent in March 1997.

In the aftermath of the election of a Likud government in Israel in May 1996 and the ensuing deadlock in Palestinian-Israeli negotiations, a gradual shift in opinion began to take place. A June 1996 poll indicated that West Bank and Gaza Strip Palestinians are almost evenly divided regarding the future of the peace process between Palestinians and Israelis. Ot those surveyed, 34.4 percent said that they were optimistic, 27.6 percent were pessimistic, and 33.3 percent thought that the elections would not affect the peace process (see Table 2.1). The more educated tended to have more pessimistic attitudes than the less educated; and the younger people were more likely to believe that there would be no change but were more optimistic overall than their elders. Note that this is a change in attitude from March 1996, when 40 percent thought that an Israeli government led by the Labor Party would be better in regard to Palestinian goals. Only 4.9 percent thought that the Likud Party would be better, and 43 percent expressed that there is no difference between the two Israeli parties.

On the final status negotiations, a similar pattern emerges. Overall, public opinion was almost evenly divided on the question of whether or not it is possible to reach an acceptable solution in the course of negotiations over Jerusalem, refugees, borders, and Israeli settlements. Around 44

Table 2.1 Attitudes on Israeli Elections, Final Status Negotiations, and Arab Summit by Selected Variables, June 1996 (weighted percentages and counts [n])

	Israeli Elections		Final Status		Arab Summit	
	Optimistic	Pessimistic	Acceptable	Unacceptable	Can Rely	Cannot Rely
Total	34.4 (336)	27.6 (270)	44.3 (432)	47.5 (464)	43.1 (419)	50.5 (491)
Region						
West Bank	29.6 (179)	31.4 (190)	39.8 (240)	53.2 (321)	40.1 (242)	54.5 (329)
Gaza Strip	42.2 (157)	21.4 (80)	51.6 (192)	38.2 (142)	48.0 (177)	44.0 (162)
Gender						
Male	33.3 (160)	31.0 (149)	42.6 (204)	52.0 (249)	36.3 (173)	60.0 (286)
Female	29.3 (174)	24.2 (119)	45.6 (224)	43.6 (215)	49.7 (243)	41.7 (204)
Education						
Illiterate–						
Elementary	38.5 (98)	27.9 (71)	50.9 (130)	35.3 (90)	55.2 (140)	34.2 (87)
Secondary–						
High School						
Diploma	35.3 (210)	27.4 (163)	43.9 (261)	49.3 (294)	41.7 (247)	53.5 (316)
College–Post-						
graduate	20.9 (25)	28.7 (34)	31.1 (37)	64.9 (77)	24.7 (29)	72.1 (85)
Age						
18–27	33.7 (119)	27.0 (95)	43.6 (154)	49.1 (174)	42.8 (150)	50.3 (177)
28–37	38.6 (98)	23.2 (59)	45.7 (116)	48.6 (123)	41.0 (103)	56.2 (141)
38–47	33.9 (57)	25.6 (43)	45.7 (77)	46.0 (78)	42.4 (71)	51.2 (86)
48+	31.4 (61)	36.1 (70)	42.5 (83)	43.9 (85)	48.2 (93)	42.6 (82)

Source: CPRS (Nablus, Jordan: CPRS, various years).

percent thought that it was possible to reach a solution acceptable to both parties, but 47.5 percent did not. In the Gaza Strip, belief in a positive outcome (51.6 percent) was higher than in the West Bank (39.8 percent). Once again, men were more pessimistic than women on this question (52.0 percent and 43.6 percent, respectively); and those with higher education levels were more likely to think that the final status negotiations would not lead to an acceptable solution than less educated respondents.

As suggested by the findings displayed above, Palestinians' future outlook could be described as a cautious blend of optimism and pessimism. These attitudes are inconsistent with those for support of the continuation of the peace process, which stood at 81.1 percent supporting and 13 percent opposing in June 1996 (see Table 2.2). Again, Palestinians in the Gaza Strip (86.3 percent) were more likely than those in the West Bank (77.8 percent) to support the continuation of the peace process; and West Bankers were nearly three times (16.8 percent) more likely to advocate stopping the process than Gazans (5.6 percent). On this question, there was no significant difference between the attitudes of men and women, but the difference between education and age levels was pronounced.

Such high support for the continuation of the peace process was reflected in the high percentage of total respondents (69 percent) who identified

Table 2.2   Attitude on Continuation of the Peace Process, Identification with Support/Oppose Camp, Amendment of National Charter by Selected Variables, June 1996 (weighted percentages and counts [n])

	Continuation		Camp		Amend Charter	
	Support	Oppose	Peace	Opposition	Support	Oppose
Total	81.1 (794)	12.5 (122)	69.0 (673)	11.6 (113)	47.6 (464)	31.9 (311)
Region						
West Bank	77.8 (469)	16.8 (101)	66.9 (403)	13.9 (84)	44.7 (270)	37.2 (225)
Gaza Strip	86.3 (321)	5.6 (21)	72.5 (270)	7.8 (29)	52.2 (194)	23.2 (86)
Gender	80.4 (385)	13.6 (65)	69.7 (333)	13.8 (66)	48.0 (230)	39.2 (188)
Male	81.7 (402)	11.6 (57)	68.7 (338)	9.3 (46)	46.9 (230)	25.1 (123)
Female						
Education						
Illiterate–						
Elementary	84.6 (216)	8.1 (21)	75.7 (193)	5.1 (13)	52.1 (133)	18.4 (47)
Secondary–						
High School						
Diploma	81.9 (488)	13.3 (79)	68.6 (408)	12.6 (75)	47.6 (283)	33.6 (200)
College–Post-						
graduate	69.6 (82)	17.9 (21)	57.6 (68)	19.9 (24)	36.4 (43)	53.5 (63)
Age						
18–27	77.2 (273)	14.4 (51)	62.6 (221)	14.5 (51)	45.7 (161)	34.4 (121)
28–37	79.7 (202)	14.5 (37)	69.7 (177)	12.7 (32)	46.2 (117)	36.1 (91)
38–47	82.5 (139)	11.8 (20)	73.7 (123)	8.8 (15)	52.8 (89)	29.4 (49)
48+	89.1 (172)	7.1 (14)	75.9 (148)	6.9 (13)	48.2 (94)	23.8 (46)

Source: Ibid.

themselves with a party or faction that supported the peace process. Of these Palestinians, 66.9 percent in the West Bank and 72.5 percent in the Gaza Strip aligned themselves with the "peace camp." On the decision by the Palestinian National Council (PNC) to amend the National Charter, a condition by Israel to continue the peace process, a little less than the plurality (47.6 percent) was in favor and a sizable percentage (32 percent) was opposed. Note again the relationships between age and education levels: the older and the less educated the respondent, the more likely he or she is to be in support of continuation of the peace process, identify with the pro-peace camp, and favor the amendment of the Palestinian National Charter.

Such high support for the continuation of the peace process but divided views on its outcome based on regional factors and future outlook is partly explained by the perception of improvement and trust (or lack of it) in the new Palestinian government and institutions. These findings suggest that there is a strong relationship between a positive or negative assessment of the domestic national reconstruction and transition to democracy efforts and support or opposition to the peace process. This observation can be measured in several attitudinal variables and tested by the strength of the relationship among these variables.

A September 1996 poll found that attitudes toward the peace process generally indicate a high level of support for its continuation (see Table 2.3). This finding is surprising given that this attitude was measured during and after a period of intense violent clashes between Palestinian civilians and security forces and Israeli military forces and settlers. Moreover, the poll also found that most Palestinians in the West Bank and the Gaza Strip think that the peace process has negatively affected the economy; and barely a majority think that it will lead to a state in the near future.

These poll results point to a possible explanation for this contradiction: support for the continuation of the peace process with Israel remains high because support for a political leadership that in turn supports the process is high. In other words, positive evaluation of the Palestinian leadership, particularly of the executive branch, is one of the most highly explanatory intervening variables in the relationship among people's perception of the economy, their expectations for the future, and support or opposition for the peace process.

Despite the high level of support for the peace process, general optimism about the future did not exceed 53 percent, while 41.6 percent of all respondents remained pessimistic.

Additional results in Table 2.3 indicate that although support for the peace process is high, there are, as usual, significant differences between

Table 2.3   Support for the Continuation of the Peace Process, Expectation for State and Future Outlook by Selected Demographic Variables, September 1996 (percentages and counts [n])

	Continuation		Expect a State		Future	
	Support	Oppose	Yes	No	Optimistic	Pessimistic
Total	69.8 (856)	24.8 (304)	50.9 (624)	33.5 (410)	53.0 (652)	41.6 (512)
Region						
West Bank	67.8 (524)	26.4 (204)	49.4 (382)	37.0 (286)	51.4 (399)	44.1 (342)
Gaza Strip	73.3 (332)	22.1 (100)	53.5 (242)	27.4 (124)	55.7 (253)	37.4 (170)
Gender						
Male	67.1 (412)	27.7 (170)	48.4 (296)	38.6 (236)	51.9 (319)	44.4 (273)
Female	72.5 (444)	21.9 (134)	53.4 (328)	28.3 (174)	54.1 (333)	38.9 (239)
Education						
Illiterate–						
Elementary	80.3 (252)	15.0 (47)	61.3 (193)	20.6 (65)	52.5 (166)	39.2 (124)
Preparatory–						
Secondary	68.8 (454)	26.4 (174)	52.1 (343)	33.6 (221)	55.1 (365)	39.9 (264)
2 Years						
College	67.7 (63)	21.5 (20)	41.9 (39)	46.2 (43)	46.8 (44)	48.9 (46)
B.A.–Post-						
graduate	54.7 (87)	39.6 (63)	30.8 (49)	50.9 (81)	48.7 (77)	49.4 (78)

Note: The "Don't Know" category has been excluded from this table, but percentages are based on the total number of responses.
Source: Ibid.

Palestinians from the West Bank and those from the Gaza Strip, between men and women, and among varying educational levels. As with many attitudinal variables, a consistent pattern of responses can be detected. That is, West Bankers, men, and higher educated Palestinians tend to be more critical and pessimistic than their counterparts.

For example, educational level of the respondents is strongly correlated with support or opposition to the peace process, expectations for statehood in the near future, and general optimism or pessimism. In nearly inverse proportion, respondents with less education have more positive views on these key issues than those with higher education levels. There is also a significant difference between men and women, but these differences disappear when educational level is controlled. In other words, women and men with similar educational levels, with few exceptions, tend to also share similar attitudes toward most issues.

Interestingly, according to this poll, which was conducted during a time of intense clashes in the Gaza Strip and in the aftermath of closures throughout Palestine, Gazans are more likely than West Bankers to support continuing the peace process, to be more optimistic, and to expect the current negotiations between Israelis and Palestinians to lead to a state. This finding is surprising but not unusual, for previous polls consistently show Gazans as more supportive and optimistic. Yet, unemployment rates in the Gaza Strip are consistently much higher than in the West Bank. Moreover, the poll represented in Table 2.3 finds that Gazans assess their economic conditions since the peace process more negatively than do West Bankers.

Overall, the majority of respondents (66.4 percent) think that the peace process has had a "negative" or "very negative" effect on the Palestinian economy. When these categories are combined, the difference between the West Bank and the Gaza Strip is nominal, as 69 percent of West Bankers and 72 percent of Gazans assess their economic conditions as negative or very negative. There is a significant difference, however, in that Gazans are more likely to think that the economy has been "very negatively" affected by the peace process, and West Bankers are more likely to assess the conditions as only "negative." Men (32 percent) are also more likely than women (23 percent) to think that the economy has been "very negatively" affected. Educational levels of the respondents, which are usually highly correlated with income levels, seem to have no discernible effect on their assessment of the economy. This could indicate that the problems of the economy (both in perceived and actual terms) are widespread, affecting all groups relatively similarly, rather than any group in particular.

These findings contradict conventional wisdom and one of the main premises of the peace process. That is, simply put, economic development will increase support for the peace process. What partly explains this contradiction, as indicated by the results of this and previous opinion polls, is that respondents' attitudes toward continuing the peace process are related to their assessment of the performance of their leadership and governmental institutions. It is the case that Palestinians in the West Bank and the Gaza Strip can be broken (analytically) into roughly two groups: those who support the continuation of the peace process and favor their government, and those who are critical of both.

A December 1996 poll found a significant rise in support for the continuation of the peace process, from 70 percent three months earlier to 78.7 percent. This rise brings the level of support to what it was before its deterioration in September 1996, after the intense and violent confrontations between Palestinian police and citizens and Israeli military and settlers.

The aftermath of these confrontations may be reflected in a significant rise in support for armed attacks against Israeli targets, reaching 40 percent in this survey; interestingly, at the same time, there is a rise in support for the peace process. In March 1996, support for suicide attacks, which took place in February 1996, was only 21 percent, compared with 33 percent in March 1995. Once again, this rise in support for armed attacks might be attributed to several factors: (1) the setback in the peace process, most directly relating to redeployment of the Israeli military in Hebron and other occupied territories; (2) the September confrontations, which were viewed as positive by Palestinians; and (3) the fact that this attitude was measured after a recent armed attack against settlers. (As found in September 1995, 19 percent supported armed attacks against Israeli civilians, which is quite low relative to the 70 percent support for attacks against settlers and 69 percent for attacks against military targets.)

As displayed in Table 2.4, there is a strong relationship between support or opposition for the peace process and attitudes toward armed attacks. It is the case that a majority (54.9 percent) of those who support the process also oppose attacks. On the other hand, 63.7 percent of the respondents who oppose negotiations with Israel express support for armed attacks. Such an opinion is also reflected in respondents' stated political

Table 2.4   Continuation of the Peace Process by Attitude Toward Armed Attacks,
(weighted percentages and counts)

	Position on Peace Process		
	Support	Oppose	No Opinion
Support Attacks	34.8 (298)	63.7 (115)	23.0 (12)
Oppose Attacks	54.9 (469)	27.5 (50)	22.7 (12)
No Opinion	10.3 (88)	8.8 (16)	54.3 (28)

Source: Ibid.

affiliation, as responses from opposition parties and groups are more supportive of armed attacks than supporters of the peace process: for example, Hamas (70.1 percent), the PFLP (59.0 percent), and Islamic Jihad (57.7 percent) compared with Fatah (32.1 percent) and the Independent Nationalists (29.4 percent).

In April 1997, support for suicide attacks was still standing at 40 percent, but support for negotiations declined to 60 percent. Support for attacks was particularly high among students and the young, reaching 45 percent. It was also high in refugee camps (45 percent) compared with cities (36 percent) and among Hamas supporters (60 percent) compared with Fatah supporters (39 percent). In a September 1997 survey, support for violence was still relatively high, standing at 36 percent. But support for the peace process rose in November 1997 to 68 percent. As noted above, such high support for the continuation of the peace process, but also growing support for political strategies and positions that contradict the basis of continuing peace process, is partly explained by a positive or negative evaluation of the Palestinian government and its institutions.

National Reconstruction

The peace process has directly affected the two dimensions of the process of national reconstruction: state building and the legitimacy of the Palestinian political order. It has given a strong impetus to the state-building process as it established, for the first time in modern history, a Palestinian National Authority in parts of the Palestinian territory. The PNA now has personal and territorial jurisdiction over all Palestinians and Palestinian-populated areas in the West Bank and Gaza (except for Hebron and Jerusalem). In addition to populated areas, Palestinian territorial jurisdiction extends to another 20 percent of the West Bank, the so-called Zone B. In this area, the PNA has complete territorial jurisdiction and functional authority, except over internal security, which is temporarily retained by Israel. In most areas of the remaining part of the West Bank, the PNA has limited functional responsibility. The Israeli-Palestinian interim agreement stipulates that once the Israelis carry out the phased further redeployments, the PNA will have complete jurisdiction over the whole West Bank and Gaza except for Jerusalem, settlements, and specified military locations.

Despite the fact that the PNA's functional jurisdiction does not, today, cover responsibility over foreign affairs, Oslo II does not impose any limitations on PLO activities in this area. In fact, the agreement authorizes the PLO to negotiate and sign agreements on certain matters with other states and international organizations on behalf of the PNA. Foreign countries are allowed to send representatives to, and open offices in, PNA areas. For example, the PLO is authorized to conclude postal agreements with foreign countries. The PNA can issue stamps and directly exchange mail with these countries. The PNA can also issue passports to Palestinians under its jurisdiction. Furthermore, it can issue "visiting permits" (i.e., visas) to people wishing to visit Palestinian areas even if those visitors do not belong to countries having diplomatic relations with Israel. Many countries have already opened offices in Gaza, Rām Allāh, and Jericho; Palestinian mail goes everywhere, and most countries recognize and accept the Palestinian passport.

The agreement also allows the PNA to build an airport, now almost complete, and a seaport, now in the planning stage. Television and radio stations have become operational. The PNA is allowed to establish power stations, dig for gas and oil, and operate a telecommunications network. The agreement allows the establishment of a strong security force made up of 30,000 men. In the West Bank, the Palestinian police can be armed with 4,000 rifles and 4,000 pistols in addition to 120 machine guns of 0.3 or 0.5 caliber and 15 light riot vehicles. In the Gaza Strip, the police force can be armed with 700 light personal weapons, up to 120 machine guns, and 45 wheeled armored vehicles. The security forces are also allowed to have ten coast guard ships.

State institutions have been established with functional jurisdiction similar to that of any other state except in the area of external security. Palestinian's sense of identity and of independence is stronger than ever after many decades of life under occupation and in exile, during which the Palestinian political "center" was subject to the harsh requirements of the Arab state system.

The peace process, however, has also had a negative impact on national reconstruction. The peace agreements have left unresolved the major issues of the conflict, including the future of Arab Jerusalem, Jewish settlements, and Palestinian refugees, in addition to the question of sovereignty over the land and the nature of the Palestinian political entity. The failure of the peace process to address these issues by postponing them to future negotiations has created serious defects in the state-building process and deepened internal Palestinian divisions regarding the legitimacy of the PNA and the entire Palestinian political order.

The current Palestinian political system, with the PLO at its center, emerged under difficult circumstances in the absence of statehood and in diaspora or under occupation. It gained legitimacy from Palestinian consensus over the goals and means of resistance and liberation as expressed in the Palestinian National Charter as amended in 1968. The legitimacy of the political center was also based on its ability to control and allocate resources. Cracks in the structure of the system began to appear in the mid-1970s when the PLO adopted the principle of the "national authority" or the independent state—that is, the two-state solution. The divisions became deeper with the rise of the Palestinian Islamic movement that saw in Islam the only source of political legitimacy. When, in November 1988, the PLO adopted the UN Partition Resolution and Security Council Resolution 242 and declared the independence of a Palestinian state in a small part of Palestine, the legitimacy of the whole political system came into doubt. The Gulf War of 1990–1991 tremendously weakened the status and legitimacy of the PLO at the regional and international levels. It became powerless in its ability to deal with and confront new challenges as it lost great sources of political and financial support. The peace process, the DOP, and the Gaza-Jericho Agreement came at a time when many were expecting the demise of the existing Palestinian political center. The PNA and its institutions were being established at that moment when many Palestinian political factions, inside and outside the PLO, were publicly expressing the view that the PNA was illegitimate. The bloody confrontation in Gaza in November 1994 between the PNA security forces and the supporters of Hamas exemplified the depth of the gulf between an existing order claiming legitimacy and challenging forces refusing to acknowledge its legitimacy.

The crisis over the legitimacy of the Palestinian political system stems from the loss of Palestinian consensus regarding national identity, territorial boundaries, and the goals and means of struggle. The old legitimacy was based on agreed-upon definitions of who the Palestinians are and what the boundaries of the Palestinian state are. It was also based on consensus of Palestine "liberation" as a goal and "armed struggle" as the means to achieve it. The new political order, conversely, revolves around a current legitimacy based on the goal of independence, state building, and the means of negotiations. "Palestine" is now defined as the West Bank and Gaza, and Palestinians are seen as primarily those living in "Palestine" and those seeking to live in it. But the new legitimacy lacks consensus, or an alternative to a consensus. The peace process that embodied the loss of consensus, and therefore legitimacy, provided at the same time a new source of legitimacy: popular will and a new mechanism to determine it— namely, elections, a subject to which we will return later.

Transition to Democracy

A close examination of the interaction among the three processes of peace, national reconstruction, and transition to democracy shows that the most successful process has been the first. National reconstruction has been less successful, while the transition to democracy has seen some reversal. The priorities and policies of the PNA and the donor community reveal a hierarchy of priorities, with peace on the top and democracy on the bottom.

The PNA's first priority has been the ending of occupation by promoting the peace process. Its second priority has been the strengthening of the capacity of the central government, with special emphasis on the creation of a strong security force. Economic development and the promotion of investment comprise a third priority, while the fourth has been the creation of state institutions.

The emphasis of the donor community on building the capacity of the PNA, rather than on supporting institutions of civil society, reveals a widespread belief that the success of the peace process requires political stability achievable only through the creation of a strong central authority. The PNA strongly advocated this view, not only because of its commitment to peace, but also because of its belief that the requirements of democracy may indeed contradict those of national reconstruction. Conceptually, of course, liberal democracy emphasizes the rights of the individual whereas nationalism places a higher value on the rights of the collectivity. But, more important, the need, in the early stage of state building, to put an end to anarchy, to assert the state's right to monopolize force, to halt political and economic dependence, and to eliminate any foreign rivals to the loyalty of the people may indeed prove to be more powerful than the need to democratize the political system.

The peace process in the early 1990s helped in easing Israeli restrictions on political activities in the West Bank and Gaza. As the process made progress, the Israeli policy became more "liberal" in dealing with the freedom of the press, free expression, NGOs, and party and factional activities and political mobilization. As the Israelis gradually loosened their grip on Palestinian life and stopped direct interference in internal Palestinian matters, a power vacuum was created, allowing a degree of revitalization in democratic life and the "resurrection" of civil society. But the peace process and the resulting emergence of the PNA also had some serious negative repercussions for the process of transition to democracy in Palestinian society and politics. It weakened the institutions of civil society and led to the adoption by the PNA of undemocratic policies aiming at "protecting" the peace process and the process of national reconstruction.

The Palestinians succeeded during the 1980s in creating social, political, professional, and popular civil institutions that fulfilled many functions, including those performed in normal circumstances by the state. Most of these institutions received the full support of the PLO, which saw in them preliminary steps toward a future Palestinian state. With the establishment of the PNA, many of these institutions became redundant. Some were already weakened by the financial difficulties the PLO faced after the Gulf War. Others were absorbed by PNA institutions and ministries when these were established in 1994 and 1995. Still others lost their top men, who left to work for the PNA.

Institutions of civil society received another blow when they lost some of their foreign financial sources. Despite hopes and expectations of increased financial allocations from donor countries and agencies to Palestinian NGOs and their projects, the opposite took place. Little, if any, money from the emergency assistance program actually went to Palestinian NGOs. The political and economic reality that emerged in the months immediately after the implementation of the Gaza-Jericho Agreement dashed liberal hopes of a smooth and peaceful transition to self-rule. Rising unemployment, economic stagnation, political violence, and Israeli closure of territories under PNA control contributed to delays in the peace process and to the weakening of the PNA. Liberal visions had to give way to a more somber assessment, and focus shifted from strengthening Palestinian civil society to building the capacity of the central government. More resources went directly to PNA institutions, bureaucracy, and security services. The shift in priorities not only weakened the institutions of civil society, it also served to strengthen the ability of the PNA to contain and, if needed, emasculate these institutions. Despite the emergence of new NGOs, taking advantage of the transitional nature of the current political phase, the ability of these institutions to provide a buffer between state and society remains uncertain and temporary at best.

Along the same lines, the PNA has tended to implement policies and programs and to enact laws and propose draft legislation that aim at strengthening its central control and coercive capabilities, at "protecting" the peace, and at asserting national agendas at the expense of liberal democratic principles and practices. The PNA dealt a heavy blow to democracy, human rights, and the nascent judicial system when it established military security courts in February 1995, invoking the hated 1945 emergency regulations under which Palestinians have been subjugated by the Israeli military occupation for over twenty-eight years. These courts were established in order to deter Hamas and Islamic Jihad from attacking Israeli targets and to show the Israeli government that the PNA was serious about combating terrorism. Several people, including opposition figures not directly involved in attacks against Israelis, were tried and convicted by these courts, sometimes in the absence of lawyers. Mass arrests of opposition leaders and activists, without charges or trials, became a routine matter after every major attack on Israeli targets. Many people complained of torture, and several suspects died in jail during interrogations.

Moreover, the PNA took repressive measures aimed at suppressing the freedom of the press, including the temporary closure of opposition papers and the banning of distribution of the mainstream *al-Quds* newspaper for publishing anti-Oslo views of opposition figures. The newspaper *al-Nahar* was temporarily banned in July 1994 for its pro-Jordanian tendencies and has been allowed to reopen only after ensuring a change in editorial direction.

Another pro-Jordanian paper, *Akhbar al-Balad,* was also banned at the same time and could not reopen. Newspaper editors have understood the message and have begun to exercise self-censorship. *Al-Quds* has refrained from publishing news stories about torture in Palestinian jails, reports by human rights organizations on press freedom, and, ironically, public opinion polls showing widespread popular opposition to PNA restrictions on press freedom. Threats have also been made against a few academic and political figures opposed to the peace process and to Arafat's leadership aiming at silencing them. At least one human rights organization and some NGOs have also come under similar pressure.

While threats and intimidation by security services may have been used to tame and coerce Palestinian newspaper editors, opposition figures, and NGO heads, proposed draft legislation—some already enacted, before the elections of January 1996 (laws reflecting similar antidemocratic mentality)—might be available to the PNA to provide legal means of coercion. In particular, the press law and the draft legislation for NGOs and political parties reveal a trend toward the concentration of power in the hands of the executive authority at the expense of society. Societal forces, including political parties, are suspected and seen as the "enemy." Research institutions, publishing houses, printing shops, and polling organizations are required to obtain permits for their activities and to submit copies of their publications to the Information Ministry. NGOs are required to seek permission before they can accept funding from foreign sources. Political parties are required to ensure that their files and mail are available for government inspection on a routine basis.

Public opinion polls indicate strong criticism of the status of democracy in Palestine. For example, a June 1996 survey found that Palestinians of the West Bank and the Gaza Strip are divided on the status of freedom of expression, an important indicator in the transition to democracy, under the Palestinian National Authority (see Table 2.5). About 48 percent of the respondents believe that freedom of expression has improved since the arrival of the PNA, while another 48 percent think it has worsened or has not changed. Palestinians in the Gaza Strip (52.1 percent) are more likely than those in the West Bank (44.8 percent) to perceive this improvement; there is no regional difference concerning those who perceive worsening conditions; but more West Bankers (20.6 percent) than Gazans (12.4 percent) note no change in the degree of this freedom since the arrival of the PNA. Similarly, 49 percent feel that people today cannot criticize the PNA without fear, and only 42 percent feel that they can. There is no significant difference between West Bankers and Gazans regarding this issue. For both of these variables, men are more likely than women to think the freedom of expression has become worse or has not changed under the PNA and to fear criticism of the PNA. There are also strong

Table 2.5 Attitudes on Freedom of Expression and Ability to Criticize the PNA, by Selected Variables, June 1996 (weighted percentages and counts [n])

	Freedom of Expression			Criticism of PNA	
	Better	No Change	Worse	Without Fear	With Fear
Total	47.6 (465)	17.5 (171)	30.5 (298)	43.9 (429)	49.1 (479)
Region					
West Bank	44.8 (271)	20.6 (125)	30.3 (183)	44.3 (268)	48.3 (292)
Gaza Strip	52.1 (194)	12.4 (46)	30.9 (115)	43.3 (161)	50.3 (187)
Gender					
Men	41.0 (197)	15.8 (76)	39.4 (189)	39.0 (187)	55.3 (265)
Women	53.5 (263)	19.1 (94)	22.2 (109)	48.9 (241)	42.7 (210)
Education					
Illiterate–Preparatory	56.5 (144)	16.6 (43)	22.4 (57)	52.0 (133)	38.5 (98)
Secondary–High School Diploma	47.6 (284)	18.0 (107)	30.4 (181)	43.6 (260)	50.6 (302)
College–Postgraduate	27.8 (33)	16.1 (19)	49.6 (59)	29.3 (35)	63.8 (76)
Age					
18–27	42.3 (150)	18.6 (66)	34.5 (122)	39.4 (139)	55.2 (195)
28–37	46.4 (118)	17.6 (45)	32.5 (83)	44.7 (114)	49.7 (126)
38–47	50.7 (86)	18.6 (31)	25.7 (43)	46.0 (77)	44.3 (74)
48+	55.9 (109)	14.5 (28)	24.6 (48)	49.8 (97)	40.4 (79)

Source: Ibid.

negative relationships between the two variables with age and education of the respondent: the older and less educated a respondent, the more likely it is that he or she thinks that freedom of expression has improved and that he or she can criticize the PNA without fear.

Related to these issues of freedom of expression and the ability to criticize the PNA without fear, the CPRS asked respondents to rate the treatment of Palestinian citizens by the police and security services. On this question, 44.3 percent of the respondents feel treatment is "good," 36.8 percent answered "fair," and 14.4 percent "bad." Although Palestinians on the West Bank tend to be more critical of the PNA and its institutions overall, 46.7 percent rate the police and security services as "good," compared with 45.5 percent in the Gaza Strip, who mostly (42 percent) assessed the treatment of citizens as "fair." Men have a more critical attitude toward the police and security services than women. There is also a strong negative relationship between education level and assessment of treatment: the more educated, the more likely to rate treatment poorly. Older respondents tend to think that the treatment is "good," and the bulk of the younger respondents think it is "fair." Refugees also gave a more favorable assessment than nonrefugees.

However, in a December 1996 poll, 42.9 percent of all respondents assess the status of democracy in Palestine as positive (compared with 33.7 percent who assessed it as fair and 22.8 percent negative); this is low compared with their evaluations of democracy in Israel, the United States, and France. Dissatisfaction with the PNA extends to other pertinent issues relating to the transition to democracy in Palestine. A sizable percentage (52.7 percent) of all respondents think that people today cannot criticize the authority without fear. This opinion is also reflected in the low percentage (27.7 percent) of respondents who think that the press is free in Palestine. Moreover, only 35.3 percent expressed their belief that Palestine is heading toward democratic rule, while only 14.7 percent think the opposite (i.e., that their government is heading toward dictatorship). As with the evaluation of the status of democracy in Palestine, certain demographic groups are more critical of the PNA: specifically, men, West Bankers, and opposition parties and groups, as well as more educated Palestinians.

Needless to say, the antidemocratic tendency in the PNA institutions goes beyond the constraints of the peace process and the requirements of national reconstruction. It is obvious that the process of transition to democracy is also affected by deeper dynamics such as socioeconomic development and political culture. Public opinion, the nature of the emerging ruling elite, and the structure of the new political system, including the electoral system, also play a significant role in the transition process.

Three different political elites provided leadership to West Bank Palestinians over the past several decades: the traditional commercial class and big clans, the national bourgeoisie, and the grassroots and popularly supported leadership of the factions and resistance movements. The traditional commercial class and landowners ruled in the aftermath of the 1948 defeat under the Jorandian monarchy. This class became loyal supporters of the Hashemites and continues to have Jordanian tendencies today. Its loyalty to the Palestinian national agenda has always been questioned by the PLO and its supporters. Nablus has been, and still is, the center of the Palestinian commercial class. The Israeli occupation in the West Bank in 1967 unintentionally led to the gradual weakening of this class. The process of the proletarianization of the Palestinian peasantry and its movement to the cities, due to Israel confiscation of Palestinian land, water policy, and the opening of the Israeli market to the Palestinian laborers, weakened the hold of the traditional commercial class over Palestinian rural society. The rise of Palestinian nationalism and the spread of the national message in the confrontation with Israeli occupation forces further weakened the hold of that class over the cities and towns. The rise of the Palestinian national bourgeoisie as a potential alternative elite gave the national movement a big boost.

The Palestinian national bourgeoisie emerged in the late 1960s and early 1970s under Israeli occupation. Its nationalist agenda made it the enemy of occupation and gradually gave it popular legitimacy. Its members came from families belonging economically to the commercial class and from urban middle-class intellectuals and professionals. This elite was the first to articulate the demand for an independent Palestinian state. By the mid-1970s, it had succeeded in convincing the PLO to adopt its position regarding statehood. But before it succeeded in organizing a grassroots support loyal to it, the new elite was decapitated by the policies of then Defense Minister Ariel Sharon, who preferred to revive a traditional rural class of landowners and elite families. By the early 1980s, the West Bankers were without a dominant elite.

A popular leadership of national activists emerged to fill the vacuum. Many grassroots, student, and professional organizations flourished in the 1980s. Some of these organizations were Islamic, though most were nationalist. The Israeli authorities played a role in the politicization of the traditional Palestinian Islamists in an attempt to weaken the nationalists. The period of the 1980s witnessed the politicization of the poor and the middle class and their mobilization in the service of organized political and paramilitary factions. It was this leadership, mostly poor and lower middle class, which led the intifada and sustained its momentum over a period of several years from 1987 onward.

The peace process in the early 1990s led to the creation of a coalition between the grassroots leadership, which effectively controlled the street, and the national bourgeoisie, which received substantial media attention. While the former had its own legitimacy derived from street support, the latter had to rely on PLO backing for legitimacy. The Oslo Agreements led to the formation of the Palestinian National Authority. This allowed the return of Arafat, some 5,000 Palestine Liberation Army (PLA) men, and several hundreds from the PLO bureaucracy. In the first few months of his arrival, Arafat sought to base his authoritarian rule on a coalition with senior PLO and PLA officials, professionals and bureaucrats from the middle class and the national bourgeoisie, and business leaders from the commercial class and the big families.

The PLO officials and the bureaucratic and professional class representing the national bourgeoisie came primarily from the returning PLO cadre and from Fatah's leadership of the middle and upper-middle class. They owed their power positions to Arafat and not to their status within the community. This political elite has been socialized in such Arab countries as Syria, Iraq, and Egypt. It has been raised with nationalist teachings and has learned to emphasize national agendas over democratic ones. A quota system, like the one employed in the PNC, was the closest they ever came to a democratic practice. The commercial class, needed in the process of rebuilding and development, poses no immediate threat to Arafat's hold on power. It commands little respect or loyalty in the street, and it had been effectively eliminated from power positions during the intifada and the years preceding it. Most of the leaders of this class had been living outside the West Bank and had returned only recently. The economic interest of the commercial class and big families and clans may not necessarily invite public participation in the political process.

The third ruling partner in Arafat's coalition is the Palestinian military. Initially, Arafat sought to marginalize Fatah in his attempt to present himself as the leader of all Palestinians—Fatah's effective participation in the ruling elite would have weakened Arafat's hold on power. The PLA poses no threat to Arafat's rule since it is apolitical: it had been deployed in several Arab countries and never had any effective unified command and control; and since it all came from the outside, it had no local loyalties to compete with the loyalty to Arafat. Arafat appointed a man with little political ambition or following as head of the national security forces. Arafat believed that a nonpartisan PLA would be more successful in maintaining security, the most essential element in the Israeli-Palestinian peace process. The bloody confrontation in November 1994, between the Islamists and the Palestinian security forces in Gaza, led Arafat to introduce changes in his ruling coalition. Fatah now was invited to become a true partner in order to confront and neutralize Hamas. Arafat's reliance on the PLA to shield him and the peace process from the Islamic opposition proved a failure. He then called upon Fatah's militia for help. Palestinian security forces were opened to thousands of Fatah activists. The number of armed Palestinian police officers increased from 8,000 to about 18,000. Most of the Fatah men had spent years in Israeli jails and had been repeatedly subjected to Israeli interrogation techniques.

Palestinian Elections: Political Participation and Legitimacy

Contrary to some predictions after the Oslo Agreements that neither the Israelis nor the Palestinian National Authority would press for elections, in the end they were indeed held and served the purposes of both. For the Israelis, because the Palestinian issue is the crux of their legitimacy, it was not enough to make peace with a narrow leadership, as had been the case with other Arab countries; they needed to make peace with the Palestinian people, to make sure that the Palestinians supported the process. For the PLO, since the old Palestinian consensus was gone, the elections were needed to give Arafat a mandate and to give legitimacy to a new political order.

Therefore, the democratic agenda has been absent, and elections should not be seen primarily as the start of the transition to democracy but, rather, in the light of their role in nation building and peacemaking. This explains the attempts to manipulate the elections to serve both Israeli and Palestinian needs, why Arafat adopted an electoral law that favored the strongest party (his own faction), and why he did not encourage the participation of opposition forces beyond a token gesture.

Elections for the Palestinian legislative council have been one of the most critical developments in modern Palestinian politics. Israelis and Palestinians agreed in Oslo II to hold elections immediately after the Israeli redeployment from the populated areas in the West Bank. The agreement called for the establishment of an eighty-two-member council (later changed to eighty-eight members) with the power of legislation covering "primary and secondary legislation, including basic laws, regulations, and other legislative acts." The council's jurisdiction covers all areas under Palestinian control today and will extend gradually to cover all of the West Bank and Gaza except for the areas subject to final status negotiations, that is, Jerusalem, settlements, and specified military locations. Separate elections for the president—or, to use the term employed in Oslo II, "Ra'ees"—of the executive authority were mandated by the agreement. The elected president is to form a cabinet of ministers from among the elected members of the council. A few unelected members may also be appointed as ministers.

Probably the most remarkable thing about the elections was the level of voter turnout, which was much higher than anticipated and reached about 70–80 percent in the West Bank and 88 percent in the Gaza Strip. Even more striking was the heavy participation of supporters of the opposition factions that had repeatedly called on their supporters to boycott the elections. CPRS findings indicate that participation by the supporters of nationalist opposition, such as the PFLP, was close to the national level, while participation by Hamas supporters reached about 60 percent. After so many years of seeking self-determination and protesting the system of appointment by the leadership, people wanted to take part in the election process and did not see any viable alternatives being offered by the opposition, which is why very few heeded the calls to boycott.

Most of the international and local monitors and human rights organizations, though critical about some aspects, reported that elections had taken place in a quiet and fair environment and that reported irregularities did not have an effect on the results. The CPRS concluded from its own observations at polling stations throughout the Palestinian territories that the elections were very well organized and generally fair and honest, especially considering the complexity of the operation and the fact that these were the first Palestinian elections ever held. This was a great achievement for the Central Election Commission, which was able, with technical and financial assistance from the European Union and very short notice, to organize and train more than 7,000 teachers to work as officials in the roughly 1,600 polling stations in the West Bank and the Gaza Strip. While there were disruptions and cheating here and there at a minor level, there was no evidence of widespread violations or that the PNA played any role in the cheating. There was no violence at all connected with the elections and no systematic intervention by either the PNA or the security services.

The results of the elections confirmed Fatah's position as the dominant force in Palestinian politics. They also showed that the small political factions had very little political support in the street: of the thirteen other political factions that ran, only one managed to get a single candidate elected. One could say that the elections dealt a major blow to all the small parties and will certainly lead them all to rethink their positions; indeed, we may even see the disintegration of many of the existing political parties.

The parties that boycotted the elections also suffered a severe setback. The large turnout of Hamas supporters at the polls reflected not only the party's failure to successfully communicate its message, but also divisions within the movement over the issue of participation in the elections; many of the leaders inside, and particularly in Amman, resisted. Confirming the poor showing of Hamas is the fact that the most prominent Hamas supporter to win a seat on the council was Imad al-Faluji, who won mainly because he was on the Fatah list. In the West Bank, the only winner close to Hamas was a member of the Masri family of Nablus, who won primarily because of his family support. The PFLP was also hit hard by most of its supporters going to the polls, despite the clear call to boycott.

In assessing the elections overall, it is useful to apply what one might call "tests of legitimacy." Four such tests are considered critical. The first is voter participation, which should reach a minimum of 55 percent, including the important participation of the opposition; in fact, as mentioned above, about 80 percent participated. Second is voter perception concerning the elections themselves; a CPRS exit poll showed that only 5 percent pronounced the electoral law as unfair, and only 4 percent judged the process itself unfair. Third is voter perception of the role of the council; most thought it would have an important role in deciding fundamental issues confronting Palestinian society. In other words, most voters believed they were participating in a real process, with only 7 percent believing the council's role to be a charade. The fourth test is the role of clan or family loyalties and whether these took precedence in the voting over political affiliation and other issues. Again, based on the CPRS exit poll, it seems clear that the most important criterion for the selection process was political affiliation, followed by the character of the candidate himself: moral qualities, religiosity, his role in the community, public service, and so forth. Family or clan considerations figured only as a third-level priority. It is for these reasons that one may conclude that the elections did indeed pass the tests of political legitimacy.

The elections may also have had a significant impact on all three processes of peace, national reconstruction, and democratization. Three highly significant, and peace-related, developments have been awaiting the holding of elections. The first has been the official transfer of powers and responsibilities from the Israeli military government and its civil adminis-tration to the elected Palestinian council. Meanwhile, and pending the in-auguration of the elected council, such powers and responsibilities were exercised by the PNA created by the Cairo Agreement. The second awaited development has been the further Israeli redeployments to commence six months after inauguration of the council, with the stipulation that such re-deployments lead to the extension of Palestinian jurisdiction to remaining areas of the West Bank except those subject to final status negotiations. While no such redeployment has taken place in the aftermath of the elec-tions due to change of government in Israel, the subject is now under dis-cussion. The third development has been the convening of the PNC to amend the Palestinian charter by removing articles that deny Israel's right to exist and other references that violate Palestinian commitments to re-nounce violence. Moreover, by providing legitimacy to the new Palestin-ian political order, created by the Israeli-Palestinian agreements, elections also extended legitimacy to the agreements themselves. However, the rules of the new political order deny legitimacy to the use of violent and non-democratic means, heretofore regarded as legitimate by the Palestinian charter. Finally, elections are expected to make the Palestinian political process more responsive to public opinion in the West Bank and Gaza. This public opinion has been clearly more supportive of the peace process, as shown above.

In terms of the impact the elections have had on the process of na-tional reconstruction, they provided the Palestinian people an opportunity, for the first time in their history, to choose their own political representa-tives. In doing so, elections granted legitimacy to the emerging Palestinian political system. They gave birth to strong political institutions and helped institutionalize a new consensus, based on modern political practices, re-placing the older and dying one. Elections have also been useful as a means of unifying Palestinians in the two geographically separate areas of the West Bank and the Gaza Strip and in integrating the Palestinians of Arab Jerusalem into the political process of national reconstruction. The Oslo II agreement describes elections as "a significant interim preparatory step toward the realization of the legitimate rights of the Palestinian peo-ple." Many Palestinians and non-Palestinians see them as an expression of popular sovereignty and a prelude to self-determination and statehood.

On the negative side, elections in the "inside"—that is, in the West Bank and Gaza—may have led to the marginalization of the concerns and institutions of the Palestinian diaspora. It is worth recalling that the origi-nal Israeli insistence on Palestinian elections, as can be seen in all Israeli self-rule proposals since Menachem Begin's 1977 proposal, aimed at creating a local Palestinian leadership that would replace, or be a rival to, the PLO. The Oslo process made elections irrelevant in this regard, as it signified an Israeli realization that the PLO was irreplaceable. Nonetheless, elections still remained useful, from an Israeli perspective, in meeting a related Israeli goal: to focus Palestinian attentions and energies on the inside and its agendas—namely, independence—thus marginalizing the Palestinian diaspora and its agendas, such as the right of return. Elections may indeed have helped accelerate the process of marginalization of the "outside," a process that the Oslo Agreements may have triggered. The elected council of the "inside" may be seen as having more legitimacy than the appointed PNC in the "outside," whose mandate might now be questioned. Other PLO institutions are likely to be weakened as their functions are gradually assumed by the new institutions in the inside and as they lose their financial resources.

Most important of all, elections may have the potential of being a liberalizing experience in which Palestinians are invited to participate in the political process. In such a participatory process, individuals, factions, and political parties may have had the opportunity to exert influence, to mobilize forces and aggregate interests, and thus improve the respect for political and civil rights and help decrease repression. In Oslo II, the Palestinians committed themselves to "open government," accountability, and separation of powers as democratic bases for the establishment of Palestinian political institutions. But one must also remember that elections might yet become the means to regulate and institutionalize dissent or, worst yet, to provide legitimacy to repression. They might have been seen by the ruling Palestinian elite as a means to obtain legitimacy and consolidate power.

The process of transition to democracy in the West Bank and Gaza faces severe challenges. The peace process will probably continue to affect it negatively, particularly as popular frustration mounts when final status negotiations are deadlocked. In the aftermath of the suicide attacks of Hamas in February 1996, and as the peace process stalled, the PNA record on human rights and respect for democratic values has deteriorated. Under pressure to deliver security, the PNA made it the most valued commodity. In the absence of progress in the peace process, and in order to keep the process alive, the PNA began to rely more and more on coercion and brute force in order to deliver security for Israelis. The security services, whose job it is to provide security, amassed a great deal of power and were given a free hand to employ it as they saw fit. Violation of basic human and political rights became widespread. The press lost whatever freedom it may have enjoyed in the past. The opposition was silenced by fear and intimidation. The judiciary, already emasculated under Israeli occupation, was weakened and its decisions ignored.

The resolution of the conflict between national and democratic agendas will depend on the way decisionmakers order the hierarchy of their priorities: Will a security-related agenda, political independence, and economic well-being continue to take precedence over political participation, accountability, and freedom of expression? Will the Palestinian National Council play a prominent role in Palestinian politics? Or will it become subordinate to the executive authority? The preceding discussion may have already provided some answers to these questions, but more clues are needed before final answers can be given.

Note

1. All the data in the text, tables, and figures in this chapter are from polls conducted by the Center for Palestine Research Studies, from 1994 to the present, under the supervision of the author. For further information or for copies of the polls, please contact Khalil Shikaki, Center for Palestine Research Studies, P.O. Box 132, Nablus, Palestine, (tel.) 972-9-238-0383, (fax) 972-9-238-0384.

3

The Oslo Agreements:
Toward Arab-Jewish Reconciliation

Moshe Ma'oz

The Oslo Agreements of September 13, 1993, and September 28, 1995, and the Hebron Agreement of January 15, 1997, have appeared to mark the beginning of a new era of peacemaking between Arabs and Jews in the Holy Land, possibly in the whole Middle East region. This has certainly been the vision and goal of the leaders of both Israel and Palestine, Yitzhak Rabin and Yasir Arafat, who, alongside U.S. President Bill Clinton, signed both Oslo Agreements (I and II) in Washington D.C.: thus the agreement of September 1995 "reaffirming their determination to put an end to decades of confrontation and to live in peaceful coexistence, mutual dignity and security, while recognizing their mutual legitimate and political rights . . . [and] their desire to achieve a just, lasting and comprehensive peace settlement and historic reconciliation through the agreed political process."[1]

To be sure, the Oslo and Hebron Agreements were approved not only by the official Israeli and Palestinian leaders, but also by the majorities in both communities in Israel, the West Bank and the Gaza Strip: the Oslo accords were initially backed by 60–65 percent and reached 75–80 percent following the Hebron protocol. Significantly, the Hebron Agreement also confirmed the Oslo Agreements and was signed by the new Israeli Likud leaders who had previously rejected the Oslo Agreements. The historical and psychological importance of this event must be stressed: for the first time in the century-old conflict between Arabs and Jews over Palestine/ Eretz Israel (or one hundred years since the first Zionist Congress in Basel, 1897), the major Israeli right-wing Likud Party gave up its ideological-political claim to the entire "land of Israel" and pragmatically acknowledged the principle of sharing the land with the Palestinian national community, led by the Palestine Liberation Organization (PLO). This major change came fifty years after the Labor movement, while leading the Jewish community, accepted UN Resolution 181 of November 1947, providing for the partition of Palestine/Eretz Israel into two states—Arab and Jewish. Tellingly, the PLO, after decades of rejection, accepted UN Resolution 181 only in late 1988, thus preparing the ground, alongside other circumstances, for adopting the Oslo accords of the 1990s.

Nevertheless, these inspiring historical accords consisted merely of a Declaration of Principles (DOP) and interim agreements regarding Palestinian self-government in Gaza and Jericho (and subsequently in other parts of the West Bank), the transfer of powers to the Palestinian National Authority (PNA), and the creation and functioning of new Palestinian institutions. These agreements by no means stipulated any provisions for a final settlement between Israel and the PLO but stated that "permanent status negotiations will commence as soon as possible, but no later than May 4, 1996, between the parties."[2]

As it happened, despite certain delays and crises caused mainly by Hamas terrorist actions, most clauses of these accords, including the Gaza-Jericho Agreement of May 4, 1994, and the Preparatory Transfer of Power Agreements of August 29, 1994, were implemented in a more or less satisfactory manner. This was mostly the case while the Israeli Labor-Meretz coalition was in power (until May 29, 1996) and before the permanent status negotiations started.

Thus, while the Israeli military and civil administrations withdrew from the Gaza Strip and parts of the West Bank, the PNA was created and included a presidency, government ministries, security networks, and an elected legislative council—all of which have formed a nucleus for a Palestinian state, at least in the eyes of the PLO.

However, several months before the scheduled commencement of the permanent status negotiations on the issues of a Palestinian state, of the status of Jerusalem, of Palestinian refugees, and of Jewish settlements, several critical setbacks occurred to the Oslo process. Among the major causes for these setbacks were the violent terrorist deeds of fanatic Palestinians, as well as the insensitive approach of Israel's new prime minister, Benjamin Netanyahu.

The first heavy blow to the Israeli-Palestinian peace process was inflicted by a Jewish fanatic, Yigal Amir, who on November 4, 1995, assassinated Rabin, Israel's prime minister and chief leader of the Oslo process. On February 25 and March 24, 1996, Islamic fanatics killed dozens of Israelis in several suicide attacks in Jerusalem, Tel Aviv, and Ashkelon, thus changing or hardening the attitudes of many Israeli Jews to the Oslo process and contributing to the election of Netanyahu in the May 29 election.

Finally, Netanyahu's unilateral actions in Jerusalem and violent Palestinian reactions have further damaged the Oslo process, notably: (1) Netanyahu's decision to open an archeological tunnel near the Temple Mount/Haram al-Sharif on September 24, 1996, which triggered severe Palestinian riots and fire exchanges between Israeli and Palestinian troops, with scores killed and wounded on both sides; and (2) the Israeli government's order to construct a new Jewish neighborhood on Har Homa/Jabal Abu Ghnaim, on the southeastern outskirts of Jerusalem, which led to yet another Hamas suicide attack in Tel Aviv on March 21, 1997, followed by acute clashes between PLO-led demonstrators and Israeli soldiers in several West Bank locations, causing more deaths and virtually bringing to a standstill the Israeli-Palestinian peace process.

Does this critical halt of the political negotiations (and security cooperation) between Israel and the PNA signify a breakdown of the Oslo Agreements and a reversal of the peacemaking process; or is it merely another temporary setback in this long and painful ordeal? What are the prospects for continuing and completing the Oslo peace process in the face of the highly sensitive and controversial issues of the permanent settlement that are due to be negotiated as the twenty-first century dawns? Is the Israeli-Palestinian peace process reversible or irreversible, and in each case, what would be the impact on Arab-Israeli relations in the Middle East?

Although this chapter does not venture to predict future developments, it mainly examines the Oslo accords and their repercussions on the peace process. First, however, the major developments in the century-old Arab-Jewish conflict in Palestine/Eretz Israel prior to the Oslo Agreements are outlined.

Asymmetry and Transposition During a Century of Confrontation

The Arab-Jewish conflict in Palestine started in the 1880s as a sociocultural clash fueled by economic disputes.[3] The indigenous Arab-speaking majority of the population—socially conservative and religiously oriented, mostly Muslim—was faced for the first time with newly arrived European Zionist Jews. Unlike the old and small Jewish *Yishuv* (community) in the Holy Land that had been apolitical and religious, submissive and adaptable to the Muslim-Ottoman system, the Zionist Jews were highly politicized, secular, socialist, and, in the eyes of the indigenous population, assertive if not aggressive.

The Balfour Declaration of November 2, 1917, and the subsequent creation of the British Mandate over Palestine in 1920 enhanced the transformation of the initial sociocultural Arab-Jewish strife into a political-national struggle as well.[4] The Jewish-Zionist national movement, which had preceded its rival Palestinian-Arab movement by several decades, professed the notion of creating a Jewish national home all over Palestine/Eretz Israel. To this end, the Zionist movement systematically expanded its venture in the country by absorbing new Jewish immigrants and refugees, mostly those fleeing the Nazi persecution and horrors during the mid to late 1930s and 1940s. While acquiring large tracts of land and building many villages and several towns, the Zionist movement also established a modern and well-organized network of national, economic, social, and cultural institutions, including well-trained paramilitary forces.

Yet the major bulk of this movement—notably, the socialist parties and groups—realizing the impossibility of fully implementing the Zionist ideology across all of Eretz Israel, adopted a pragmatic policy regarding the dispute with the Palestinians. This policy culminated in the adoption of the aforementioned UN Partition Resolution (i.e., Resolution 181) of November 29, 1947, which provided for the establishment of two states in Palestine: Arab and Jewish.

By contrast, the mainstream of the Palestinian-Arab national movement, led by the Mufti al-Hajj Amin al-Husayni, was both ideologically and politically uncompromising toward the national aspirations of the Zionist Jews.[5] Employing political pressure, economic measures, and armed violence, this Palestinian leadership endeavored to curtail, undermine, or destroy the Zionist venture, but it totally failed. For although it represented the majority of the population and enjoyed the backing of neighboring Arab and Muslim countries, the Palestinian-Arab movement substantially lagged behind its Jewish-Zionist opponent in cohesion, organization, motivation, and performance. And, unlike the Zionists, the Palestinian leadership rejected the 1947 UN Partition Resolution and subsequently—with the help of irregular fighters from neighboring Arab countries—launched guerrilla warfare against the Jewish community in Palestine. Those Arab fighters, however, were no match for the highly motivated, better trained, and more organized Jewish Haganah forces. Indeed, though they were initially poorly equipped, these forces were able first to defeat the irregular Arab fighters and then, during the 1948 war, to ward off five regular Arab armies that had been dispatched to abort the creation of the new state of Israel.

Following the 1948 war, the Arab-Jewish conflict was essentially transformed into a confrontation between Israel and the Arab states,[6] while the Palestinian community disintegrated and dispersed or remained in three regions of Palestine Israel—the West Bank (under Jordanian rule), Gaza (under Egyptian control), and Israel—as well as in Lebanon, Syria, and the Persian Gulf.

For a long period, they were either incapable of, or prevented by their host states from, reorganizing as a national community. But scores of young Palestinians were organized and employed by a few Arab states or were permitted in the 1950s to launch guerrilla/terrorist attacks against Israeli citizens and economic projects. In 1964 the Arab League created the Palestine Liberation Organization, which, under Egyptian guidance, operated against Israel and became an umbrella structure for the various Palestinian guerrilla groups. Among those, the group Fatah was the most authentic Palestinian force; first set up in the late 1950s under Arafat's leadership, it became in the late 1960s the dominant group in the PLO, now also under Arafat's chairmanship.[7]

In its National Charter of 1964 and 1968, the PLO articulated its extreme anti-Zionist ideology and strategy and its commitment to the destruction of Israel by means of military struggle. To be sure, these militant positions of the PLO, accompanied by guerrilla actions inside Israel, contributed to deepening anti-Arab sentiments and to demonizing the Palestinians as bloodthirsty terrorists in the eyes of many Israeli Jews.

The occupation of the West Bank and the Gaza Strip by Israel in the Six Day War of June 1967 spurred on the revival of both Palestinian nationalist feelings in the occupied territories and Jewish nationalist and religious adherence to these territories (Judea and Samaria in their definition). Therefore, with the renewal of the bicommunal confrontation between Jews and Arabs in Palestine/Eretz Israel after June 1967, the Israeli Jewish community was now greatly superior to the Palestinians—demographically, politically, economically, and militarily. This imbalance of power furthered the gradual transposition of attitudes whereby more Israeli Jews continued to ignore or deny the national aspirations of the Palestinian Arabs, while the latter gradually adopted a more pragmatic position toward Israel.[8]

The political radicalization among Israeli Jews stemmed not only from Jewish nationalist and religious attachment to the occupied territories, but also from genuine and deeply rooted security concerns—enhanced after the 1973 war—as well as from social and economic developments and interests. For example, members of the lower classes of Israeli society were interested in keeping Palestinians working in unskilled professions in Israel in order to facilitate their own upward mobility. In addition, more and more Israelis, particularly among the post-1967 younger generation, became accustomed to regarding Judea and Samaria as part of Israel, and some of them moved to new neighborhoods and settlements in these territories where they were offered cheaper housing subsidized by the government.

Indeed, the Israeli Labor governments, and certainly those of the Likud, contributed—directly or indirectly—to enhancing the notion of a "Greater Israel" in Eretz Israel at the expense of the political aspirations of the Palestinians. While the West Bank was officially named "Judea and Samaria," Israel's Labor governments for several years after 1967 ignored the reality of a Palestinian people or of a Palestinian nationalism. And although

Prime Minister Rabin publicly acknowledged the existence of a Palestinian problem for the first time in 1974, he placed its resolution within the context of an Israeli-Jordanian settlement. He and other Labor leaders, though not advocating the annexation of the West Bank and Gaza to Israel, declared time and again that in any peace settlement Israel should never return to the pre-1967 borders, never agree to the establishment of a Palestinian state in the West Bank and Gaza, and never redivide Jerusalem, Israel's capital, which must remain unified under its sovereignty.[9]

Accordingly, East Jerusalem was formally incorporated into Israel, and new Jewish suburbs were constructed on pre-1967 Arab territories north, east, and south of Jerusalem. In addition to creating several Jewish settlements along the Jordan valley, to serve strategic security concerns, the Labor governments permitted the rebuilding of Jewish villages in the Etzion bloc (on the Bethlehem-Hebron route), which had been a Jewish area prior to the 1948 war, as well as the town of Qiryat Arba, adjacent to Hebron, and a small Jewish quarter within Hebron. These latter ventures were influenced partly by the memory of the old Jewish quarter in Hebron that had been destroyed in 1929, when dozens of its Jewish inhabitants were massacred by Arabs, and partly by the pressures of the National Religious Party (NRP), a coalition partner of the Labor Party, and of Gush Emunim, a new Jewish religious-nationalist and militant movement.[10]

Evidently, the Gush Emunim movement not only expanded its membership and its radical political activities after the Likud Party came to power in the 1977 Israeli election, but it also became the Likud government's major vehicle for settlement activities throughout Judea and Samaria, aiming at de facto incorporation of these regions in Israel.

Under the dynamic leadership of Ariel Sharon, first as agriculture minister and subsequently as defense minister, some ninety new Jewish settlements (with 22,000 inhabitants) were constructed in the West Bank between 1977 and 1984, in addition to twenty-four settlements (with some 600 people) built during the Labor governments' terms in office. (The most recent figure is 140 Jewish settlements, with some 150,000 inhabitants.)

Simultaneously, while Sharon greatly endeavored to suppress Palestinian institutions and evict Palestinian leaders in the territories by means of administrative measures, he periodically overlooked the illegal actions of Gush Emunim activists or of other militant settlers against innocent Palestinians. These developments and events possibly contributed to the emergence of an anti-Arab Jewish terrorist group for the first time since 1948. In 1980, Jewish terrorists planted explosives in the cars of three Palestinian mayors—Bassam al-Shaká of Nablus, Karim Khalaf of Rām Allāh, and Ibrahim Tawil of Al-Bīrah—severely wounding the first two. During the first half of 1984, Jewish militants shot several unarmed Arab students in the Hebron Islamic College, tried to blow up the mosques in

Jerusalem's Haram al-Sharif, and planted explosives in the city's Arab buses. It is true that these Jewish terrorists were arrested and tried in Israeli courts, while several Likud ministers—notably, Foreign Minister Moshe Dayan and Defense Ministers Ezer Weizman (in the late 1970s) and Moshe Arens (in 1983–1984)—adopted strong measures to stop the violent activities of the militant Jewish settlers.

At the same time, however, the Likud governments by and large did not seriously attempt to negotiate a political settlement for the West Bank–Gaza territories with the locally elected nationalist Palestinian leaders, despite the commitment of Israeli Prime Minister Menachem Begin in the Camp David Agreement of 1978 to permit the "Palestinian Arabs to participate in the determination of their own future."[11] No wonder, then, that the Palestinian community in the West Bank and Gaza—in reaction to the Israeli occupation, the appropriation of Arab lands, the establishment of Jewish settlements, the annexation of East Jerusalem, and the like—underwent an accelerated process of political radicalization and national crystallization. These developments were manifested, on the one hand, by anti-Israeli demonstrations, strikes, and terrorism and, on the other hand, by creating or cultivating such national institutions and public organizations as elected municipalities, the Palestinian National Front, the National Guidance Committee, universities, hospitals, and newspapers, as well as associations of students, women, physicians, engineers, and other groups. Under the guidance of several radical political leaders, attempts were made to mold these institutions and associations into an infrastructure for a Palestinian state while mounting their struggle against Israeli occupation. Ironically, these Palestinian activities resembled the earlier Zionist campaign against the British Mandate and were possibly facilitated by the democratic norms of the neighboring Israeli society.

To be sure, for pragmatic reasons, several West Bank nationalist, pro-PLO leaders were interested in negotiating a political settlement with Israel for the territories, including the creation of a Palestinian state next to Israel. But, with a few exceptions, Israeli government leaders evaded recognizing, let alone cultivating and negotiating with, these nationalist-pragmatic Palestinians.

Significantly, the PLO command in the "diaspora" (initially in Jordan, then in Lebanon, and finally in Tunisia) strongly discouraged the West Bank leaders—even using threats and smear campaigns—from negotiation with Israel or from building national institutions for a would-be Palestinian state. The PLO was deeply concerned lest the West Bank–Gaza politicians would emerge as an alternative leadership and come to terms with Israel, while ignoring the PLO's interests.

As we know, the PLO's ideological and strategic aims had been to liberate the whole of Palestine from Israeli occupation by means of a military struggle and to establish there a Palestinian state under its sole leadership. Failing to achieve these aims and considering Israel's military superiority over the Arab states, however, the PLO since 1974 has gradually changed its extreme policy in favor of a new pragmatic strategy[12]—namely, the establishment of a Palestinian state on the West Bank and Gaza in coexistence with Israel. Although the PLO accepted resolving the conflict with Israel by political means, until 1988 it had neither renounced the use of military means or terrorism nor recognized Israel's right to exist. In contrast with the exception of a few left-wing activists, most Israeli Jews continued to consider the PLO a terrorist organization that could not be a partner for negotiations.

Significant changes in the positions of many Israeli Jews regarding the Palestinians, and of the PLO leadership regarding Israel, emerged only in late 1988, largely under the impact of the Palestinian intifada.[13] This popular nationalist uprising against the continued Israel occupation that erupted on December 9, 1987, in Gaza and the West Bank (and continued for several years) caught both Israel and the PLO by surprise and, along with U.S. pressure and other factors, induced both sides to adopt more pragmatic policies toward each other.

The aims of the intifada leaders and activists, with the exception of the Muslim militant organization Hamas, were to liberate the West Bank and Gaza and to create a Palestinian state alongside Israel. The PLO was influenced by such positions, but it was also concerned lest the intifada leaders should negotiate a political settlement with Israel without its major participation. Managing in due course to control and direct the intifada and to utilize its impact on Israel and the world, the PLO adopted unprecedented pragmatic decisions. In November 1988, the Palestinian National Council (equivalent to the PLO's "parliament") announced the establishment of a Palestinian state, inter alia, on the basis of UN Resolution 181 of November 29, 1947. And, in December 1988, at the special UN Assembly meeting in Geneva and in a subsequent press conference, Arafat also acknowledged UN Resolutions 242 (of 1967) and 338 (of 1973), recognizing Israel's right to exist and renouncing terrorism.

These historic decisions clearly reflected the culmination of the transformation of the mainstream Palestinian nationalist movement from totally rejecting both the Jewish national movement and Israel to finally accepting them.

As for the mainstream of the Jewish national community, which had conversely moved since 1948 from accepting the Palestinian nationalist movement to rejecting it, by late 1988 more than half of the Israelis agreed to start a dialogue with the PLO, and certainly with the Palestinians on the West Bank and Gaza. But even after late 1988, most Israeli cabinet ministers in the National Unity government continued to oppose negotiations with the PLO, to ignore Palestinian national aspirations, and to create more Jewish settlements in the territories.

However, in May 1989, having been induced by the intifada, by U.S pressure, and by Israeli public opinion, the Israeli Labor-Likud government suggested negotiating a political settlement for the West Bank and Gaza with representatives of both the local Palestinians and the Jordanian government, on the basis of the Camp David autonomy plan. Fortunately for the Israeli government, then under Yitzhak Shamir's premiership, various regional and global developments facilitated its request that only Palestinians from the West Bank and Gaza should participate within a joint Jordanian-Palestinian delegation at the Madrid Peace Conference (opened on October 30, 1991). The PLO was formally excluded from that conference after it had been greatly discredited and weakened, owing to its previous support of Iraq's invasion of Kuwait. Despite the PLO's attempts to control and instruct the "inside" Palestinian delegation, the latter, enjoying domestic support and international prestige, could perhaps, under suitable circumstances, reach a settlement with Israel without PLO participation.

Yet the Israeli-Palestinian negotiations at Madrid encountered severe obstacles, even after the ascendancy of Rabin and his Labor Party in the June 1992 Israeli elections. One of the major obstacles was created by the Palestinian delegation's insistence that the interim Palestinian self-government should also include East Jerusalem, in addition to the West Bank and Gaza, as a first stage in the establishment of a Palestinian state.

Paradoxically, Prime Minister Rabin, who had opted for years to reach a settlement with the "inside" Palestinians in conjunction with Jordan, found himself negotiating with the "outside," "terrorist" PLO at the secret Oslo channel, as Arafat appeared now to be an easier negotiating partner:[14] because of its political and financial weakness and its fear of being left out of a possible Israeli-Palestinian settlement, the PLO was prepared to make far-reaching concessions to Israel, provided it was recognized by Israel as the official Palestinian representative.

On the one hand, the PLO agreed neither to include East Jerusalem in the interim agreement nor to have an Israeli commitment regarding the nature of the permanent settlement, namely, a Palestinian state. On the other hand, the PLO was the only organization with solid military and civilian institutions capable of exercising political authority, of curbing the local Palestinian opposition groups (most notably, Hamas), and of combating their terrorist activities against Israel.

As for the motives of Arafat to strike this deal with Israel, he expected to be rescued from possible oblivion, to become the chief Palestinian authority in the territories while still representing the Palestinians in exile, and to gain international recognition and financial support from the West, particularly the United States.

The Israeli Labor Government, the PLO, and the Oslo Process

As already indicated, the Oslo Agreements of 1993 and 1995, in their grand principles, represented a historical and psychological breakthrough in Israeli-Palestinian relations. For the first time, the two rival nationalist communities mutually recognized each other's legitimacy and national-political aspirations and committed themselves to working together for peaceful coexistence in the partitioned land of Israel/Palestine.

But even though the historical asymmetry in the positions of the two nationalist communities was repaired, the imbalance between them has remained vast in many respects. For instance, the Oslo Agreements enabled the powerful Israeli state to virtually dictate most of its terms to the vulnerable Palestinian organization, but they retained a substantial disequilibrium in the strategic goals of the two parties. The Israeli Labor government, owing to domestic constraints and lingering concerns (and possibly a shortsighted vision), imposed a gradual open-ended and multistage agreement, with no commitment to the final outcome concerning the crucial issues of a Palestinian state, Jerusalem, Jewish settlements, and Palestinian refugees. By contrast, the PLO, while inevitably accepting this interim open-ended agreement, has continuously stressed its strategic aim of establishing a Palestinian state on the West Bank and the Gaza Strip with its capital in Arab/East Jerusalem.

Whereas pronouncing this strategic goal has been vital for legitimizing Arafat's role and for justifying Oslo I and II, the PLO possibly had certain reasons to believe that the Israeli Labor-Meretz government, despite its official position, would eventually agree to meet Palestinian expectations. For one thing, several Labor and Meretz ministers did not conceal their anticipation that a Palestinian state would be created on the West Bank and Gaza in the final stage of the Oslo process. Such a formula has for years been included in the Meretz Party's program, while the Labor Party decided on April 25, 1996, to erase from its own platform a long-standing objection to the creation of a Palestinian state.[15]

Labor Minister Yossi Beilin went even further by initiating (in early 1994) and agreeing (in November 1995) with Abu Mazen (a.k.a. Mahmud Abbas), Arafat's deputy, on a blueprint for the permanent settlement: creation of a Palestinian state on the West Bank and Gaza with certain border alterations and with its capital in Al-Quds (the Arabic name for Jerusalem) in the Arab suburb of Abu-Dis on the eastern outskirts of Jerusalem.[16] According to several polls, about half of the Israelis supported such a formula, especially the creation of a Palestinian state on the West Bank and Gaza.

To be sure, Israeli public support for the Oslo process and for a future Palestinian state remained solid or grew as long as personal security was maintained, Palestinian terrorism was curbed, and the agreements with the PLO were orderly implemented and bore benefits to Israel. Indeed, as mentioned above, the Oslo accords were carried out fairly well, while the PLO established its ruling institutions and the Palestinians democratically elected their legislative council (on January 20, 1996). In addition, the Oslo Agreements considerably improved Israel's regional position: Israel signed a formal peace treaty with Jordan (on October 26, 1994), followed by the establishment of economic and consular relations with other Arab states—Morocco, Tunisia, Qatar, and Oman. Israel also benefited economically and diplomatically by the growing international investments and the increasing sympathy among the world community, including some Muslim countries. Consequently, by late 1995, there appeared to emerge a sense of cautious optimism regarding the Oslo process among both Israelis and Palestinians, while various teams and sections among them were cooperating to advance common interests and mutual understanding in the fields of business enterprises, academic research, educational and cultural issues, and the like. Even some Jewish settlers initiated or participated in Israeli-Palestinian dialogues.

The Anti-Oslo Backlash

Unfortunately, the unique currents of mutual cooperation and trust between Israelis and Palestinians, as well as the constructive momentum in implementing the Oslo Agreements perhaps toward creating a Palestinian state, did not gain further impetus. In fact, since late 1995, they have suffered a series of crucial setbacks at the hands of anti-Oslo elements, Palestinians and Israelis alike. In addition to their strong opposition to the Oslo process on ideological-religious and/or nationalistic-chauvinistic grounds, these elements became increasingly concerned, even alarmed, vis-à-vis the productive results of that process. Their uncoordinated reactions—notably, terrorist deeds, as well as omissions and miscalculations by both Israeli and Palestinian leaders—contributed to obstruct the Oslo peace process since early 1996 and bring it to a standstill by March 1997.

Among the Israeli Jewish population, the opposition to the Oslo Agreements embraced extreme right-wing parties and groups and their followers, Gush Emunim, the Settlers Council, the NRP, the Tzomet Party, and initially also the Likud Party. This collective opposition strongly rejected the Oslo Agreements and the notion of a future Palestinian state for various motives and reasons: ideological convictions regarding Eretz Israel or Greater Israel and the unity of Jerusalem under Israeli sovereignty; security concerns regarding Palestinian terrorism and its strategic menace to Israel; and deep apprehensions regarding the fate of the Jewish settlements on the West Bank and the Gaza Strip. Consequently, these right-wing groups launched, in mid-1995, many efforts and subsequently a concerted campaign against the Labor-Meretz government and its peace policy. For example, settlers illegally attempted to expand their scope of habitation while a few rabbis issued religious edicts calling Israeli soldiers to disobey orders to remove Jewish settlements in the territories.[17] In addition, public protests were organized and intercity traffic was obstructed by militant Jews, who also heckled and threatened Labor leaders, particularly Prime Minister Rabin. At political rallies he was labeled "traitor" and "murderer," and in posters he was depicted wearing the Nazi SS uniform. This smear campaign possibly motivated or encouraged Yigal Amir, a fanatic right-wing Jew, to assassinate Rabin during a peace rally in Tel Aviv on November 4, 1995.

The subsequent enormous wave of sympathy for Rabin and support for the peace process in Israel, in Arab countries, and in the international community did not last too long. Palestinian enemies of the Oslo process, notably Hamas, continued their efforts to disrupt the negotiations through a series of bloody terrorist actions, which greatly contributed to reverse pro-Oslo, pro-Labor support among Israeli Jews.

Already in 1995—in April, July, and August—the Hamas organization launched a series of attacks in Israel, causing many Israeli casualties. The PNA adopted tough measures against this organization, rounding up hundreds and sentencing several members, while starting to cooperate with the Israeli security services in combating terror. Simultaneously, Arafat attempted, and partly succeeded in, confining Hamas actions to political means and co-opting a few of its activists within the PNA. But he also released from detention many Hamas suspects and attended the funeral of one of their "martyrs."

At any rate, the preventive and security measures of the PNA and of Israel could not abort the two devastating suicide attacks by Hamas in Jerusalem and Tel Aviv on February 25 and March 3, 1996, killing and wounding dozens of Israelis. These attacks were allegedly carried out in revenge for the killing by Israeli agents of Yahya Ayyash, the mastermind behind the wave of Hamas suicide bombings against Israel in previous years. And although the PNA subsequently became more successful in preventing further Hamas attacks for about a year, these two violent actions created a cumulative effect among the Israeli Jewish public and influenced the Israeli national election campaign. Many right-wing Israelis accused Arafat of cooperating with Hamas and not fulfilling his commitment to change the notorious Palestinian National Charter.

Benjamin Netanyahu, the Likud leader and the contending candidate to Labor's Shimon Peres for the position of prime minister, used these issues, specifically Hamas terrorism, in his election campaign. Harping on the failure of the Labor Party's Palestinian policy, he vowed to bring "peace and security" to Israel, rejected the Oslo Agreements and the PLO, but did not outline a clear alternative policy. On the eve of his election on May 29, 1996, however, Netanyahu did reluctantly undertake to talk to the PLO and honor the Oslo process, but he advocated implementing the agreements in a much slower, "safer," and tougher way than did Labor.

Indeed, Netanyahu as prime minister continued the Oslo process at a slow pace, while attempting to drive a tough bargain, particularly regarding the Hebron issue, which was finally settled in January 1997. Similarly, he met Arafat for the first time only on September 4, 1996 (there were more meetings later), and he made other gestures such as increasing the number of Palestinians allowed to work in Israel from 25,000 to 35,000 (eventually to 60,000), releasing the remaining Palestinian women terrorists from Israeli jails in early 1997, and undertaking to withdraw the Israel Defense Forces from a further 9 percent of the West Bank (including only 2 percent of Zone C, which is fully under Israeli control).

By contrast, however, adhering to the Likud ideology and to the new government's guidelines, Netanyahu stated time and again his objection to the establishment of a Palestinian state and to the redivision of Jerusalem (namely, not to relinquish Israel's sovereignty over any part of united Jerusalem), and he vowed to continue Jewish settlement activity in Jerusalem, Judea, and Samaria. Indeed, the new Israeli cabinet lifted the previous administration's ban on new construction of settlements and adopted measures to limit, if not eliminate, PNA activities in East Jerusalem.[18] Furthermore, in order to demonstrate Israel's determination to control the eastern part of Jerusalem and to continue building Jewish housing there, in September 1996, Netanyahu ordered the opening of the Hasmonean tunnel near the Temple Mount/Haram al-Sharif and, in March 1997, the start of construction of a new Jewish neighborhood on Har Homa/Jabal Abu Ghnaim. As we know, these unilateral actions provoked violent reactions and terrorist actions by Palestinians, as well as clashes between Palestinian and Israeli troops, causing many deaths on both sides. Israeli senior officials accused Arafat of giving a the green light to Hamas to carry out terror attacks. At any rate, the Har Homa construction brought about a breakdown of the Palestinian-Israeli Oslo process, drew worldwide condemnation of Israel, and considerably worsened Arab-Israeli relations.

The Arab states in North Africa (Morocco and Tunisia) and in the Persian Gulf (Oman and Qatar) froze or diminished the economic and semi-diplomatic relations they had established with Israel after the signing of Oslo I and II. King Hussein of Jordan, Israel's veteran Arab ally, was deeply offended that Netanyahu had not consulted him before the opening of the Hasmonean tunnel and also criticized him for the Har Homa venture. Subsequently, the king demonstrated his support for Arafat and the emergence of a Palestinian state. President Hosni Mubarak of Egypt, the first Arab country to make peace with Israel, complained that he had been misled by Netanyahu, who promised him to pursue the Oslo process energetically. Egyptian, Palestinian, and other Arab leaders also complained about the arrogant and condescending attitude of Netanyahu when referring to Arab regimes and affairs. Syrian leaders issued severe threats, accompanied by displays of military power, in reaction to Netanyahu's proclaimed refusal to withdraw from the Golan in the framework of an Israeli-Syrian settlement. Finally, even the Clinton administration manifested in various ways its criticism of Netanyahu's insensitive and damaging handling of the Oslo Agreements and has urged him, and Arafat, to revive and actively pursue the peace process.

In response to the U.S. inducement and to Egyptian and Jordanian criticism, and possibly aware of Israel's international isolation and diminishing foreign investments, Netanyahu pronounced his new policy in April 1997: to negotiate and reach with the PNA a permanent settlement within six months, instead of the two years stipulated by the Oslo Agreements. On the face of it, this new proposal appears to be merely an unserious gimmick in view of the crucial problems that ought to be negotiated: borders with the Palestinian entity, Palestinian refugees, Jewish settlements, and the status of Jerusalem. And, as we know, negotiations over the Hebron Agreement alone lasted more than six months. Yet the Hebron protocol, as well as several utterances by Netanyahu and his adviser Bar Ilan and other Likud leaders, indicates that the prime minister has possibly relinquished the notion of a Greater Israel and has increasingly acknowledged that a Palestinian state will eventually emerge. Furthermore, according to a public poll conducted in February 1997, some 50 percent of Israelis accept the idea of a Palestinian state and 71 percent think that a Palestinian state will emerge before 2010.[19] Therefore, if a right-wing leader like Netanyahu agrees to the establishment of a Palestinian state as a permanent settlement, he is likely to obtain the support of most Israelis, as was demonstrated in the Hebron Agreement and earlier during "the Begin syndrome," when Israel withdrew from Sinai following peace with Egypt.

Conclusion

Theoretically, it may be possible for Netanyahu to reach a permanent peace settlement with the PLO, provided he invites the Labor Party and its new head, Ehud Barak, to form a national unity coalition and government. This will have to be done along common guidelines regarding the settlement of the Palestinian issue, for example, creation of a demilitarized Palestinian state on some 70 percent of the West Bank with certain municipal links to the Arab sections of Jerusalem. In addition, the Jewish settlements along the "green line" and in the Etzion bloc, as well as the Jordan valley, will be annexed to Israel, while Hebron's Jewish enclave and Qiryat Arba will enjoy an autonomous municipal status and will be linked to Israel by a special road. The Labor Party is likely to accept such a formula, as it is roughly compatible with its own agenda. Many members of the Knesset (MKs) of Likud—including Rafi Eitan's Tzomet Party and David Levy's Gesher Party, Shas (a.k.a. Sephardim), Yisrael Ba'aliya (Russians), and the Third Way—could be persuaded to endorse this plan. And whereas the NRP and several other right-wing MKs from Likud will certainly move to the opposition, the majority of the Knesset and of the Israelis (70–80 percent) will support such a formula.

Yet the crucial question is whether or not Netanyahu will accept such a plan and invite Barak to form a national unity government. It would appear that Netanyahu's blueprint for a final settlement with Arafat is substantially different from the above-mentioned formula. He presumably visualized a limited or constrained Palestinian entity in the Gaza Strip and in the mountain highland towns of the West Bank and their surroundings, comprising up to 50 percent of Judea and Samaria. This region is to be divided into two or three enclaves and/or cut by Israeli-controlled roads and pierced by Jewish settlements, which should remain under Israeli sovereignty. Greater Jerusalem must remain united, also under Israel's sovereignty, with free access to all religions and a special role for Jordan in Haram al-Sharif, or the Temple Mount.[20] To be sure, such a blueprint is compatible with the security concerns and strategic concepts of Netanyahu and his narrow right-wing coalition, and it is likely to be approved by most of them. Netanyahu possibly believes that he can get away with this plan while withstanding U.S. and European pressures. Consequently, unless he is forced or persuaded otherwise by the United States, he is not likely to accept Barak's formula or to form an alliance with the Labor Party (which, in turn, is not likely to endorse Netanyahu's plan). Concerning Arafat and the Palestinians, Netanyahu probably thinks that they will have no choice but to accept his blueprint, for if they reject it, they will be left with control over merely 40 percent of the West Bank.

Arafat, of course, has flatly rejected both plans and insists on the creation of a Palestinian state in the whole West Bank and the Gaza Strip, with its capital in Arab East Jerusalem. From his perspective, the Jewish settlements should be evacuated or partly remain under Palestinian sovereignty. He may nevertheless accept a formula similar to the joint blueprint of former Labor Minister Beilin and his own deputy, Abu Mazen; for example; the establishment of a (demilitarized) Palestinian state on the West Bank and the Gaza Strip along the pre-1967 green line, with certain border alterations, which will essentially address main security concerns for Israel and include many Jewish settlements. And while the Palestinians will have an extraterritorial corridor through Israel from the Gaza Strip to the West Bank, their capital, Al-Quds, will reside at Abu-Dis and will be linked to the Arab section of Jerusalem. This section, in turn, will be municipally autonomous under an umbrella city council, supervising both Israeli and Palestinian sections. Haram al-Sharif will continue to enjoy special status under Palestinian or Jordanian-Palestinian jurisdiction, while in the latter case, the Palestinian state will be linked to Jordan in a confederal system.

Arafat can probably convince most Palestinians in the West Bank and Gaza to acknowledge such a solution, which renders them some 90 percent of the West Bank. However, he will have great difficulties in accepting and "selling" to his people the so-called Barak formula whereby the Palestinians will have their state on only 70 percent of the West Bank. Still, there is a fair chance that Arafat may nonetheless negotiate such a formula under certain conditions, such as leasing to Israel the Jordan valley for twenty-five years, having some sovereign rights in East Jerusalem, and creating a Palestine capital nearby. Even then, Arafat is likely to encounter strong opposition from among his own Fatah movement, certainly from Hamas and conservative Muslim sections. He may survive such opposition by using his security apparatus, on the one hand, and by improving the socioeconomic conditions of his people, on the other.

Surely Arafat cannot negotiate or accept Netanyahu's blueprint, even if it provides for the creation of a Palestinian state (instead of an autonomous entity). He may be unable to control the violent opposition by sections of Fatah, particularly by Hamas. By 1998, Hamas had greatly increased the number of its members and followers to 40–45 percent of the population, owing to the long stalemate in the PLO's negotiations with Israel. A final settlement with Israel along Netanyahu's plan is likely to ignite a Hamas-led Palestinian popular rebellion against Arafat and certainly a violent guerrilla/terrorist campaign against Israel. This will surely provoke sharp Israeli reprisals and bring about the final collapse of the Oslo process, serious damage to Israel's relations with Egypt and Jordan (as well as with the international community), and a crucial setback to the prospects of Arab-Jewish reconciliation.

Notes

1. The full text of the Oslo II Agreement appears in *Near East Report* 34, no. 22 (October 9, 1995). The full text of the Hebron Agreement is in *Near East Report* 41, no. 2 (January 27, 1997).
2. *Near East Report* 34, no. 22, October 9, 1995, p. 120.
3. For a detailed study of the origins of this conflict, see N. J. Mandel, *The Arabs and Zionism Before World War I* (Berkeley: University of California Press, 1976).

4. See, for example, J. C. Hurewitz, *The Struggle for Palestine* (New York: W. W. Norton and Co., 1950).

5. For a detailed study, see Philip Mattar, *The Mufti of Jerusalem Al-Hajj Amin Al-Husayni and the Palestinian National Movement* (New York: Columbia University Press, 1988).

6. See, for example, Ilan Pappe, *The Making of the Arab-Israeli Conflict: 1947–1951* (London: Tauris, 1992).

7. For detailed studies of this development, see H. Cobban, *The Palestinian Liberation Organization* (New York: Cambridge University Press, 1984); and S. Mishal, *The PLO Under Arafat* (New Haven, Conn.: Yale University Press, 1986).

8. For detailed studies, see, for example, Moshe Ma'oz, *Palestinian Leadership in the West Bank* (London: Frank Cass, 1984); and Emile Sahliye, *West Bank Politics Since 1967* (Washington, D.C.: Brookings Institution, 1988).

9. Cf. Mordechai Nisan, *Israel and the Territories: A Study in Control, 1967–1977* (Ramat Gan, Israel: AMS Press, 1978).

10. On Gush Emunim, see, for example, M. Peleg, *Mi-Gush Emunim ve-ad Kikar Rabin* (in Hebrew) (Tel Aviv: Hakibutz Hamenchad, 1997).

11. W. B. Quandt, *Camp David, Peacemaking, and Politics* (Washington, D.C.: Brookings Institution, 1986), p. 379.

12. See Cobban, *The Palestinian Liberation,* p. 62.

13. On the intifada, see, for example, F. R. Hunter, *The Palestinian Uprising* (Berkeley: University of California Press, 1991); Z. Schiff and E. Ya'ari, *Intifada* (in Hebrew) (Tel Aviv: Schocken, 1990); and Muhammad Nasr, *Al-Intifada* (in Arabic), published by the author (n.p., n.d.).

14. For details, see, for example, K. Aggestam, *Two-Track Diplomacy: Negotiations Between Israel and the PLO Through Open and Secret Channels* (Jerusalem: Hebrew University Press, 1996); and Yossi Beilin, *Touching Peace* (in Hebrew) (Tel Aviv: Yediot Ahronot, 1997).

15. See *Middle East Journal* 51, no. 4 (autumn 1996): 583.

16. See Beilin, *Touching Peace,* pp. 167–175; and *Ha'aretz* (Tel Aviv), February 22, 1996, and March 19, 1996.

17. *International Herald Tribune,* August 26–27, 1995.

18. *Middle East Journal* 51, no. 1 (winter 1997): 97; *Journal of Palestine Studies* 26, no. 1 (autumn 1996): 116–118.

19. *Ha'aretz,* May 1, 1997; Y. Alpher, *The Netanyahu Government and the Israeli-Arab Peace Process: The First Half Year,* no. 4 (London: Institute for Jewish Policy Research, 1997), pp. 4, 9.

20. Cf. Dore Gold, *Jerusalem* (Tel Aviv: The Jaffee Center, Tel Aviv University, 1945), p. 41; and *Yediot Ahronot* (Tel Aviv), June 5, 1997.

4

The Anglo-Irish Peace Process: Obstacles to Reconciliation

Paul Arthur

So why has the crisis in Northern Ireland not been resolved, either by a compromise settlement or genocidal carnage? The answer is simple. There has been no resolution because the violence has not been intolerable. By whatever calculus communities compute their interests, the price of compromise is still thought to be greater than the cost of violence.

—John Darby, 1986

In August of 1994 when the Irish Republican Army (IRA) announced a total cessation of violence, it refused to use the word "permanent" with regard to the cease-fire. When the Combined Loyalist Military Command (CLMC) reciprocated with its announcement on October 13, 1994, the command made it clear that its cessation was dependent on the IRA not returning to war. The CLMC statement announced that it was ceasing all operational hostilities because it had received "confirmation and guarantees in relation to Northern Ireland's constitutional position within the United Kingdom." By contrast, the IRA's announcement demonstrated no such confidence. It stated that a "solution will only be found as a result of *inclusive negotiations*. Others, not least the British Government, have a duty to face up to their responsibilities" (emphasis added). The peace was fragile from the outset. The thrust of this chapter is to look at the more fundamental barriers to peace that have to be displaced before one can examine the mechanisms that will assist in inducing attitudinal change.

The approach of this chapter is modest. It accepts that a "peace agreement is merely one element of a larger peace process, an element that may create some new opportunities but hardly alters all aspects of the conflict."[1] In other words, it recognizes that we need to have a proper sense of timescales in approaching peace processes. It was Gerard Manley Hopkins who wrote in 1879: "and when Peace here does / house / He comes with work to do, he does not come to coo, / He comes to brood and sit." We too need to be conscious of the number of actors involved, of the status (actual and perceived) each one holds, and of our own propensity to rely on conventional wisdom. Finally, following Robert Rothstein, we need to put particular emphasis on the "contextual situation created by the structural conditions" in analysis of the Anglo-Irish conflict.[2] This chapter considers the current peace process in the context of factionalism, memory, and victimhood; in the role played by prestigious third parties in nudging the parties toward peace; and in the need to address relations between Great Britain and Ireland. First, however, we must recognize the (unconscious) barriers that the Western political tradition places in the path toward reconciliation.

It was Kader Asmal, the South African cabinet minister, who, in citing Antonio Gramsci, reminded us of an older political tradition:

> If the old order is dying and the new is not yet born, can there be reconciliation simply through an assertion that new structures and new arrangements will be set in place? Is reconciliation between victim/survivor and the overlord possible on the basis of a Caliban and Prospero relationship, between master and servant?[3]

Ultimately, reconciliation is about much more than simple institutional restructuring. Barely a decade after the defeat of the Nazis, Hannah Arendt addressed similar concerns through the power to forgive and the power to promise:

> The possible redemption from the predicament of irreversibility—of being unable to do what one has done though one did not, and could not, know what he was doing—is the faculty of forgiving. . . . In contrast to forgiving, which—perhaps because of its religious context, perhaps because of love attending its discovery—has always been deemed unrealistic and inadmissible in the public realm, the power of stabilization inherent in the faculty of making promises has been known throughout our tradition.[4]

We should note that nowhere in her treatise on forgiveness does she mention forgetting:

> Instead, she argues that forgiving is truly an act of freedom. Revenge—the alternative to forgiveness—is merely a reaction that stands in contrast to the unpredictable and unexpected character of forgiveness. . . . Forgiveness sets aside revenge . . . [T]he only really viable—and therefore moral—option is to identify, thereby remembering, the villainy of the past, but then to displace this legacy of inhumanity to the margins of societal concern.[5]

This suggests that one of the important elements in any peace process is a concern for healing, an area that has not received its due regard in the Anglo-American system.

The second way in which the Western political tradition impedes progress toward reconciliation is its inattention to what Rothstein calls the "subjective and elusive." This chapter asserts that more attention should be paid to the significance of symbolic capital and to our capacity for mythmaking:

> Man's political life is more intimately an expression of the general quality of his imaginative life than we are in the habit of noticing. And those who are concerned with man's imaginative life are therefore concerned with the area in which his political concepts are shaped. Are shaped: they do not shape themselves, but are shaped in his imagination, not only by man's immortal destiny and the metaphysical questions to which it gives rise, but also by the particular contexts of nation, doctrine, class and race. . . . [T]he study of politics must neither neglect the fact that man is an imagining and myth-making animal, nor fail to make explicit allowances for the necessary entry of imagination and myth-making into the study itself."[6]

The Irish conflict is redolent of a huge capacity for mythmaking. It is one of the major elements that has sustained the conflict; and unless we address it wherever it appears, we will learn (with Lionel Trilling) that unless "we insist that politics is imagination and mind, we will learn that imagination and mind are politics, and of a kind that we will not like." In the political economy of reconciliation, we must not forget the paradox of our emotional inability to forgive politically and our tremendous capability to use symbols and myths in a potentially destructive manner—or at least to sustain us through serious communal crises.

The Context of Decision

It is not too difficult to chart the breakdown of the first phase of the Irish peace process. The reasons are all too familiar: historic mistrust, a sense of communal "memory," factionalism, and victimhood. I will examine these in turn and try to put them into some comparative perspective. Above all we need to keep our eye on timescales because they remove the euphoria of the quick fix. One way in which we can approach this is to consider a very simple question: When did the Anglo-Irish peace process begin?

The received wisdom is that it was launched on December 15, 1993, when the British and Irish prime ministers launched their Joint Declaration. It was a piece of tortuous syntax that defies textual exegesis. One of its more astute commentators, David Goodall, had been a major player in

Anglo-Irish diplomatic relationships and one of the architects of the Anglo-Irish Agreement of 1985. Understanding the nuances, the actors, and the dynamics of the conflict, he notes the skillful drafting and the abundance of coded language that "laid a veneer of unanimity over what are still divergent and in some respects directly conflicting interests." Hence it is

> a minor diplomatic masterpiece . . . [which] is not a formal agreement or treaty setting the framework for a comprehensive constitutional settlement; it is a political statement of attitude and intent directed primarily at the IRA. The two heads of government have carefully shelved all the difficult long term issues . . . in order to make a bid for an IRA cease-fire.[7]

In the short term, they succeeded. For virtually the first time in Anglo-Irish relations, they were using the language of "inclusion" and "process," and this was enough to enable the IRA to renounce violence and to permit Sinn Fein into the democratic process.

But it is important to remember that the Joint Declaration had its own preplay in the form of secret meetings and exercises in track-two diplomacy. Shortly after the publication of the declaration, Sinn Fein produced its own record of its secret communications with a British government emissary.[8] *Setting the Record Straight* traced a line of communication back to mid-1990. The document is indicative of the fragility of the peace because it illustrates the mutual animosities. There had been negotiations in previous cease-fires; those in 1974–1975 had sapped IRA morale and led to a change in leadership. It was that selfsame leadership that was now in command. It needed to be convinced that the present negotiations would not be a rerun of the past—an assurance given on January 12 and March 23, 1993. For his part, Prime Minister John Major accepted as "a working assumption" that the IRA had renounced violence for good three months after the August cessation, and his officials began a series of bilateral talks with Sinn Fein. It was assumed that talks with ministers would follow later.

Another version of the preplay leading to the current peace process consists of the talks that had been conducted between Sinn Fein and the major nationalist constitutionalist party, the Social Democratic and Labour Party (SDLP), during 1994. These talks had occurred in the aftermath of an IRA public relations disaster—the Enniskillen bomb in November 1987—when eleven innocent civilians were blown to bits as they commemorated their dead of two world wars. The SDLP took advantage of Sinn Fein's psychological weakness with a series of meetings with the group beginning in the following March. Although the talks broke down in September, their significance should not be underestimated. It was the first time that Sinn Fein policies had been closely scrutinized by a party with the same ends of Irish unity. The SDLP invoked the ghosts of the republican past to challenge the latter's claim to be the heirs of nonsectarianism. In that respect, the dialogue had an educative effect and shifted the debate away from moral certitude. Over the next few years, republicans were to open their doors to concerned members of the Protestant community who sought to point out the errors of the armed struggle. As well, the dialogue rehearsed many of the issues that were to surface in the Joint Declaration. Finally, the debate about self-determination was moved from its theological plinth and placed firmly in the harsh realities of the late twentieth century.

A third aspect of the preplay was the influence of exogenous forces. One commentator, Tim Coogan, has suggested that we can trace the gestation of the peace process to the pope's visit to Ireland in 1979, when he challenged so publicly the morality of the armed struggle.[9] That may or may not have impacted republican supporters, but it is an indication that they were moving from the interstices of a sect into a more mature political movement that was conscious of changes in global conditions. This maturation can be noted in particular in Sinn Fein's attitude toward developments in Europe. Throughout the 1980s, it had been hostile toward the European Union (EU); and yet in its discussion document *Towards a New Ireland* (1992), it recognized that traditional sovereignties were eroding, that jurisdictions were in flux, and that boundaries were altering. It alluded to the demand for political democracy in Eastern Europe, to German reunification, to economic restructuring under EU integration, and to an Irish republicanism that "has its roots in the crucible of Europe during the great French Revolution. It saw the political and economic transformation of Europe as providing a golden opportunity for Ireland to finally resolve its British problem."[10]

The EU played an important role in the immediate post-cease-fire period. Indeed, it is probably true that external actors have played the crucial role in keeping the process in some sort of shape. In the autumn of 1994, the European Commission created a Special Task Force to look into further ways in which it could give practical assistance to Northern Ireland and the border counties to assist in the peace process. It produced the "Delors package" (also known as the Peace and Reconciliation Programme), which would run for five years with a budget of ECU 300 million (300 million European currency units) for the first three years, with financing for the final two years subject to review. This program is particularly important because it attempts to target projects at a grassroots level.

Just as important was the role of Bill Clinton's administration in the pre–cease-fire period. Despite objections from the British government and his own Justice and State Departments, early in 1994 President Clinton gave the Sinn Fein president, Gerry Adams, a visa to visit the United States—his first in over twenty years—to address the prestigious American

Committee on Foreign Policy. Adams had forty-eight hours in media nirvana, and nowhere did he give an unequivocal renunciation of violence. That was a matter of some embarrassment to his hosts and to President Clinton. It damaged Anglo-American relations and infuriated the wider population. Despite that—but after the IRA cease-fire—he was able to visit the United States on another two occasions during 1994, and Sinn Fein was permitted to raise funds here. In addition, the United States continued to court investment for Ireland. In May 1995, President Clinton hosted a major investment conference in Washington, D.C., to be followed by a more modest affair in 1996. In late 1995, he made a historic visit to Britain and Ireland, which had the effect of injecting more dynamism into the peace process at a time when it was bogged down in the decommissioning issue. Within hours of his visit, the British and Irish governments held a hastily called summit in which they announced the launch of a "twin-track" process to make progress in parallel on the decommissioning issue and on all-party negotiations.

Such external support and pressure was critical in sustaining the idea of peace, especially after the collapse of the first IRA cease-fire, by transforming the context and, hence, the conflict:

> By definition, intractable conflicts cannot be resolved. Still, they can be transformed into tractable ones that are, in principle, capable of resolution. The only way to do this is to construct a context that includes the sacrificially expelled other. It is here that public peace processes play a crucial role.[11]

Factionalism

The cease-fires arrived after a long gestation. They were influenced by endogenous and exogenous factors and were sustained by (track-one and track-two) diplomacy. Moreover, they occurred within a process of constructing an alternative political discourse on the age-old Anglo-Irish relationship. This process begins with an ambiguity about the relationship between politics and violence, and it descends into the idea of politics as a zero-sum game. The very acceptance of "process" is an acknowledgment that politics need not be static. From such modest beginnings, a new vocabulary begins to emerge. If this is the case, it represents a remarkable shift in attitudes against the accretions of a malign history.

One of those accretions has been the effect of factionalism in the politics of Northern Ireland. Cynthia Enloe reminds us that ethnic conflict "can be irreconcilable and thus most harmful to nation-building when each of the chief contestants is politically underdeveloped. Fraught with internal dissent and suspicion each community is incapable of presenting leaders who can negotiate and institutions that can accurately represent the community's views."[12] Enloe could have had Northern Ireland in mind when writing this, because it was a polity that existed under a form of permanent factionalism. To some extent, such factionalism had been encouraged by the system of proportional representation introduced at the founding of the state. But that had been abolished by 1929 and factionalism continued. At its most basic level, the nationalist community was represented by physical force and constitutional traditions.

In the unionist community, the position was slightly more complicated. There were interdenominational divisions in Protestantism that ensured that that community did not enjoy the same communal solidarity as their Catholic neighbors. More important, they divided on their attitude toward the constitutional future of Northern Ireland. Richard Rose has categorized them as "ultra" and "allegiant";[13] Owen Dudley Edwards as the "fearful" and "confident" Protestants;[14] Paul Bew and colleagues refer to "populist" and "antipopulist" unionists;[15] and Jennifer Todd writes of the "Ulster British" and the "Ulster Loyalist" traditions.[16] The checklist illustrates the "singular *lack* of confidence in its own efficacy and power" of a community that was "historically dominant, well organized and successful in so many walks of life."[17] As John Whyte notes, it "is because Protestants distrust Protestants, not just because Protestants distrust Catholics, that the Ulster conflict is so intense."[18]

These divisions within unionism were reflected as late as May 30, 1996, when elections were held for a Northern Ireland Forum. Whereas nationalists were divided between Sinn Fein and the SDLP, there was a five-way split in unionism between the Ulster Unionist Party (UUP), the Democratic Unionist Party (DUP), the United Kingdom Unionist Party (UKUP), the Progressive Unionist Party (PUP), and the Ulster Democratic Party (UDP). The PUP and UDP were the political representatives of the loyalist paramilitaries and remained fully committed to the peace process. On the other hand, the DUP and the UKUP believed the process to be a sham and an attempt to appease republican extremists. That placed the largest party, the UUP (24.2 percent), in the invidious position of having to decide on which side to jump. To support the fringe parties would alienate the UUP's more powerful rivals in the DUP, and that could have a malign effect when the UUP next stood for election. So the UUP's response at that stage was procrastination, and that slowed the dynamic of the peace process.

Factionalism has had a more insidious effect on political life than simply shaping election results. From a survey of Belfast residents and politicians conducted in 1966—that is, before the present troubles broke out—Ian Budge and Cornelius O'Leary produced a circular argument that politicians perceived their electors to be more extreme than was the case, hence their need to appear to be extreme to ensure reelection. The result was that the electorate assumed that conditions were worse than they had imagined:

> Certainly a majority of Unionist adherents and councillors—seconded by the press—wished in 1966 to make conciliatory moves towards the Catholics . . . which if carried through might have defused the imminent crisis. But moderate councillors were discouraged and conservatives strengthened by an overestimate of intransigence among the population: while the resultant failure of the moderate leaders to act strongly reinforced popular impressions of Unionist intransigence and immobility.[19]

It is important to remember the degree to which Northern Ireland has operated as a demotic culture. A demotic culture suggests that power emanates from the bottom up, in that elites pay close attention to the views of their grassroots supporters. This kind of dependency on the demos has been prevalent in Northern Ireland for historical and sociological reasons. From the seventeenth century, Protestants have indulged in a form of "public banding,"[20] whereby they refuse to place their trust in the state security apparatus but rely instead on local arrangements. Moreover, a population of 1.5 million, contained within a tiny landmass, has a phenomenal degree of elected representation—twelve members of Parliament at Westminster, fifty-two in the Northern Ireland Parliament at Stormont, and several hundred local councillors elected to seventy-three local authorities. In such a "face-to-face" society, politicians are in constant contact with their electors.

This demotic culture is particularly the case in the Protestant community, where denominational differences have ensured that no one church can speak on the behalf of all Protestants. In his study of Presbyterians and the conflict, John Dunlop writes of the religion's democratic ethos and its mistrust of centralized power in contrast to the hierarchical and authoritarian nature of Catholicism. He writes too of a "People of the Word" who "do not live easily with studied ambiguity,"[21] hence their great suspicion of documents like the Joint Declaration. At a structural level, this attitude has meant a huge amount of local autonomy and an inordinate influence in the political realm for the deeply conservative, interdenominational Orange Order. As a result, political leadership has been lacking, and politicians have taken their lead from their perceptions of how much the market will bear. This has led to an absence of risk taking and the promotion of procrastination.

This need not necessarily have a negative effect on a peace process, however. If the "bottom" is prepared to take risks for peace, then it has the capacity to produce political realignment. The forum elections of May 1996 may be the earliest indication that such a realignment is under way. The fringe loyalist parties that had campaigned on a platform promoting peace garnered a sufficient number of votes to take part in the multiparty negotiations. On the nationalist side, Sinn Fein did remarkably well with 15.5 percent of the vote, largely as a consequence of being committed to a peace process. These two examples demonstrate that that which was insidious in the past could be inverted to act as a catalyst for change.

In this respect, the loyalist and republican parties assumed the role of what Byron Bland calls "transcenders."[22] He cites a number of examples. One occurred in January 1976, when eleven workers were held up by gunmen in a rural area in Northern Ireland. When they were asked if there were any Catholics in the group, the assumption was that this was a loyalist paramilitary group. The single Catholic worker made a move to step out, but one of his comrades tried to hold him back. The message was one of commonality. Nevertheless, the Catholic man stepped out, and the gunmen (who were in fact IRA) murdered the other ten:

> "Transcenders are many things—people, actions, events, gestures, metaphors, dreams, and visions. In Northern Ireland, the non-sacrificial stories in the Gospels are central. The form is not important. It is the task they accomplish that is important: *they connect what violence has severed.*"[23]

On many occasions in the multiparty talks that ensued from the Forum elections, the fringe parties continued to play this role, pushing the historically constitutional parties toward compromise and engagement with the other side.

Memory

> It is possible that there is no other memory than the memory of wounds.
>
> —Czeslaw Milosz

Literary critic Denis Donoghue makes the distinction between official and unofficial history:

> History is only one way of being significant. Memory gives the unofficial sense of history, effects an order not sequential but agglutinative. That is why we never ask our memories to line up rationally or sequentially, like soldiers on parade: they obey our orders, but not always or in the form we prescribe.[24]

History has been used in an applied sense in the Irish conflict. When modern Sinn Fein and the IRA were resurrected in 1969, they claimed to be the direct descendants of those who led the rising in 1916 against British rule; and they, in turn, were the direct descendants of the United Irishmen who had attempted precisely the same in 1798.

The 1798 rebellion was led by Wolfe Tone, a Protestant and the architect of a rhetorical nonsectarian republicanism. Tone wrote in his book *Life* that his means were to "unite the whole people of Ireland, to abolish the memory of all past dissensions, and to substitute the common name of Irishman in place of the denominations of Protestant, Catholic and Dissenter." This has had a powerful resonance in a country riven by religious conflict. A cult developed around the memory of Tone more than forty years after his death. According to Marianne Elliott, his *Life* was

> the first nationalist reading of Irish history, a reading that was to become the gospel of Irish republicanism. The elements of that gospel, stripped of its American and French terminology, are that the Catholics are the Irish nation proper; Protestant power is based on "massacre and plunder" and penalisation of the Catholics, reducing them to slavishness, which the Catholic Committee finally broke in 1792.[25]

That message had a certain seductive charm in republican Belfast and Derry in the 1970s and 1980s. Tone's grave at Bodenstown became a place for national pilgrimage. To this day, it remains a holy place in republican martyrology and attracts annual commemorations.

Of course, republicanism was about "armed struggle," and Tone's legacy may not have been so benign. In one respect, he was the perfect archetype. He had no real sense of projection, and his message "was almost empty of positive content. Breaking the connection with England, and the eradication of English influence in Ireland, were the obsessive concerns. What would succeed independence was hazy indeed, especially in social and economic terms."[26] In addition, he "contributed the notion of the Republic (especially as epitomised by its Army, the repository of civic virtue and authority) and in general favoured the movement's totalitarian strain."[27] The year 1798 (and 1916) represented heroic failure and a form of religious nationalism based on martyrology. The leader of the latter, Patrick Pearse, described Bodenstown as "the holiest place in Ireland; holier to us even than the place where [St.] Patrick sleeps in Down. *Patrick brought us life but this man died for us . . . the greatest of all that have died for Ireland.*"[28] According to Pearse, Tone bequeathed a gospel of Irish nationalism that "armed his generation in defense of it," as was apparent in 1916.

I have lingered on Tone and Pearse because they represent the iconography of Irish republicanism. Both had been engaged in armed struggle, and both have been used to justify the contemporary campaign of violence. Their followers have worked on the assumption of splendid failure within a characteristic Irish time frame that inclines "Irishmen to a repetitive view of history and . . . such a view inclines them—perhaps in defensive wariness and from fear of failure—to prize the moral as against the actual, and the bearing of witness as against success. The *locus classicus* of this cast of mind is the Proclamation of the Republic on Easter Monday 1916."[29] This recurring sense of timelessness reinforced by "the Christian view of God as standing outside time entirely," this sense of timeless justice, "spreads in all directions in Ireland, north as well as south, to fundamental law as well as natural rights";[30] and it enables Irish revolutionaries to elide time, to choose from the past to validate or invalidate actions of the present. In this century, the 1916 rebellion marks the crucial event that explains all others, as Adams has no doubt:

> [The IRA] today takes its historical and organizational origins from the forces which engaged in the Easter Rising of 1916, though one can trace its ancestry much further back if one wishes. But the circumstances which shaped the support for the IRA are above all the experience of the barricade days from 1969–72. These days are of continuing importance not just in terms of the IRA but because they saw the development of tremendous communal solidarity, more than a memory of which remains today.[31]

Memory again—that umbilical link between 1916 and the barricade days of the 1960s and 1970s.

Victimhood

Northern Ireland operated under not only an underdeveloped and demotic culture, but also an *intimidatory* one. When protracted violence erupted in 1969, the IRA was unprepared. It lacked the resources to defend its community; paradoxically, that meant a stronger sense of communal solidarity because often it was the general public rather than a revolutionary elite that organized the barricades to defend the areas of Catholic west Belfast against an onslaught launched by Protestant mobs, with police complicity in some cases. It was in this milieu that a new revolutionary generation began to assert itself. It started with several assets, the most crucial being that "the whole process was so *natural* as to be beyond comment." Attitudes were to be more important than weapons, and that was to be the key to republican strategy: "Nothing had to be imported, nothing fashioned by ideologues, nothing sold to the people, nothing secretly arranged because of events. All that was needed was to exploit the existing reality."[32] That reality was based on a memory of past oppressions and the nature of an intimidatory culture with its emphasis on territoriality and vigilance. Settler (Protestant) vigilance, whether in the form of loyalist mobs or locally recruited militias (official or otherwise), "taught the natives that power and self-assertion were the property of those who could successfully inflict violence."[33] The result was a circularity of violence whereby "vigilance of power perpetually generates the symptoms of rebellion it purportedly guards against; while rebellion on the principle of collective responsibility validates the anxieties of the dominant."[34]

The Protestant tradition of "public banding" reflects this sense of public insecurity. Public banding reasserted itself during the final Home Rule crisis with the creation of the Ulster Volunteer Force and the establishment of a Provisional Government. In more recent times, sections of Protestant Ulster perceived the civil rights campaign as a challenge to their existence and entered into a form of public banding because they believed that state power could not monopolize coercive relationships. In that situation, "the whole system is one of threatened violence in which the state is a feeble pivot between its ostensible supporters . . . and the natives."[35]

Given these circumstances, it is not surprising that in modern times, Northern Ireland has "generated the most intense political violence of any part of the contemporary UK, the highest levels of *internal* political violence of any member-state of the European Community, and the highest levels of internal political violence in the continuously liberal democratic states of the post-1948 world."[36] Nearly 2 percent of the population of Northern Ireland has been killed or injured since the late 1970s, leaving the auditors to conclude that being "'second to Lebanon' is an unenviable classification."[37] Nor is it surprising that the people of Northern Ireland suffered from "'a political economy of helplessness,' a victim-bonded society in which memories of past injustice and humiliation are so firmly entrenched in both communities and the sense of entrapment so complete that the hunger strikes [of 1980–1981] are a metaphor for the entrapment of the larger society."[38]

The hunger strikes serve admirably as a paradigm of the Northern Ireland conflict. Ten republican prisoners took their own lives through starvation in a demand for political status inside the prisons. They were following in a tradition in which twelve republicans had already starved to death earlier in the twentieth century for their beliefs. It was a practice that flourished in pre-Christian times in Ireland and derives from the ancient Irish (Brehon) Laws that recognized and strove to regulate the rite of "fasting against a person of exalted state in order to enforce a claim against him." The alternatives for the exalted person were threefold: the first was to concede the claim; the second to start a counterfast; and the third was to let the hunger striker starve himself to death. None of these was congenial. Like the 1916 rebels, the prisoners in 1981 had gone into battle not to win but to die. Their campaign was seeped in martyrology and religious symbolism: Sinn Fein's plea for a vote to save a prisoner's life; the graffiti of a dying hunger striker being comforted by the Virgin Mary with the message "Blessed are those who hunger for justice"; the prisoners using their bodies as social texts, in the act of refusal, i.e., refusing to eat, wash, smearing body and cell with excrement, acts which not only violate conventional notions of cleanliness and dirt, but are shockingly redolent of the purification by putrefaction of the flesh, as with the early Christian anchorites (which one might add is embodied in the text and discourse of Irish Catholicism).[39]

Also symbolic was their supporters' sense of the theatric, with the hunger strikers portrayed in crucified postures, the prison's barbed wire being transformed into crowns of thorns and prison blankets into burial shrouds. Above all, there was the place of religion, with Mass as a "real sacrifice" and source of comfort and strength to the prisoners. And at the heart of the Mass lay the Eucharistic prayer, with the memorial acclamation of the people, a version of which reads, "Lord, by your cross and resurrection / you have set us free. / You are the Saviour of the world."

On the day that the first hunger striker died, the IRA killed a police officer. At his funeral, the clergyman asked rhetorically: "Where does the real agony lie? Is it with those who use the threat of the choice of death or with those who have no choice?" This perception, according to Padraig O'Malley, "once again reaffirmed Protestants' sense of their own victimhood and helplessness, invalidating their grievances, making meaningless the deaths of their coreligionists who gave their lives for the protection of the state, reminding them of the perilous state of their existence."[40] In that respect, the hunger strike emphasized that Northern Ireland is a society without a sense of empathy. Protestants had their own "chosen traumas"; and both communities had fallen back on a mechanism that characterizes traumatized national groups—what John Mack calls the "egoism of victimization":

> The egoism of victimization is the incapacity of an ethno-national group, as a direct result of its own historical traumas, to empathize with the suffering of another group. It is analogous to the narcissism or self-centredness of some individuals who see themselves as having been so hurt or deprived in the past that they can attend only to their own needs, feeling little or no empathy for the hurt they inflict upon others. Similarly, ethno-national groups that have been traumatized by repeated sufferings at the hands of other groups seem to have little capacity to grieve for the hurts of other peoples, or to take responsibility for the new victims created by their own warlike actions. Victims kill victims through unendingly repeated cycles that are transmitted from one generation to another, bolstered by stories and myths of atrocities committed by the other people, and by heroic acts committed in defense of the nation and its values by one's own.[41]

"Top-Down" Versus "Bottom-Up" Tactics

The changing Anglo-Irish relationship since the 1980s has been the motor that has altered the Northern Ireland conflict. In August 1969, the British government produced a Joint Declaration (signed by the British and Northern Ireland prime ministers) that said that "responsibility for affairs in Northern Ireland is entirely a matter of domestic jurisdiction. The United Kingdom Government will take full responsibility for asserting this principle in all international relationships." Clearly, this statement was aimed at the Irish government, and it was no accident that the leader of the UUP, James Molyneaux, alluded to it in his contribution to the House of Commons debate on the Joint Declaration between the British and Irish governments in 1993. He wondered whether the prime minister could assure his party members that "the drift from that position over the past 20 years will be halted under his premiership." On the other hand, the SDLP leader, John Hume, described the 1993 declaration as "one of the most comprehensive declarations that had been made about British-Irish relations in the past 70 years." He placed his comments in a context in which the "British-Irish quarrel of old, the quarrel of sovereignty, has changed fundamentally in the evolution of the new interdependent and post-nationalist Europe of which we are members, but the legacy of the past is the deeply divided people of Ireland."

These two statements encapsulate the gap between contemporary unionism and republicanism. The former wants to return to the certainties of the status quo ante. With the imposition of direct rule in 1972, republicans had lost their Parliament and government overnight. The signing of the Anglo-Irish Agreement in November 1985 (without any consultation whatsoever with the unionist leadership) demonstrated a decisive shift in the locus of power from London and Belfast to London and Dublin. It fell well short of joint authority, but it suggested that Anglo-Irish relations were much less asymmetrical than in the past. The failure of the unionist people to overthrow the agreement represented a seminal point in British-Ulster relations. For the first time in their history, unionists had failed to overturn a major decision of a British government. In 1912–1914, they had succeeded in amending the Third Home Rule Bill; in 1974, they had successfully rejected the imposition of a power-sharing government and of a Council of Ireland. The Anglo-Irish Agreement represented a historic failure, a failure compounded by joint decisions of the two governments in the following years. Thereafter, the two governments worked on the assumption that they were dealing with a three-stranded relationship: within Northern Ireland; between north and south; and between the peoples of Britain and Ireland.

All of this has highlighted the essential powerlessness of the unionist people. Admittedly, their Parliament members held the balance of power in the latter end of the Major premiership, but that was both negative and short term. The best that they could hope for was a slowing down of the Anglo-Irish process, and that was a long way from the heady days of

1921–1972. Now they were conscious of being a tiny minority within the United Kingdom and of being virtually friendless in Parliament. Their new position raised questions about the nature of their political leadership and about political elites generally. The Anglo-Irish process was teaching them to distinguish between endogenous and exogenous elites. When Hume told his annual party conference in 1980 that not only were they not in government but they were not even in opposition, he could have been speaking for all political leaders in Northern Ireland. From the 1980s, the locus of power lay at Westminster, assisted by the incremental influence of Dublin. The SDLP had input through Dublin, but unionist leaders did not enjoy the same luxury. One outcome was the replacement of Molyneaux by David Trimble as leader of the UUP in September 1995. Reverend Ian Paisley remained as leader of the DUP, but the electoral thrust of his party and his own (essentially negative) powers were diminishing. This trend has remained, as Paisley has kept his party outside the multiparty talks process since the summer of 1997.

The Anglo-Irish Agreement, the Joint Declaration, and the Frameworks Document of February 1995 (which placed flesh on the bones of the Joint Declaration) were all top-down initiatives brought about by the frustration of the British and Irish governments over the unwillingness of the endogenous elites to forge a common way forward. These did not claim to be final settlements but were no more than a tiny step toward (to quote from the Declaration) "the development of an agreed framework for peace." The two governments were anxious to avoid the problem of unattractive initial offers and, in relation to the three-stranded approach, had devised the formula that "nothing is agreed until everything is agreed." The introduction of this formula was indicative of the sensitivities involved; both governments were conscious that they were dealing with a people used to a bottom-up approach, so they were careful not to pitch their ambitions too highly. The Heads of Agreement document published in January 1998, while nudging the parties forward, continued to reflect this concern. A pointed acknowledgment of the people's role is the simultaneous referendums to endorse the Good Friday Agreement reached on April 10, 1998, by the two governments and the parties engaged in the peace process.

Increasingly, the two governments came to acknowledge the Hume dictum that "the legacy of the past is the deeply divided people of Ireland." This comment can be read as a direct challenge to the republican tradition, although there is evidence to suggest that there were elements within the Sinn Fein leadership that were ready to meet it. Jim Gibney, an influential insider, had stated as early as June 1992 that a British "departure must be preceded by a *sustained* period of peace and will arise out of negotiation."[42] A similar view was expounded by Hume at his party conference in 1995 when he spoke of "the real healing process [that] will take place and *in a generation or two* a new Ireland will evolve" (emphasis added). Here at least was some sense of realism and proper timescales from one side of the divide. It explains too why the IRA did not respond more positively to the Joint Declaration for more than eight months. In the first place, it needed greater clarification of the meaning of the declaration; and second, it needed to bring its rank and file with it. That was one reason Sinn Fein published *Setting the Record Straight* in January 1994 and called a special delegate conference in July. In the meantime, the leadership had been traveling the length and breadth of Ireland to explain its reasoning. It also explains the IRA's refusal to use the word "permanent" regarding the cease-fire and why it was not prepared to countenance any weapons decommissioning prior to inclusive meaningful talks. Initially, when the IRA sought clarification of certain aspects of the declaration, the British view was that it was a freestanding document that needed no further comment. Sinn Fein demurred. After a standoff, the government agreed in May 1994 to answer twenty questions put to it by Sinn Fein through the Irish government. Question 18(a) asked specifically: "The British Government has called upon Sinn Fein to renounce violence. What does this mean?" The response was a fudged reiteration of paragraph 10 of the Joint Declaration.[43] Sinn Fein assumed that the very absence of violence and its democratic mandate were enough to ensure entry into all party talks.

Instead, the secretary of state produced a further clarification of this issue in the United States in March 1995, one month after the publication of the Frameworks Document, which had received a fairly hostile welcome from the mainstream unionist parties. This address was dubbed the "Washington Three speech" because it contained three elements on decommissioning: the acceptance of the principle of disarmament; the modalities by which it could be achieved; and the necessity to make some gesture of decommissioning as an act of good faith prior to entering negotiations. Loyalist and republican paramilitaries balked at the inclusion of this third point. They saw it as the imposition of a new precondition and that to accept it was to surrender. This was to be the major hurdle blocking the peace process until the International Body on Decommissioning—under the direction of former U.S. Senator George Mitchell, with the assistance of General Jean de Chastelain of Canada and former Finnish Prime Minister Harri Holkeri—proposed a compromise. The Mitchell Report issued on January 22, 1996, was careful to make the point that "the peace process cannot be achieved solely by reference to the decommissioning of arms" (para. 51). In that respect, it got the British government off the hook on which it had impaled itself. Nevertheless, and in spite of the breakdown of the IRA cessation, republicans have managed to keep their structures intact. It may be that it was necessary to return to violence to do just that. But at least one valuable lesson had been adhered to: the leadership ensured that it kept its rank and file in touch and went to great lengths to avoid a split. Splintering of republican movements has been a tendency in Irish history and had occurred twice since the 1970s.

Unity within republicanism was paramount for two reasons. An undisciplined return to the armed struggle could unleash a campaign more vicious than heretofore. Second, the leadership was conscious that if it were to enter negotiations, it would have to rely on its powers of persuasion rather than the barrel of a gun. Adams was aware of the direction in which he wanted to take republicanism. He was engaged in a "New Departure." His manifesto, *The Politics of Irish Freedom,* admitted that since the 1930s, there had been no real effort to map out "what type of republic was aimed at. . . . We could not free the Irish people. We could only, with their support, create the conditions in which they would free themselves." He accepted that in the past, "the republican movement was a separatist movement with radical tendencies. In its current embodiment the radical tendency is for the first time in control."[44] It was this tendency that persuaded the 1986 Sinn Fein annual conference to end abstentionism to the Irish Parliament (supported by the General Army Convention of the IRA), to enter into talks with the SDLP in 1988, and to pursue the path of peace in the 1990s.

Republicanism had been suffering from a presentational problem in that the IRA campaign was too "successful" insofar as it was able to inflict disproportionate damage on the civilian population and to establish exchange relations with the state. But it was not powerful enough to secure victory. We can put this into a comparative context by borrowing from the literature on emancipatory movements and on the mythopoeic in politics. The former allows for "the politics of the moral moment [where] the defects of society are interpreted as failures of the State" and where discourse is examined as a "combination of narratives and texts, in the context of transcending projects. They take on an independent life of their own whether from above, in the form of the discourse of the state, or below, in an antidiscourse directed against the state."[45] The latter undermines ordered jurisdictions and stable networks by downgrading "conventional knowledge while claiming superior moral insight." The point of departure for contemporary emancipatory movements "is not equality but *victimhood.* This is what distinguishes them from 'old' social movements which fought for equality or greater participation. Today it is the 'negativised other' which takes the moral measure of the whole." The IRA fit this model.

It shared with the bulk of the Irish people a reading of history as conquest and dispossession with a loss of patrimony and a historic sense of grievance. Theirs was not

a world of choice from which some had been excluded but a universe of
meaning in which insight is inspired by victimhood and confrontation
[where] inversionary discourse is a means of altering prevailing boundaries and jurisdictions on the ground and in the mind. If *they reject ordinary claims and demands and remain aloof from negotiation and the bargaining that accompanies democracy* the intent is to create moral and
symbolic capital in opposition to economic capital.[46]

There is a whole Irish literary tradition devoted to the creation of such capital. It can be found in some of the poetry arising with the dispossession of
an entire caste after the Elizabethan conquest in the seventeenth century. It
can be found in the Irish strategem of wrapping itself in ambiguity; it can
be found even in the context of political violence. Successive Irish rebel-
lions could never hope to defeat the might of British rule, hence the concept
of splendid failure within a characteristic Irish time frame. The 1916
Proclamation of the Easter Rebellion, for example, alluded to the fact that
the uprising was the seventh call to arms in the previous three centuries. It
was a vindication of the current generation and an exercise in calculated
martyrdom that would create the climate for a new generation to continue
the struggle. Similarly, Adams made the connection between 1916 and the
"barricade days" after 1969. It was another step along the road to national
liberation begun by Wolfe Tone. It was part of a narrative—"the universal
desire to make sense of history by retelling the story to ourselves."

> [Narratives] can serve to release new, and hitherto concealed possibili-
> ties, of understanding one's history. . . . [T]he contemporary act of
> rereading (i.e., retelling) tradition can actually disclose uncompleted nar-
> ratives, which open up new possibilities of understanding.[47]

The last significant act in the politics of the moral moment was the
second hunger strike in 1981. The mythopoeic at its heart lies in a definition of myth as "a strategic mode of consciousness whereby we seek to
negate a real world that has grown intolerable in order to transform it into
an imaginary world which we can tolerate." Here was a classic example of
the great power of endurance. Because sacrifice obeys the laws of myth,
not politics, it can "operate on the assumption that victory can only spring
from defeat, and total rejuvenation of the community from the oblation of
a chosen hero or heroic elite."[48]

One of the messages of the hunger strike was that republicanism could
tap into an emotional groundswell of public opinion. Republicans transferred this into electoral support, and within a few years Sinn Fein was
capturing 40 percent of the Catholic vote. Its tactic of violence and the bal-
lot box, however, was proving to be contradictory in that it was finding it
difficult to broaden its constituency. This was the case in the Irish Republic, where it was taking less than 2 percent of the vote, a matter of some
embarrassment for those who claimed to be in the vanguard of the move

for Irish unity. In any case, Sinn Fein's constituency within Northern Ireland was showing signs of war weariness and a distaste for some of its operations. In addition, loyalist paramilitaries were becoming more pro-active, so that by the 1990s, they were killing more people than republicans: in just over a year, they had killed thirteen Sinn Fein activists or supporters. Republicans were aware too of shifts in government thinking. The secretary of state, Peter Brooke, had declared in November 1990 that Britain no longer had any selfish strategic or economic interest in remaining in Northern Ireland. Both he and his successor, Sir Patrick Mayhew, were implying that if there was a renunciation of violence, there would be a place at the negotiating table for Sinn Fein. *Setting the Record Straight* illustrates that violence had at least succeeded in establishing a communicative dimension. And there were signs that a strong Fianna Fail–Labour coalition, returned to office in January 1993, was to give the conflict a high priority with the promise that it would contribute to the peace process based on the principle of equal treatment for both sides. Finally, Hume and Adams opened up a private dialogue from April to September 1993 in which they moved beyond a stale reiteration of Irish nationalism to use the language of accommodation by recognizing that any "new agreement is only achievable and viable if it can earn and enjoy the allegiance of the different traditions of this island by accommodating diversity and providing for national reconciliation."

All of these statements and movements were part of the choreography that enabled the signing of the Joint Declaration to be followed by the two cease-fires. But something more profound had happened than a greater convergence of interests. It was a fundamental change in republican attitudes because republicans were prepared to enter into sustained negotiations with the British government and the unionist parties, well short of the victory they had anticipated. They were beginning to think in terms of a logical project: How do you shape a new Ireland? The republican movement was preparing to abandon a revolutionary and sacrificial ideology, to move beyond a victim-bonded society to a "society-in-becoming." They no longer enjoyed the certitude of a closed organization; and in their various dialogues, the concealed intentions of myths were being exposed—a distinction was being made between a utopian and an ideological concept of myth, between the inclusive and the exclusive:

> A positive hermeunetics offers an opportunity to salvage myth from the abuses of doctrinal prejudice, racist nationalism, class oppression or totalitarianism. And it does so in the name of a universal project of freedom—a project from which no creed, nation, class or individual is excluded.[49]

In short, republicans were facing up to the challenge that their mission was not simply about "an active remembering which reinterprets the suppressed voices of tradition," but that they had to develop "an *anticipatory memory* capable of projecting future images of liberation drawn from the past."[50] In other words, they were facing up to the challenge put to them by the SDLP in September 1988 when that party urged the need to challenge the old realities by political dialogue and an end to violence against fellow Irish people.

Nor should we forget that when the loyalists announced their cease-fire, they went to some lengths to offer their abject apologies for their serious crimes and misdemeanors. Using the language of repentance, they marked the way forward by apologizing to the loved ones of innocent victims and expressing abject remorse. Over time, such sentiments encouraged Sinn Fein leaders to begin the process of transcendence in language of repentance and progress. Speaking at a rally commemorating the twenty-fifth anniversary of Bloody Sunday, Martin McGuinness referred to the IRA's atrocities at Enniskillen and Shankill Road and said:

> We know there are two roads before us. One is the road to further conflict and the other is the road to the negotiating table. We have declared ourselves in favour of travelling to the negotiating table. There is nowhere else for us to go.[51]

What Is to Be Done?

The onward march of peace processes is not irreversible. One has to think only of the rate of progress in the Middle East and in South Africa to validate this point, although, interestingly, the quality of political leadership was demonstrated in the latter at a time of real crisis. There were serious security breaches in South Africa with the massacres at Boipatong in June 1992 (which left fifty-eight people dead) and at Bisho in September (with twenty-eight killed and more than two hundred injured). Despite these atrocities, and despite the huge misgivings of the African National Congress (ANC) about the role of the security forces, Nelson Mandela continued to exercise remarkable leadership. After Boipatong, the ANC enunciated fourteen preconditions before it would reenter talks; those were reduced to three following Bisho to enable the process to continue. This raises the question of the creation of a "strong center" in favor of peace, an issue to which we shall return below.

Some attempt has been made in Northern Ireland to manage expectations. In June 1995, the Foundation for a Civil Society organized a three-day seminar for some three hundred opinion formers in Belfast. "Reconciliation and Community: The Future of Peace in Northern Ireland" addressed the following issues: building trust (the negotiation process);

demobilization and reintegration; policing in a postconflict situation; beyond negotiations (coexistence and community); memory and acknowledgment (exploring a common history); and dependency and interdependency (new economic and political realities in transitional societies). The seminar drew on the experiences of those who had been involved in similar peace processes in South Africa, the Middle East, Central America and the former Soviet bloc. What was particularly important was that the participants were addressing representatives of all the main political traditions, as well as the paramilitaries and government representatives. In April 1998, the foundation also held a workshop in Northern Ireland for one hundred key community activists.

Following the bomb at Canary Wharf and the IRA's return to a campaign of low-intensity violence, the situation was not completely hopeless. The loyalist cease-fire remained (largely) intact, and their political leaders showed remarkable vision. One reason they managed to be constrained was that the political parties that voiced their concerns had an important political role to play in multiparty talks, and their supporters remained true to the peace process. After eighteen months of a cessation of violence, the wider population may have shuffled off their sense of fatalism. The popular commitment to moving the process forward, in combination with the promise of more favorable treatment by the new Labour government of Prime Minister Tony Blair and the new Fianna Fail–Progressive Democrat coalition government of Bertie Ahern, pushed the IRA to a reinstatement of its cease-fire on July 20, 1997, eighteen months after it had called it off. In return, Sinn Fein was promised entry into the substantive phase of multiparty talks on September 15, following a meeting between a Sinn Fein delegation and the secretary of state on August 8.

The inclusion of Sinn Fein in the negotiations alongside seven other parties (the UUP, the SDLP, the PUP, the UDP, Alliance, the Women's Coalition, and Labour) created the opportunity for a settlement based on inclusive dialogue. In January 1998, the two governments issued their joint Heads of Agreement paper, offering the broad outline of political arrangements designed to give each side a portion of its demands. Although the language by which new north-south institutions were described was considered a step away from the stronger terms of the Frameworks Document, and although the document was coldly received by Sinn Fein, the process of negotiation continued, uninterrupted by the temporary suspensions of the UDP and Sinn Fein for murders carried out by their affiliates in contradiction to the principles delineated in the Mitchell Report. Set upon a tight deadline for completion based on the program of simultaneous referendums north and south of the border, and upon elections to a shadow northern assembly all before the height of the marching season in Northern Ireland, the talks were concluded with a marathon thirty-six-hour session that ended on April 10, 1998. The result was a sixty-four-page comprehensive document, an act of transcendence calling for the creation of a new assembly in the north, new north-south cooperative bodies, a Council of the Isles, a bill of rights and a rights commission, an international body to consider police reform, judicial changes, and the phased release of paramilitary prisoners, among other things.

This process of negotiation would not have been possible had not the British, Irish, and U.S. governments remained onboard despite periodic discouraging events and invested so much in the process. Much, in fact, depended on the British general election of May 1997. At the end of the Conservative government's seventeen-year tenure, parliamentary arithmetic at Westminster left it reliant on the continuing support of the nine UUP members of Parliament to stay in office. In turn, the UUP was conscious that if it made any concessions on decommissioning, it would be attacked by its rivals in the DUP and the UKUP and could suffer in the next elections. In these circumstances, it becomes difficult to construct a strong center in the manner of South African or, to a lesser extent, Middle Eastern experience.[52]

Labour's overwhelming victory—followed by a change in government in the Irish Republic a few weeks later—changed the political landscape dramatically. The British government was no longer dependent upon Ulster Unionist support. The UUP had done sufficiently well not to have to worry too much about its DUP and UKUP rivals; in any case, it did not need to worry about any further elections before 1999. The two new governments placed a high priority on renewing the peace process and devoted extensive resources to seeing the negotiations through to agreement. The two prime ministers invested their own prestige and commitment in the process. Blair, for example, made his first policy speech outside London in Belfast and, in an effort to reassure the unionist community, reiterated the pledge regarding consensus as a basis for Northern Ireland's constitutional status; Northern Ireland would remain part of the United Kingdom into the foreseeable future. Over the eight months of talks, the two prime ministers met with each of the parties repeatedly and negotiated many of the details personally. Both Blair and Ahern flew to Belfast to conclude the deal and participated directly in the final two-day session, contributing to the sense within the talks that the moment was ripe for agreement and that "the hand of history" was pushing the process forward.

President Clinton too was actively involved in the negotiations process, although more as an exogenous facilitator than as a direct mediator. While I have mentioned above the U.S. contribution in the preplay leading up to the cease-fires and in keeping the momentum toward peace going in the face of setbacks, the United States also played an important role in the final months leading up to the Good Friday Agreement, from hosting representatives of all the parties in Northern Ireland and the republic that chose to participate in the St. Patrick's Day festivities to President Clinton's 4:00 A.M. phone calls to talks participants in the last hours of the historic final session. Though the Clinton administration's early engagement with the politics of Northern Ireland seemed, on the basis of its willingness to confront the traditional ostracism of Sinn Fein, weighted in favor of republicanism, it became more balanced and measured in its approach, cultivating the respect of parties on both sides of the divide as a neutral force for peace. In this regard, Clinton can be regarded, as can Blair and Ahern, as "transcenders," those who overcome historical divisions and encourage others to transcend the problems of memory, distrust, or the "egoism of victimhood."

In the interregnum between the signing of the Good Friday Agreement and the referendums to endorse or reject the deal, it is difficult to say what the future holds for Northern Ireland. It may be that the obstacles to reconciliation are too deeply embedded in the cultures and politics of Northern Ireland. Nevertheless, an opportunity has arisen to test whether cooperation can occur only between friends who can empathize with each other or whether the Western political tradition can reshape its myths and produce a process of reconciliation, forgiveness, and healing sufficient to transcend the villainy of its past.

Notes

1. Robert L. Rothstein, "After the Peace: The Political Economy of Reconciliation," Inaugural Rebecca Meyerhoff Memorial Lecture, May 1996 (Jerusalem: Harry S. Truman Institute, Hebrew University), p. 20.

2. Ibid., p. 18.

3. Kader Asmal, *Victims, Survivors, and Citizens: Human Rights, Reparations, and Reconciliation* (Cape Town, South Africa: University of Western Cape, 1992), p. 11.

4. Hannah Arendt, *The Human Condition* (Chicago: University of Chicago Press, 1958), pp. 236–247.

5. Byron Bland, *Marching and Rising: The Rituals of Small Differences and Great Violence in Northern Ireland* (Stanford, Calif.: Center for International Security and Arms Control, Stanford University, 1996), p. 13.

6. Conor Cruise O'Brien and William Dean Vanech, eds., *Power and Consciousness* (New York: New York University Press, 1969), p. 211.

7. David Goodall, "Terrorists on the Spot," *Spectator,* January 1, 1994, p. 1676.

8. Sinn Fein, *Setting the Record Straight* (Dublin: Sinn Fein, 1994).

9. Tim Pat Coogan, *The Troubles: Ireland's Ordeal, 1966–1995, and the Search for Peace* (London: Hutchinson, 1996), pp. 325–326.

10. Sinn Fein, *Towards a New Ireland* (Dublin: Sinn Fein, 1992).

11. Bland, *Marching and Rising,* p. 12.

12. Cynthia Enloe, *Ethnic Conflict and Political Development* (Boston: Little, Brown, and Co., 1973), pp. 169–170.

13. Richard Rose, *Governing Without Consensus: An Irish Perspective* (London: Faber and Faber, 1971).

14. Owen Dudley Edwards, *The Sins of Our Fathers: Roots of Conflict in Northern Ireland* (Dublin: Gill and Macmillan, 1970), pp. 64–70.

15. Paul Bew, Peter Gibbon, and Henry Patterson, *The State in Northern Ireland, 1921–72: Political Forces and Social Classes* (Manchester: Manchester University Press, 1979).

16. Jennifer Todd, "Two Traditions in Unionist Political Culture," in *Irish Political Studies* (Galway: PSAI Press, 1987), pp. 1–26.

17. Sarah Nelson, *Ulster's Uncertain Defenders: Protestant Political Paramilitary and Community Groups and the Northern Ireland Conflict* (Belfast: Appletree Press, 1984), p. 177.

18. John Whyte, "Catholic-Protestant Relations in Countries Other Than Ireland," in J. B. Early, ed., *Sectarianism: Roads to Reconciliation* (Dungannon: Three Candles, 1975), p. 278.

19. Ian Budge and Cornelius O'Leary, *Belfast: Approach to Crisis. A Study of Belfast Politics, 1613–1970* (London: Macmillan, 1973), p. 355.

20. Cf. David Miller, *Queen's Rebels* (London: Gill and Macmillan, 1977).

21. John Dunlop, *A Precarious Belonging: Presbyterians and the Conflict in Ireland* (Belfast: Blackstaff, 1995), p. 84.

22. Bland, *Marching and Rising.*

23. Ibid., pp. 10–11.

24. Denis Donoghue, *Warrenpoint* (London: Jonathan Cape, 1991), p. 124.

25. Marianne Elliott, *Wolfe Tone: Prophet of Irish Independence* (New Haven, Conn.: Yale University Press, 1989), p. 310.

26. Oliver MacDonagh, *States of Mind: A Study of Anglo-Irish Conflict, 1780–1980* (London: Allen and Unwin, 1983), p. 75.

27. Ibid., p. 89.

28. Elliott, *Wolfe Tone,* p. 416; emphasis added.

29. MacDonagh, *States of Mind,* p. 13.

30. Ibid., pp. 6–7.

31. Gerry Adams, *The Politics of Irish Freedom* (Dingle: Brandon Books, 1986), p. 52.

32. Bowyer Bell, *The Irish Troubles: A Generation of Political Violence, 1967–1992* (New York: St. Martin's Press, 1993), p. 41.

33. Frank Wright, *Northern Ireland: A Comparative Analysis* (Dublin: Gill and Macmillan, 1987), p. 130.

34. Ibid., p. 124.

35. Ibid., p. 122.

36. Brendan O'Leary and John McGarry, *The Politics of Antagonism: Understanding Northern Ireland* (London: Athlone, 1993), p. 8.

37. Ibid., p. 16.

38. Padraig O'Malley, *Biting at the Grave: The Irish Hunger Strikes and the Politics of Despair* (Belfast: Blackstaff, 1990), pp. 8–9.

39. David Apter, *Democracy, Violence, and Emancipatory Movements: Notes for a Theory of Inversionary Discourse* (Geneva: United Nations Research Institute for Social Development, 1997), p. 75.

40. O'Malley, *Biting at the Grave,* p. 182.

41. John Mack, "The Psychodynamics of Victimization Among National Groups in Conflict," in Vamik D. Volkan, Demetrios A. Julius, and Joseph V. Montville, eds., *The Psychodynamics of International Relationships,* vol. 1, *Concepts and Theories* (Lexington, Mass.: Lexington Books, 1990), p. 125.

42. Quoted in Coogan, *The Troubles,* p. 339; emphasis added.

43. The British and Irish governments reiterated that the *achievement* of peace must involve a permanent end to the use of, or support for, paramilitary violence. They confirmed that, in these circumstances, democratically mandated parties that establish a commitment to exclusively peaceful methods and that have shown that they abide by the democratic process are free to participate fully in democratic politics and to join in dialogue in due course between the governments and the political parties on the road ahead.

44. Adams, *The Politics of Irish Freedom,* pp. 8 and 162.

45. Apter, *Democracy,* p. 20.

46. Ibid., p. 23; emphasis added.

47. Richard Kearney, *Narratives* (Manchester: Manchester University Press, 1988), p. 272.

48. Ibid., p. 223.

49. Kearney, *Narratives,* p. 275.

50 Ibid., p. 270.

51. *Derry Journal,* February 4, 1997.

52. Adrian Guelke, *Improving the Political Process: Peace by Analogy* (London: British Irish Association, 1994), p. 1319.

5

Seeking Peace amid the Memories of War: Learning from the Peace Process in Northern Ireland

Duncan Morrow

When is a sheep not a sheep? Certainly when it's a wolf. There are many stories in Western culture warning us to beware of the wolf disguised, reminding us not to be taken in by its devious ways. Red Riding Hood found out the hard way, of course. Although she had her doubts, it took her some time to realize that the changes to her grandmother's appearance were not simply in her imagination. Unfortunately, clarification came a bit late. And in some versions of the story, there isn't even a woodcutter who arrives to cut her out again. In the story of the three little pigs, the need to spend the time building your house with impenetrable walls emerges as the primary lesson.

These allusions matter in Northern Ireland. Indeed, to enter into that atmosphere is to enter into some of the atmosphere that has bedeviled the peace process in Northern Ireland since 1994. How do you negotiate if your opponent is not the gentle lamb he or she presents himself or herself as, but is indeed a voracious and untrustworthy carnivore? The answer, of course, is to keep your own wolflike capacities in reserve, just in case. In doing so, however, you confirm to your opposite numbers that you are no herbivore yourself. To distort, if only slightly: When is a peace process not a peace process? When behind the surface offers of peace lies a strategy to take you by surprise and destroy you. When it's just another way to beat you.

Of course, there is nothing new in fear and mistrust at the outset of peace processes. Indeed, if there is no fear and mistrust, there may be no direct need for such efforts. The goal of any peace process must be, however, the serious intention of abolishing the wolves forever. In Northern Ireland, where peace in all of its current conceptions means the possibility of all people continuing to live together, it matters particularly. The

111

commitment to enter a peace process depends on a real willingness of the people there to get rid of their own defenses in the long run and a belief that the "other" is like-minded. What I want to suggest here is that unless at the core of the Northern Irish peace process there is a negotiating partnership that grasps the need to break the self-perpetuating, indeed escalating, cycle of wolves, the underlying pattern of fear and mistrust will reassert itself.

Until now, Northern Ireland has not yet entered on that kind of process. Any recognition of the need to take the teeth from its own wolves has been lacking. People personally profess a wish for some risks, but when it comes to voting or taking those risks themselves, pessimistic common sense reasserts itself.

There is much talk among the conflict-resolution fraternity about whether peace processes have to be built from the "bottom up" or whether they are elite-led or "top down." Consociational theory depends on the capacities of leaders to make deals. Leaving aside objections about the democratic deficit in consociationalism, the capacities of political leaders in atomized modern societies to "deliver" are strictly limited. I wish to suggest that whether they are approached in a top-down or a bottom-up manner, peacemaking remains rooted in the obvious: a commitment by the partners to reduce the grounds for fear and mistrust that obstruct any serious possibility of peaceful coexistence or better. From this core, we can move outward to encompass ever more distant groups. Without a commitment to reconstitute existing relationships, peace processes degenerate into the mutually exclusive assertion of "rights," each held to be inalienable.

This in itself incurs finding out things about ourselves that we may not know, accept, or even believe are regarded as threatening. Crucially, and painfully, the "security" that protects one side threatens the other. The social or political sequence in which specific actions occur is ultimately less important than the cultivation of a consistency in trustworthiness that exposes the skepticism of the other as groundless and self-defeating. Without this goal, negotiations take place on quicksand, without any clear limiting floor to fear with all of the resultant calamities.

Something Rotten in the State

In an important historical survey of intercommunal relations in the north of Ireland in the nineteenth century, Frank Wright points out that any simple colonial economic relationships that existed between Protestant settlers and Catholic Irish natives in preindustrial northeast Ireland had largely disappeared by the beginning of the twentieth century.[1] Catholics and Protestants competed in the same labor market in the sense that both could expect the same wages for the same work.

What had not changed, indeed what had modernized, was the relationship of distrust and fear that had been endemic between Catholics and Protestants in many rural districts since the arrival of Protestant settlers in the seventeenth century. Those relationships were instead imported into the growing urban areas in religiously segregated ghettos. Slow economic equalization did not of itself create better intercommunal relations but reproduced the old enmities for a very different age. As wages equalized, so discrimination was justified by and maintained hostility. Many important industries became religiously segregated. Higher Catholic unemployment became endemic. Lower economic inequalities fueled greater resentment about the political and social barriers that remained. The rising Catholic middle class developed its own infrastructure, based on separate schools and extending into separate economic relationships, especially in rural districts. In effect, two parallel subsocieties based on Catholic/Protestant rivalry emerged. Fear and mistrust between them was institutionalized for the modern age and became the dominant theme of political and social life throughout Northern Ireland.

As the franchise was extended, Protestants, in a minority everywhere in Ireland except Inner Ulster, became increasingly aware of their absolute dependence on their connection to the British Imperial Parliament if they were not to be politically delivered to a Catholic majority. When the campaign for Irish Home Rule grew in the 1870s and 1880s, politics polarized along religious lines. Threatened by minority status in an Irish setting, Protestant liberals increasingly found accommodation with traditional conservatives in support of the union with Great Britain.

Irish Home Rule was understood in most of Ireland as a matter between England and Ireland. But within the north, it crystallized the deep internal sectarian political divisions. If nations are first defined by what they are not, two nations, both claiming the right to determine the state, were defining themselves anew in opposition to each other but without clear territorial boundaries between them. Both signaled their willingness to resort to arms to defend their cause. Although a Home Rule Act was finally passed in 1913, it had not been implemented when World War I broke out and was shelved for the duration. The momentum that stemmed from the Easter Rising in 1916 and rows over conscription in 1917 polarized opinion and exposed the seriousness of the divisions on the island of Ireland. But Britain's capacity to act to defend areas of ongoing influence, the six northeastern counties, and its unwillingness to insist that Ireland be treated as a whole meant that the new border was not between Ireland as an island, and Britain, as a different island, but between nationalist, overwhelmingly Catholic Ireland and Britain, including the Protestant industrial northeast of Ireland.

The implications of this polarization, which achieved independence for the twenty-six mostly Catholic counties in Ireland, were little short of catastrophic for nationalists in the six mostly Protestant counties. Northern nationalist ties to the source of their political muscle and Catholic opinion outside the six northeastern counties were juridically cut, and any attempt to retain or revive them was treated as treason by their Protestant neighbors and political rulers. Only British military cooperation with republicans could have changed the outcome substantively.

Northern Ireland's legitimacy was grounded in the doctrine of national self-determination for unionists, "the majority." Implicitly, however, the doctrine denied a large minority the same right. Someone had to be the minority. Realpolitik in 1920 dictated that Northern nationalists would be assigned that role. The principle of national self-determination was used as a reason to justify the partitioning of the island into two. Britain ceded all of Ireland except where British rule could rely on sufficient local support for the establishment of broadly stable order. "Sufficient support" meant, in effect, sufficient numbers of unionists, overwhelmingly Protestants. Where there were any gray areas, such as in the two counties of Fermanagh and Tyrone, the balance of political power fell in favor of unionism.

National self-determination as a doctrine might not matter, except that both unionists and nationalists to this day rely on it as their fundamental legitimizing principle. Each group's right to national self-determination *is* democracy. For unionists, Irish republicans deny the democratically expressed will of the majority in Northern Ireland by adopting violence, while for many nationalists, the partitioning of Ireland represents an antidemocratic violation of the self-determination of the Irish people. National self-determination can no more resolve Northern Ireland now than it could in 1920. It cannot be granted to one without simultaneously denying it to another. Northern Ireland represents a great pardox of democracy: one group's democracy is another group's tyranny. Woodrow Wilson's great liberal principle of democratic state legitimization, national self-determination, ends up not as liberation, but as imprisonment in fear and mistrust, both returning in repeated cycles.

Given its own devolved Parliament, Northern Ireland developed as a quasi-independent regional unit, whose party structure, political obsessions, and historic memories emphasized its difference, rather than its similarity, to the rest of the United Kingdom and Ireland. Irish nationalists outside the north came to recognize the real limits to their ability to change events inside the north and substituted rhetorical gestures for substantive policy. Both Britain and Ireland covertly distanced themselves from the previous front line of their hostility, creating in Northern Ireland a pressure cooker of unresolved fundamental differences. Britain and the Irish Republic normalized their own relationship by distancing themselves from their problem children in Northern Ireland, who went on experiencing the cycles of confrontation from which the 1920–1921 settlement largely freed the rest of the island. To use a metaphor from a more recent age, Northern Ireland was treated much like the Chernobyl nuclear reactor: insulated (badly) with concrete and left ignored in the hope that the problem would resolve itself.

Permanent unionist majorities and the monopolization of all political power by Protestants served to underline the sense of otherness with which Catholics were regarded by the politically powerful in Northern Ireland.[2] Power resided somewhere else. For the Catholic working class, in contrast to Protestants, the Northern Irish state offered no structural hope of redress for grievances. Exclusion from the structures of power could not be attributed to the market, it was something more profound. Catholics, whether voting or not, were expressly excluded from the paths of political power. The rituals and symbols of the state were organized to highlight their exclusion.

Catholic alienation and hostility itself, then, justified underlying Protestant paranoia about long-term Catholic intentions. Unionists could not accept the equal citizenship of those who sought the state's destruction. Instead, they adopted extradraconian measures to enforce state security. Eternal Protestant suspicion again meant that Catholics could never forget their second-class status. It is this cycle, and the relationships on which it is built, that constitutes the core of the Northern Ireland conundrum. At any time, even at times of relative calm, this cycle can be reactivated.

In the 1960s, many believed that a period of more permanent tranquility had arrived. At the latest by 1971, it was clear that in spite of widespread goodwill at the outset, campaigns for civil rights had become enmeshed in the most vicious cycle of sectarian fear and resentment to hit Northern Ireland since 1920. When violence broke out in Northern Ireland in 1969, both Britain and Ireland found that their distance from the pressure cooker had allowed them to develop their own bilateral relationship but at the cost of dealing with Northern Ireland as unknown foreign territory.[3]

The explosion of political violence in the 1970s reemphasized the absence of any common bond between nationalism and unionism. In the course of the escalation, both sides found ever greater evidence to justify their fear and mistrust of their opponent's intentions. Of course, large numbers of people, the vast majority, eschewed any direct involvement in political violence, but all were affected by it and all were required to decide on the validity of each particular act of terror and the policy of the state in opposing it. Even among those who would claim to consistently oppose all nonstate political violence, Protestant tolerance of strict security measures by the police and army, whose sharp edge was inevitably focused on Catholic areas where Irish Republican Army (IRA) support was strong, contrasted with deep Catholic ambivalence, even among moderates, about the real independence and fairness of the security and criminal justice system in dealing with Catholics in these areas, especially after internment without trial was introduced in 1971 and after unarmed civilians were shot dead by British soldiers in Derry in 1972. The inability of Catholics to wholeheartedly back the police refueled Protestant suspicions of the reliability of Catholics, while the resistance among Protestants to any open critique of the security forces fueled Catholic doubts about the reality of any justice within Northern Ireland.

In 1972, direct British rule from Westminster was imposed. Direct rule, although now in existence for over twenty-five years, has always been treated as a temporary expedient. While it alleviated the worst of the immediate pressure, it provided no mechanism for creating greater legitimacy for political authority in Northern Ireland and dragged the British government back into direct engagement with Irish nationalism for the first time in fifty years. At the same time, continuing Protestant majorities elected unionist representatives, meaning that no deal could be struck on a strict British/Irish nationalist basis without implications about and for the majority of the Northern Irish population.

If there are lessons to be learned from this period, they are complex ones. First of all, all solutions based on the principle of national self-determination in the northeast of Ireland are likely to leave a bitter minority, whichever way they are resolved. Events in the 1960s showed that surface tranquility secured by domination that always remains incomplete generates the next round of bitterness.

Second, alternatives to national self-determination are not widely available. Any such solutions cannot be generated under conditions of permanent fear. Contemplating living and cooperating with others is not made easier when those others appear to be "wolves." The rationality of pluralism is not the rationality of the frontier. Politics becomes, as one writer put it, "hectic but hopeless."[4] Asking people to vote for generosity to their neighbours before security for themselves appears to many like asking turkeys to vote for Thanksgiving.

Third, all peace processes that seek to escape from the cycle of fear and mistrust without creating an absolute victory for one side over the other require a leave-taking from national self-determination in its crude form. The logic of single-group domination is the logic of ethnic cleansing in Northern Ireland. Peace proposals that cannot leave behind the purist logic of nationalism for a more nuanced form of interstate living quickly become part of the domination/resistance cycle, another twist in a zero-sum game.[5]

The Structure of the Northern Ireland Conflict: Some Peculiarities

Northern Ireland has long been compared with South Africa and the Middle East and, latterly, with the former Yugoslavia and the edges of the former

Soviet Union.[6] The parallels in structure, imperial history, social impact, and intractability, to name but a few, are obvious.

But comparison highlights both similarities and differences. For theories of peacemaking or conflict resolution, the differences are often more interesting than the similarities. Unlike South Africa, there is no consensus in Northern Ireland that any peace deal will end with a transfer of power from the existing power group, nor is there any agreement that the present system is fundamentally illegitimate in the sense of apartheid. On the other hand, unlike the Middle East, there is no acceptance that this is war, where the outcome is separation and Israelis and Palestinians negotiate as foreign powers. Separation would still feel like defeat. Unlike Bosnia, Northern Ireland has not yet suffered ethnic annihilation.

The primacy of the communal division in Northern Ireland politics has been a fixed point for centuries. Social life is overwhelmingly organized on a divided basis. Recent demographic statistics show a sharp trend toward separated living in both urban and rural areas.[7] Schools, churches, sports, newspaper readerships, and traditional cultural activities—the core of an anthropological notion of "culture"—are separated. People are generally not well informed about the worldview in the other community. Territorialism, manifested as a sense of communal ownership of particular urban districts and in a divided market in land ownership, is widespread.[8] Where changes occur in local population balances, there are often serious tensions. Clashes over marching in recent years are only some of the symptoms.

At the same time, Northern Ireland is formally mixed. People share town centers, universities, and some workplaces. Nevertheless, the traditional mechanism of dealing with discomfort on issues of division is to steer clear of them in public. Businesses and government have sought, under pressure of legislation, to create neutral environments, but attempts to build sustainable relationships across the traditional divide have largely been concentrated in small-scale voluntary, community, or educational ventures.[9]

Peace processes that do not recognize the deeply rooted nature of social division will necessarily appear naive. Yet, the development of policies and structures for securing equity, diversity, and interdependence represent the long haul of peace in Northern Ireland. There has been considerable discussion about whether social integration must precede or follow political integration. While it is certain that political stability is vital for these developments, it appears to be less important where such possibilities emerge and more important that they emerge. What is critical is that a core of stability at both social and political levels is established that acts as a counterweight to the power of fear and mistrust in a fragile context.

Northern Ireland is characterized by political ambiguity. It is a "place between states" in the sense that it has become distinct in itself and yet is tied to places beyond the immediate six-county area. One of the results of this is a consistent blurring of the distinction between "internal" and "external" parties to the conflict. Yet clear definitions of internality are central to the rights of each group under international law, while understanding the relation of the parties to each other is crucial in defining what constitutes a "third party" to negotiations, and they are also central to the political debate. Unionists regard the Republic of Ireland as an external state with no jurisdiction to act on or say anything about the internal affairs of Northern Ireland. Peace is possible when the claim is removed. It is a primary assumption of nationalist politics that Britain is ultimately a "foreign" power, expressed in republican propaganda as an "occupying force." Peace is a matter for Irish people, to be resolved, as nationalist rhetoric usually expresses it, "on this island," thereby implicitly denying a role to Britain beyond Ireland.

Unlike the crisis in the Middle East, the formal distance between the British and Irish governments and the internal groups and parties in Northern Ireland is not a matter of international relations between states (as between Israel and the United States), but a matter of degree as much as of boundary. Until partition, neither Protestants nor Catholics regarded themselves as in some sense a separate nation from the British or Irish outside the six counties. De facto, Britain retains final responsibility in Northern Ireland. Republican ideology sees Britain as the enemy, downgrading any responsibility to make an independent relationship with unionists. The Republic of Ireland is also not fully external to Northern Ireland in that it is tied to it by its constitutional claim, in the deep sense of Irish nationality that binds north and south together for many Catholics, and by the fact that many institutions, indeed most Catholic and nationalist ones, treat Ireland as a ritual and organizational unity. Since the Anglo-Irish Agreement, the right of the Republic of Ireland to some role within Northern Irish affairs has also been recognized in international law. The political elite of both Britain and the Irish Republic are, however, nearly entirely separated from Northern Ireland. They do not rely on Northern Irish people for their position, and the political rewards for individual politicians of focusing on Northern Ireland are small. British and Irish "involvement" is thus crucially blurred. The result is an increasing critical distance on the emotions of conflict as one leaves Northern Ireland and a decreasing level of direct interest.

Expectations and legitimacy in negotiations depend on a clear understanding of the rights and responsibilities of each player. All Northern Irish peace strategies include all current residents of Northern Ireland, but few do so exclusively.[10] Unionist visions of peace do not deny Catholics the right to live in Northern Ireland but insist on absolute acceptance, at least for the time being, of the Britishness of Northern Ireland by nationalists.[11]

Nationalists project a future Ireland in which Protestants will have a place but one politically detached from Britain.[12] The ambiguities about who should be at the table and in what capacity, then, preclude all-inclusive dialogue, especially if the agenda is determined within Northern Ireland because someone feels that somebody is there who should not be or somebody is not there who should be. A commitment to seek peace is therefore derailed before the invitations are sent out because the invitation list is seen to presuppose a particular outcome.

Explicit statements by both governments about a permanent and stable role for both governments in all negotiations have been rare, in part because Britain fears unionist uproar and Ireland would be seen to have abandoned the republican dream entirely. Since the Anglo-Irish Agreement of 1985, however, the Anglo-Irish dimension has de facto become established, although the Frameworks Document of 1995 accepted that internal arrangements for Northern Ireland were a purely British responsibility. Ambiguity about responsibilities and duties also means, however, that at crucial moments, both the Irish and British governments can retreat from responsibility into feigned disinterest. But the recent growth in explicit external interest in Northern Ireland, particularly that of the United States and the European Union, is predicated on a clear Anglo-Irish axis guaranteeing the core of the process and ensuring that foreign actors are not drawn to sides in a war but behind an agreed strategy. In the absence of a clear statement that the Anglo-Irish framework is permanent yet clearly distinct from a nationalist stitch-up, the addition of external powers has been seen by unionists as strengthening pan-nationalism and an interference in the internal workings of the UK.[13]

In an academic sense, peacemaking theories that assume a primary role for "internal" actors lose their focus when these definitions are not clarified.[14] How far will or can a British government, with or without Ireland, act without the immediate consent of the local population in Northern Ireland? The Anglo-Irish Agreement of 1985 certainly suggests that Britain has some autonomy in this regard. Distinctions between top-down and bottom-up approaches to peacemaking depend logically on being clear about what constitutes the top and the bottom of the scale. Currently, there are at least two versions of top-down approaches to peacemaking, depending on whether the British and Irish governments are understood as "external," or the top of the scale. If the governments constitute the driving force behind top-down models, what is their relationship to the middle of the scale, presumably politicians operating within Northern Ireland, and how does the existence of a middle level impact their relationship to those at the bottom, presumably the people of Northern Ireland?

A third aspect of the situation in Northern Ireland is the importance of liberal democratic principles of legitimation.[15] Notions of "justice" central to the claims of both unionists and nationalists in Northern Ireland are contending within the same Western frame of reference. Expectations of the state continue to be broadly liberal democratic, at least in the sense that failure is measured by the distance by which the state fails in its task compared with some notional liberal democratic ideal. In spite of recurrent controversies, the press and academia remain unencumbered by any serious restrictions. Although Northern Ireland has remained poorer than other parts of the UK, it has traditionally been richer than other parts of Ireland and is by no means the poorest part of Europe, let alone elsewhere. Assumptions about the bureaucracy, the tax and welfare regimes, the formalities of the law, and open and secret elections correspond to basic expectations throughout the UK and large parts of northwest Europe. In short, and here all comparison with Eastern Europe breaks down, the state continues to be measured by the limits of the rule of law and a free press, including the European Convention of Human Rights.

However, if liberal democracy acts as the source of legitimation for all political actors, it does so in an ambiguous way. The doctrine of national self-determination as used by both nationalists and unionists is a fight to construct a winning majority. Liberal democracy in mixed territories crumbles where one group is seen to openly use a threat of coercion against another. This is the case in Northern Ireland.

Because it forms the language of the conflict, the meaning of "democracy" in nationally disputed territories is therefore a core issue at dispute. Each claims the right to Max Weber's definition of "statehood": the monopoly of legitimate force in a territory. The more each group tries to enforce its use of violence, the more it is seen to be illegitimate by its opponents. Conservative theorists of democracy such as Joseph Schumpeter and Giovanni Sartori have long dismissed the notion of a "common good" as utopian even under more promising circumstances,[16] but the absence of agreement on common procedures makes even procedural democracy, with its focus on minimum individual rights, unachievable. Both unionists and nationalists maintain that procedural democracy in the wrong hands ends up as communitarian tyranny. Thus liberal democratic procedures exist yet constantly fail, and the constant temptation to turn to antidemocratic practices is ironically justified as defending some ultimately democratic ideal.

What is liberal democracy between competing national groups? If procedure is primary, then the construction of majorities, as well as the shape of the border, is central. Northern Irish parties have thus mostly adopted variations of the majority rule concept and compete over whether new proposals for settlement should be subject to Irish or Northern Irish assent. Conversely, if there are minimum values at the core of democracy, such as the establishment and protection of the dignity of all people, then liberal democracy cannot be established by procedure alone and may be antithetical to nationalist competition. Are there minimum levels of equal inclusion in outcomes and not only in procedures before a democracy is worthy of its name? The definitional dispute matters if it is to be argued that a solution devised and imposed by governments without electoral mandates in Northern Ireland nevertheless creates a more inclusive "democratic" outcome than domination created by local electoral majorities.

I want to look at three results of the ambiguity about what constitutes democracy. First, antistate or extrastate violence in Northern Ireland takes place within the context of a political system that is formally committed to legal and political rules recognizable throughout Western Europe. Giving full and equal recognition to groups that legitimize violence—notably, the IRA but including loyalists—immediately risks legitimizing other extralegal violence in Northern Ireland and starting a revenge cycle the only law of which would be might is right. Abolition of the rules of democratic behavior destroys Weber's primary definition of the state as the monopoly of legitimate violence on which all Western states depend for legitimizing the use of regulated and legal force to fight chaotic violence. Peace processes in liberal democracies must be geared to improving the legitimacy of the state, not on pretending that there can be any neutrality on extrastate violence.

Second, the liberal democratic self-definitions of both the Republic of Ireland and the United Kingdom have had important beneficial effects, providing clear external grounds by which the actions of all of the figures in Northern Irish affairs, including the two states, can be called to account. By maintaining a view of democracy that subordinates majority rule below universal dignity, both British and Irish governments are pushed and can push others into a common defense of basic norms of behavior. Furthermore, the self-imposition of democratic limits on their own behavior limits the means by which Ireland or Britain will prosecute any disputes between them to peaceful diplomacy. Unlike Serbia and Croatia in the Balkans or Turkey and Greece in Cyprus, neither state has ever used divisions in Northern Ireland as an excuse to have a proxy war. No peace process would be served by reducing the insistence on liberal democratic limits. Instead, the common commitment to them must be enhanced.

Third, normal liberal democratic forms, especially decisionmaking by electoral majorities and notions of the rule of law, are constantly compromised by the history of Northern Ireland, wherein the state has been rooted in the acceptance of only part of the population. The gap between the rule of law and tyranny has been reduced as the instruments and agents of law have been dragged into the conflict and used extraordinary powers primarily against the marginal community. The insight of divided societies is that liberal democratic forms need much more than majorities to foster free societies. Majority rule, as Alexis de Tocqueville knew, need not necessarily produce inclusive outcomes.[17] The irony for the Northern Irish is that the very stability of Britain and the Republic of Ireland allows them to be ignorant of the potential risks of simple parliamentary majorities and makes all of the closest parliamentary comparisons absolutely useless for Northern Ireland.

The permanent crisis of legitimacy in Northern Ireland has blurred the sharp formal distinctions between the violence acceptable under conditions of peacetime and those under war. Is violence against the British state and its agents "crime" and its agents criminals under law, or does the absence of consent on the part of Northern Irish nationalists justify war in which the proponents are soldiers? Crucial distinctions dissolve. If life in Northern Ireland justified or justifies the level of terror threatened and carried out over the last three decades, then international terrorism by all relatively deprived groups can probably be justified endlessly throughout Europe and North America. Democracy can deal with terror only once it ceases to be terror and the terrorists have equal, not greater, weight with all others. However, IRA and loyalist self-understanding depends on a legitimacy in their campaign granted by a state of war. Prisoners are not criminals but prisoners of war, and the police are not the law but an arm of an illegitimate state.[18] By 1994, however, the war logic of loyalist paramilitaries had almost reduced the category of "legitimate target" to the level of any vulnerable Catholic. If this is not crime, what is?

The end of war implies direct negotiation between armies who sue for peace, but the insistence that having armies was wrong in the first place makes such discussions impossible for those who insist on the democratic method. Disarmament at the end of a war applies to all sides equally. Under the rules of democracy, no state can treat legal and illegal arms equally, but this clashes with the IRA's insistence that its war was not crime. Demands for a decommissioning of terrorist weaponry appear indistinguishable in some nationalist eyes from insisting on defeat before negotiations and an unwillingless to take seriously the deeper legitimacy of the struggle, especially as legal weapons are overwhelmingly held on the Protestant side. All of these questions are formally insoluble unless the notion of democracy in Northern Ireland is expanded far beyond the model defended by unionists, allowing more flexibility among those who have supported extrastate violence to come in from the cold. Ultimately, it has to be expanded to ensure the dignity of all people in some way that encompasses their nationality securely.

Purely procedural ideas of democracy in areas of disputed rights to national self-determination result in a crippling ambiguity in categories crucial to political stability where clear distinction is necessary: internal/external, democracy/tyranny, force/violence, law/terror, war/peace. Ultimately, there can be no ambiguity between them, but all attempts by one side to impose their version on the other by force take us further from a universal democracy and point to a political meltdown. The restoration of viable distinctions between these categories by means other than violence becomes the crucial task prior to the establishment of agreed procedures.

Toward a New Settlement

By 1972, the British government concluded that unionist domination of political authority was no longer functional and began to search for a wider consensus for political institutions. Attempts to create a pluralist Northern Ireland based on the sharing of executive power between unionists and nationalists failed in 1974 when a strike of Protestant workers paralyzed key industries and forced the unionist participants in the experiment to withdraw.[19] Although the British government resumed direct political responsibility, British parties were anxious to avoid Northern Ireland becoming a party political issue among them. Britain was nevertheless unavoidably responsible for security policy, focused against the IRA. At the same time, the British sought to devise a political framework that could gather the support of both nationalists and unionists simultaneously.

Seeking to be neutral while saturating Catholic areas with unwanted troops proved difficult. The potential crisis inherent in this situation crystallized with the IRA hunger strikes of 1981.[20] Britain clearly needed a partner with credibility on the nationalist side, but nationalists in Northern Ireland needed guarantees against unionist domination or sabotage. When the New Ireland Forum of 1984 suggested that constitutional Irish nationalism was moving away from an insistence on a united island, the potential for wider cooperation grew. Although Margaret Thatcher rejected the proposals of the forum, the rise of Sinn Fein as an electoral force concentrated minds in London. The signing of the Anglo-Irish Agreement in 1985 indicated British acceptance of the view that effective security and minimum legitimacy among nationalists could be secured only in cooperation with the Republic of Ireland. By stabilizing relations with nationalists, however, the agreement threatened to destabilize relationships with unionists. During 1986, there was massive, though unsuccessful, unionist opposition to Irish involvement.

Unlike power sharing, the agreement survived unionist protest. Its status as an intergovernmental treaty made it immune to local opposition. Crucially, Britain and Ireland had now accepted a new status as active political participants in the internal affairs of Northern Ireland. The success of the policy depended not on locals, but on the governments: Britain was governing with the active opposition of most of those in Northern Ireland who called themselves British. In effect, the government also underlined the revocation of Stormont, confirming that simple rule by majority in Northern Ireland was untenable. The Irish Republic had officially conceded that Irish unity would come about only with the consent of the people of Northern Ireland, effectively isolating Sinn Fein. While the agreement fell short of joint sovereignty—the United Kingdom retained all sovereignty while Ireland remained constitutionally committed to unity—both unionists and republicans regarded it as a definitive shift away from fundamental aims.[21]

There were now two forms of consociational government of Northern Ireland on the table, driven by different levels of political authority: the Northern Ireland–driven power-sharing model that had failed in 1974 and the intergovernmental model of 1985 that survived but that suffered from the effective exclusion of Northern Irish people in its operation. While the Anglo-Irish Agreement was therefore vulnerable to political alienation from below, it had the one virtue of being free from the paralysis of Northern Irish politicians who had failed to deliver their supporters on the ground for anything other than monocultural solutions.

Two clear tracks emerged for Northern Irish political development after 1985. On the first track, both governments sought to draw unionists back into the political process, culminating in talks among constitutional parties in the early 1990s. Amid considerable acrimony, the talks ended inconclusively with unionists accusing John Hume, the leader of the largest nationalist party, the antiviolence Social Democratic and Labour Party (SDLP), of sabotage. On another track within Irish nationalism, Hume engaged in private discussions with the leader of Sinn Fein, Gerry Adams, between 1988 and 1993, giving rise to considerable unionist fear. Hume argued that the British government was neutral on the union and that IRA violence was the primary obstacle to persuading unionists or the British to any Irish unity. He further argued that in the event of a cessation of IRA violence, the British might act as "persuaders" to "an agreed Ireland." In September 1993, Hume and Adams announced that they had come to an agreement on the conditions that could end IRA violence. These conditions have never been made completely public, creating considerable anxiety among unionists.

Events moved quickly in the autumn of 1993, spurred on by a serious upsurge in intercommunal terrorism. The Irish foreign minister, Dick Spring, published seven principles for a new deal that included a rejection of all coercion and an emphasis on consent.[22] Unionist satisfaction that the republic's government had apparently accepted some unionist principles was undermined when, in apparent contradiction of assurances given in the House of Commons, it became clear that the British government had held face-to-face meetings with members of the IRA.[23]

The atmosphere surrounding the British-Irish Inter-Governmental De-claration made at Downing Street in December 1993 was therefore volatile. The governments were able to take some satisfaction from the support the declaration got from the SDLP and the muted response from the Ulster Unionists. In essence, the Downing Street declaration repeated much of the Anglo-Irish Agreement of 1985. The British government as-serted that it had no "selfish strategic interest in Northern Ireland" but de-clared its willingness to uphold Northern Ireland until a majority voted for change. It accepted the right of the Irish people to make a deal, but only if agreement was "freely given," concurrently north and south. The Irish government also promised to seek change in the Constitution of the Irish Republic as part of an overall settlement. Significantly, however, all groups currently supporting the use of political violence could join nego-tiations on the way forward once they showed their intention to abide by the democratic process.

The significance of a British Conservative prime minister and a Fi-anna Fail Irish prime minister putting their names to a joint document was not lost on those with a sense of history. For the first time since 1920, all democratic political parties in both Britain and Ireland outside Northern Ireland were behind the same political strategy. The weight of this top-down axis now bore down on the IRA and Sinn Fein. After eight months of procrastination, and despite official rejection of the document in July 1994, an IRA cease-fire was called on August 31, 1994.

The Ceasefires and the Emergent Process

After 1994, the "peace process," involving Sinn Fein and eventually the loyalist paramilitaries, replaced the "talks process," based on talks among constitutional parties only. The origins of the peace process in the Hume-Adams dialogue meant that unionists greeted the cease-fire with deep sus-picion. Behind the lamb or sheep of the cease-fire, they continued to see the wolf of unreformed IRA goals and tactics. Martin McGuinness, a lead-ing light in the Sinn Fein leadership assumed by everyone to be high up in the IRA command, insisted that the IRA was calling a cease-fire from a position of strength. McGuinness was for unionists the same figure who in 1986 had declared that "our position is clear and it will never, never, never, change. The war against British rule must continue until freedom is achieved." The refusal of the IRA to declare the cease-fire "permanent," preferring instead the description "complete cessation," was regarded by unionists as evidence that the cease-fire was a tactical maneuver rather than a change of heart. Fears of secret deals or understandings between the

British government and Sinn Fein were widespread. While nationalists rejoiced and dismissed unionist concerns as groundless,[24] unionists called for clarifications from the IRA and for a commitment to a referendum in Northern Ireland before any constitutional changes were made.[25]

Reacting to this, John Major announced that there would be no changes to the constitutional position of Northern Ireland without a referendum in Northern Ireland.[26] Sinn Fein responded tersely, given that most of its goals prima facie appeared unlikely to be ratified in a Northern Ireland referendum. When Albert Reynolds, the prime minister, told a London newspaper that he did not expect Irish unification to come about in this generation,[27] McGuinness retorted that "this problem can be solved an awful lot quicker than that." By October, however, guarantees to loyalist paramilitaries were sufficient to reassure them that no secret deal had been made, and on October 13, they announced their own cease-fire on the premise that "the Union is safe."[28]

Interpreting the situation was fraught with difficulties. On the one hand, the main unionist parties continued to warn about the underlying threat from nationalism, pointing to the absence of permanence and pan-nationalist consensus among Sinn Fein, the SDLP, the Irish government, and Bill Clinton's administration. On the other hand, the loyalist paramilitaries felt confident enough to announce a cease-fire on the basis that the union was safe. What did the republican movement expect to get out of the peace process? Had it moved from unreconstructed anti-Britishness to a more pragmatic position, and was this true of the whole movement?

The most glaring absence within the peace process was of any clear and reliable relationship between nationalists and unionists in Northern Ireland. Unionist suspicion of Hume and jealousy of his political success and international standing were palpable. A Hume-Adams agreement had not translated into a Hume-unionist understanding. Indeed, Hume-Adams appeared to have no strategy to include unionists. At its heart, it still seemed to regard unionists as an outpost of Britishness that could be "put down" at whim by the British government. Many unionists reasoned that they were being offered a cease-fire by the IRA with one hand only in order to be persuaded of the IRA's goals by the British. If this was the heart of the deal, then unionist defensiveness seemed justified. In the absence of any indication of the true nature of IRA demands, the space for paranoia expanded.

From the outset, the only stable British-Irish axis in the peace process ran through the governments in London and Dublin. No other partnership existed across the lines of unionism and nationalism. In effect, the peace process was premised on the capacity of Britain and Ireland together to reduce the room for maneuver of their respective traditional clients. At the same time, there was little indication that either Dublin or London understood the centrality of their own relationship or that they had the capacity to persuade, let alone dictate to, groups in Northern Ireland. The whole peace process depended, then, on the capacity of the top-down axis to enforce its model of international cooperation on unwilling local players, many of whom would resist such a model permanently.

By October 1994, the process appeared to be gathering speed. However, both governments insisted that local politicians must resolve the fundamental differences. They appeared to pin their hopes on the cease-fire creating the conditions for a rapprochement within Northern Ireland. Yet days after the IRA cease-fire, Major ejected the Democratic Unionist Party delegation from his office. This contrasted sharply with the handclasping of the leaders of the strands of Irish nationalism on the steps of the Dail. The absence of any unionist ownership of the peace process meant that peace was not universally regarded with unconfined joy. After the Anglo-Irish Agreement and the revelations about secret talks with Sinn Fein, unionists regarded all Anglo-Irish processes as dedicated to their demise. The SDLP's and now, apparently, Sinn Fein's close relationship to Dublin did not encourage them to take a more generous view. The structure of the Dublin-London partnership was regarded by unionists as fundamentally skewed against them, because Britain had declared itself neutral whereas the Irish Republic acted as a guarantor for nationalists. Nor was equality in this matter easy to achieve without the ceding of joint sovereignty, something that was absolutely ruled out by all unionists. Negotiating this imbalance was also difficult. Major's announcement of a Northern Irish referendum and the so-called triple lock guarantee on the process was quickly dubbed a unionist veto by Sinn Fein.

By attempting to place Northern Irish parties at the center of the process, Britain found itself tacking between unionist and nationalist concerns, while Ireland was unable to reassure unionists of its intentions without risking losing Sinn Fein from the new consensus. The absence of permanence ensured that the fear of entrapment was never removed from unionists. The begrudging response and attempts by the British government to alleviate it were then read by nationalists as evidence of hopeless immobilism on the part of unionists and a lack of vision and generosity on the part of the British. On the nationalist side, there was much talk of the courage involved in agreeing to the cease-fires. This was the long-awaited grand gesture. However, the British government, far from persuading unionists, spent all of its time trying to reassure unionists that they would not be forced into a United Ireland. Whether nationalists really expected the British government to try to persuade unionists out of their country or not, trust in the process began to ebb away even among nationalists.

Negotiating the Peace

The cease-fires of course represented a stepping back from war. There is little doubt that, after twenty-five years, Northern Irish people had tired of violence. In and of themselves, the cease-fires were popular. But tranquility in the short run still did not guarantee safety from the wolves over time. As one unionist remarked, "everything may be on the table, except the guns that are under the table."

Eventually, neither side believed that its opponent had given up its ultimate intent of enforcing its own version of national self-determination. More specifically, there was very little evidence that either side had given up its own version. So in a sense, the others were correct to be wary. In this context, the definition of peace remained fundamentally unaltered: the first move in any peace process must be made by the other, by "them." "We," the innocent, are ultimately powerless. Neither side could distinguish between making the decisive gesture and losing. No gestures were made, and the other's intransigence was blamed. Centrally, the cease-fires remained within the zero-sum game.

The mistrust crystallized as a series of themes, all of which barred the way to negotiations. Four issues came to dominate the agenda: the decommissioning of paramilitary weapons, the future of paramilitary prisoners, the right to march, and the nature of consent. Behind all of them was a concern to shape the process in an image likely to affect the result and to set in place a series of guarantees that would limit the range of possible outcomes, ensuring that the cliché that "everything was on the table" at the negotiations would have only formal status. Each of the preconditions was itself a negotiation about the end destination, and everybody knew it.

While intergovernmental pressure may have brought about the cease-fires, the lack of coordinated expectations about priorities and strategies beyond the Downing Street declaration and the different political pressures on the British and Irish governments meant that they had no clear agreement for the post-cease-fire period except to "encourage dialogue." As time went by, it was clear that local issues could quickly derail the intergovernmental consensus and that the governments had no reliable mechanisms for resolving their own differences. Under the 1985 agreement, Britain, as the sovereign state, consulted Ireland on many issues but retained final responsibility. There was therefore every possibility that the consultation would annoy unionists while the decision would annoy nationalists. The Irish government also seemed ambiguous about whether it had any intention or capacity to recommend amendment to the Articles of the Constitution that laid claim to Northern Ireland. Thus the core British-Irish axis was deeply uncertain in crucial areas.

Uncertainties at the top of the top-down strategy were ruthlessly exposed when the governments tried to hand back power to Northern Irish politicians. Unresolved "issues" between the governments became chasms of people unhappy about dealing with one another. Both governments were weakened further as Reynolds fell from office in late 1994, putting Fianna Fail into opposition in Dublin while the Conservative Party's capacity to act independently of the Ulster unionists and its own ultra-unionist rump in Parliament collapsed. By early 1997, Northern Irish politics was characterized by a weak, almost inert Anglo-Irish structure and by a politics made in the anger of the streets as the wolves bared their teeth.

The specific issues as they arose exposed the problem. The decommissioning of paramilitary weapons became the most divisive. For the IRA, as for loyalist paramilitaries, to promise to decommission before talks meant a signal that it had been defeated, and it also signaled an a priori acceptance of the illegitimacy of its war. Although formally committed to disarmament, most constitutional nationalists sought to underline the commitment to peace in the present and turn a blind eye to the continuing presence of weaponry in the short run. Unionists had a much more direct fear that guns unused in the present would be used in the future. The British government supported the unionist position when it added decommissioning to the preconditions for negotiation (the so-called Washington Three condition). The publication in a Dublin newspaper of evidence that the initials TUAS used by the IRA in the "TUAS" document on which the IRA cease-fire had been predicated did not mean "Totally Unarmed Strategy" but "Tactical Use of Armed Strategy" strengthened their conviction that this was a fundamental issue.[29] However, the categoric refusal of the IRA to countenance decommissioning in advance of talks in effect presented an ultimatum to the governments that the future of the peace process itself depended on no insistence on prior decommissioning.

Each government had a different understanding of the implications of giving in on this point. The Irish government believed that once the talks began, Sinn Fein would be forced to compromise, and it was therefore anxious to put no obstacles in the way of negotiations. The British government was both anxious not to undermine its own long-term opposition to terrorism and aware that the unionists would not attend talks without decommissioning. The failure of the governments to agree meant that decommissioning split the core axis on British/Irish lines. Meanwhile, unionists alleged that the Irish government was in the pocket of the IRA, while Britain was blamed for intransigence by nationalists.

Hence, the governments set up an International Body on Decommissioning in late 1995 under U.S. Senator George Mitchell, which came up with the ingenious formula of parallel decommissioning and a series of principles to which all parties would have to sign up if they wished to be party to negotiations. These principles included a commitment to paramilitary disarmament and a commitment to oppose any agreement by peaceful means only. There was considerable speculation that the conditions would prove impossible for the IRA. But when Major announced, while officially accepting the Mitchell Report, that elections would be required before negotiations,[30] the resulting disarray in the London-Dublin relationship was embarrassingly public. When the IRA ended its cease-fire at Canary Wharf two weeks later, many nationalists blamed the British government for intransigence. When talks began in June 1996 without Sinn Fein, they became immediately bogged down over decommissioning, an issue that goes to the core of the difficulty of mutual recognition.

The issue of prisoners and the victims of violence highlighted all the same issues of the legitimacy of political violence in Ireland and the right of the state to take revenge for, or punish, crime. Perhaps no single issue better encapsulates the agonies involved in ending conflicts and the potential at the end of conflicts that have not been finally won or lost for unresolved business to continue to drive a desire for compensation, punishment, and revenge. Prisoners are crucial to the self-sacrificial and heroic understanding of the paramilitaries and enjoy enormous respect within the camp following. However, although amnesties may follow wars, and many expected generosity in this regard, democratic governments that have legitimized locking people up on the basis that the actions were crimes have considerably more difficulty in squaring the circle. A struggle that has ended without final victory or defeat leaves the revenge cycle incomplete. Many, individually and collectively, are left with the sense of unfulfilled punishment, as well as a sense that the victims are left to suffer while the criminals go free. The anguish of the victims of paramilitary violence in a small community also exercised a powerful hold on the emotional ties of the community. Should those who have commited acts of violence but never been caught now be pursued? Should their actions—for example, the murder of police officers, taxi drivers, or civilians—be excused as acts of war, or are they culpable homicide? Although remission for paramilitary-related crime was increased, the number of prisoners released remained small, and there was no move to remove the criminal record. Republican anger was particularly deep when the British justice system appeared to make an exception for a British soldier found guilty of killing a young unarmed Catholic joyrider.

Emotional though the issue of prisoners was, the question of marching became the most potent vehicle for crisis. The Orange Order (and associates) is an exclusively Protestant organization that makes an explicit tie between religious liberty and the union with Britain. During the period of unionist domination from 1921 until 1972, the Orange Order was widely perceived to be the cultural backbone of unionist cross-class politics. Every year, the order holds thousands of marches throughout Northern Ireland, and marches through Catholic areas have long proved controversial during times of tension. The capacity of marches to get through is used by hard-line Protestants as a litmus test for their capacity to control the streets.

In the 1990s, and especially during the cease-fire, efforts to block marches through Catholic areas increased. Controversy over the issue escalated dramatically at Drumcree near Portadown in 1995, when a serious breakdown was averted by successful mediation. When the police tried to block a repeat performance in 1996, Orangemen throughout Northern Ireland manned roadblocks and stopped the free movement of traffic. As the crowds grew in Portadown, the crisis deepened, and in the face of widespread civil unrest, the Royal Ulster Constabulary (RUC) reversed its decision and forced the march through the Catholic area, beating back protesting Catholics who had not previously been involved in any civil disturbance. The results were serious rioting in Catholic areas, complete alienation from the police, and a withdrawal of all trust in the neutrality of the British government.

The crisis brought to a head all of the issues we have looked at in this chapter. Behind the Catholic residents, the Orange Order saw a plot to remove them entirely from the street. Defeat at Drumcree was turned into Custer's last stand. The presence of the leadership of the unionist parties at the event increased the close identification of the political parties with Orangism. In classic populist demagogic style, the unionist parties and the Orange Order created a crisis and disowned any responsibility for the civil disobedience, intimidation, and rioting that resulted. For Catholics, the support of the unionist parties for the events of Drumcree sent out a message that peace talks were a charade.

The British government's insistence that it had no say in the decisions that were purely matters of policing was widely regarded as technically accurate but politically absurd. The ability of the Orange crowds to alter police policy was regarded by all outside unionism as evidence that the rule of law in Northern Ireland was ultimately a question of Orange mob rule. The Irish government openly attacked the lack of evenhandedness in the policing. Among nationalists, the argument that there was a moral difference between policing and terrorist violence got increasingly short shrift. The hatred of the RUC stoked up another stumbling block of enormous proportions for any further negotiations. Instead of new distance on nationalism, the peace process was threatening to polarize nationalisms into open ethnic warfare. The failure of the state to impose any overriding notion of universal law at Drumcree left a potentially catastrophic vacuum.

Conclusion

"Reconciliation," according to the concise *Oxford Dictionary,* means "to make friendly again after an estrangement" and "to make acquiescent or contentedly submissive to something previously disagreeable." Both senses of the word can be applied to Northern Ireland. Nevertheless, there is a crucial difference between the two meanings. Classical peacemaking focuses on the first definition, with its emphasis on mutual friendship and the making of new relationships on all sides. Politics, especially after an estrangement, has often seen reconciliation in the second sense, as something the loser in a conflict must do to come to terms with reality. We must be very clear about what we mean by reconciliation if we are not to reduce it to a bland, noncontentious, and meaningless cliché.

Each party in Northern Ireland is happy to understand reconciliation as the offer to their opponents to reconcile themselves to their own defeat. Reconciliation, however, is what the others must do. The leadership of neither unionism nor nationalism has been able to demonstrate any serious capacity to address the concerns of their opposite numbers. Leadership easily becomes reduced to the articulation of grievances in which the concerns of the others are undervalued and the sense of injured innocence on one's own side is heightened. Reconciliation entailing the reestablishment of friendship as the primary goal is the theoretical, yet usually pious, hope of many but the political program of few.

National self-determination as the primary political goal applied to Northern Ireland is poison. It offers no automatic place for the loser, can be established only by successful violent deterrence, and, especially in the context of Irish history, generates resistance, not passivity, and no "reconciliation as friendship." The claim to one's right to self-determination means the implicit exclusion of the other. It is unfortunately also the most likely form of politics to be generated among paranoid and bitter people. The dynamics of Northern Irish politics in which two uncompromising, de facto fundamentalist positions battle it out for dominance, using whatever means are available to ensure victory, are visible again.

Without a partnership at the heart of a peace process that can inspire sufficient trust across the traditional split to hold the political center together in times of trouble, there is no peace process. The Hume-Adams partnership certainly ended IRA violence for a time, but it never generated a vision of a common future with unionists. The absence of a partnership axis with a final political commitment to reconciliation in Northern Ireland remains the core political problem. The only serious alternative possibility that such an axis might emerge lies in a renewed commitment to a pluralist outcome in Northern Ireland by the British and Irish governments, which might generate over time a new political and social climate in which it is unnecessary to resort to fundamentalist national self-determination to protect key interests. The problem lies in the fact that the political connection to and interest in Northern Ireland is an indirect, sometimes even peripheral one. Such pacts as the Anglo-Irish Agreement and the British-Irish Inter-Governmental Declaration can be signed by strong governments, but long-term commitments to pluralism in Northern Ireland are ultimately subordinate to the parliamentary arithmetic for weak governments.

Nevertheless, the fact that Northern Ireland's unionists and nationalists do battle in order to belong to societies that have established stable liberal democratic values at the heart of their identity means that their behavior is a constant challenge to their respective "mother" states. By far, the best long-term hope for reconciliation in Northern Ireland not based on dominance or exclusion lies in the importance for both states of defending those core principles. When the alternatives are potentially massive civil unrest and political responsibility and economic costs ultimately borne by these states, it does mean that there are clear interests, even if they are distant in the immediate day-to-day calculations of political parties.

Certainly, this has been the long-term trend of relationships since 1972. Since then, no British government has been prepared to countenance a return to failed unionist domination. They have also been unwilling to attempt to integrate Northern Ireland into the United Kingdom in a complete sense because of the permanence of government/nationalist confrontation such a move might entail. Instead, the British government has made numerous declarations of its own neutrality and the "lack of any selfish strategic or economic interest in Northern Ireland." The real changes in Anglo-Irish policy have come from the Irish side, which has moved from integral Irish nationalism in 1966 to a recognition of the need for Northern Irish consent, repeated in 1985, 1993, and in the report of the Forum for Peace and Reconciliation in 1996. The next step for the Irish government is a shift away from the remnants of the doctrine of self-determination to a determination to promote equity, diversity, and interdependence in Northern Ireland and protection of both nationalist and unionists equally under a value-based understanding of liberal democracy.

Ironically, all of these ideas are already contained within the Frameworks Document published by the British and Irish governments in the course of the cease-fires in 1995. The document foresaw continued partition in Ireland and north-south joint bodies to reassure nationalists. The British also proposed a complex balancing network of power sharing within Northern Ireland. Unionists rejected the document because of its insistence on north-south bodies with executive powers and the apparent drift toward permanent growth in the Irish, as opposed to the British, dimension. This was in spite of the fact that they were offered the so-called triple lock on the deal, whereby nothing would be finally agreed without the express consent of the Northern Irish parties, the British and Irish Parliaments, and a Northern Irish referendum. Ultimately, the permanance of an Irish dimension needs to be stated by Britain, while the limitations of such a dimension will have to be accepted and publicly acknowledged by Ireland.

Nevertheless, the document contains the makings of a clear framework within which, after fine-tuning and negotiation, two nationalities could be fully protected within one system. Its Achilles' heel lies in the insistence of the governments on Northern Irish consent. Here the unwillingness of the two governments to take the level of responsibility for political development in Northern Ireland coincides with clear arguments about democratic deficit. Here also may be a role for international pressure. Certainly, there needs to be an argument made for the long-run determination of both Britain and Ireland that all political solutions should be multiethnic. The implication must be that Britain and Ireland are in this for the long haul.

The Anglo-Irish Agreement showed that, within certain limits, local consent is not necessary for effective management. If imposed management that maintains a semblance of liberal democratic pluralism is the only short-term alternative to participative ethnic violence, then there is no alternative. If the top-down pressure coming from Dublin and London is sufficiently resolute, then fighting for Ireland by attacking the Irish government and fighting for Britain by fighting the British government become the order of the day and immediately counterproductive. The opportunity costs of political violence, the alienation of one's own key support base, are hugely raised.

Ultimately, some sort of societal reconciliation is necessary within the six counties. Ideally, responsibility should be handed back to local politicians. However, the magnanimous-sounding but ultimately pernicious idea that "everything is on the table for negotiations" needs to be quashed. In fact, only a very narrow range of options is feasible if ethnic domination is not to be the order of the day. Currently, neither unionists nor nationalists in private believe that their best options are available, but their continued presence on the table acts as a serious destabilizing factor. Sinn Fein campaigned in the June 1996 elections on the slogan of "No return to Stormont" (the pre-1972 Parliament), while unionists used the specter of a coerced united Ireland to frighten their supporters at will. Neither is feasible, desirable or likely, but neither is ever finally killed off for those who fear them.

After Drumcree, it is clear that developments in intercommunity cooperation can succeed only if those participating can be sure of state backing in the face of intimidation. In other words, bottom-up paths to peace can contribute to success only if a basic minimum of top-down stability is achieved. Northern Irish politicians appear unwilling to deliver top-down agreements that guarantee both British and Irish identities in Northern Ireland. The Anglo-Irish framework also cannot do so if the Irish component is still suspected of harboring an agenda close to that of Sinn Fein. A clear and very firm joint British-Irish approach, which will probably fall short of full joint sovereignty, still appears the most promising. Furthermore, it is something that could be given complete international backing.

The primary task in reconciliation in Northern Ireland is neither a top-down nor a bottom-up momentum, but the establishment of an axis that breaks the intercommunal divisions. The establishment of a basic floor to people's fears, the slaying of the most dangerous wolves, is the primary task. The Hume-Adams deal never achieved this, no matter what the intent of its authors. Ultimately, this may now be a matter of demonstration by those who have some freedom of maneuver, the governments, rather than by those trying to persuade turkeys to vote for what just might still be Thanksgiving. The key is to establish a solid core from which to work outward rather than to decide whether to work with the local elite or the grassroots. This core can grow simultaneously or in some erratic manner at the level of high politics, local community relations, or in the structures of public and private industry. What is crucial is that a stability at the core of the rivalry between Irishness and Britishness in Northern Ireland is established, which can then lessen and eventually stabilize the enormous well of fears. In the absence of this core, this functional model of a new relationship between competing and hostile nationalisms, all efforts at reconciliation are weak and vulnerable.

Postscript, 1998

When asked in the late 1970s about the consequences of the French Revolution, the then–Chinese premier Chou En-lai replied that it was "too early to tell." One of the perils of political analysis is the constant stream of events that changes the ground from which judgments are made.

Six months after completing this chapter, and to the surprise of many, the majority of Northern Ireland political parties signed a new political agreement on Good Friday, April 10, 1998. The deal as it emerged sought to provide a new basis for British and Irish people to live together in Northern Ireland. Northern Ireland's existence was again made dependent on the support or consent of the people of Northern Ireland alone. Devolved powers to Northern Ireland are envisaged as leading to unionists and nationalists sharing executive authority over a wide range of social and economic matters. Majorities in a new assembly will be qualified to ensure that all votes will require the support of a minimum proportion of nationalist and unionist support. New bodies were established to develop joint policy between Northern Ireland and the Republic of Ireland in a number of limited areas. This gesture to nationalist aspiration was balanced by making the new bodies subject to the authority of the Northern Ireland Assembly and the Irish Parliament and by the alterations of the territorial claim to Northern Ireland by the Constitution of the Republic of Ireland. In addition to this constitutional superstructure, the Good Friday Agreement foresaw a bill of rights, the release on license of all paramilitary prisoners within two years of its coming into force, and a commission to examine the future of policing for Northern Ireland. The agreement said little on decommissioning, but the support of the main unionist party, the Ulster Unionist Party, for the deal was only secured when Tony Blair, the British prime minister, assured the party leader that he would not be forced to sit in cabinet with Sinn Fein before decommissioning.

The role of the British, Irish, and U.S. governments in securing the deal was pivotal. At times, the sheer scale of the task seemed too much for Northern Irish politicians to carry. There is little doubt, however, that the personal attendance of the British and Irish prime ministers in the final crucial days of the talks underlined the seriousness with which the task was being undertaken in London and Dublin. Ultimately, the unionist leadership was enabled to sign the deal by the carrot of Blair's personal commitments and by the stick that rejection of Blair and his powerful New Labour government would isolate unionism in an even deeper manner than previously. Strategically organized telephone calls by President Clinton appear to have given the same message to doubting republicans. Nonetheless, there was no doubt that the core of the agreement remained the determination of the wider British and Irish communities, rather than the political drive of unionism or nationalism in Northern Ireland. On Good Friday, the unstoppable force of British and Irish will moved the immovable objects of political leaders in Northern Ireland.

The structures envisaged by the Good Friday Agreement confirmed that Northern Irish divisions could not be wished out of existence by democratic rhetoric. The "specialness" of the unionist-nationalist relationship was recognized at every point. Assembly resolutions required either a 60 percent majority or a majority among both nationalists and unionists voting. Northern Ireland was recognized as a part of the United Kingdom but with very special cross-border relationships. The dangers inherent in that historic relationship were obscured in a complex set of checks and balances at every level. No power was given or taken away without a balancing arrangement. Few communities of 1.5 million people have more levels of government.

From the early days, the peace process had been made subject to a referendum on the outcome. A top-down deal was not exposed to the glare of bottom-up politics. The ensuing public debate on the agreement circled around the same fears that had bedeviled the process from the outset. In general, the deepest reservations were in unionism. The lack of any clear commitment to decommissioning and the establishment of a policing commission were regarded by many on the unionist side as further evidence that ground had been given to republicanism. The fact that the constitutional status of Northern Ireland was more firmly guaranteed by the Irish Republic than ever before, combined with the recognition by Sinn Fein of the existence of Northern Ireland, was regarded as less significant than the establishment of north-south bodies. The very loose structures of Protestant political culture lent themselves well to populism. On the other hand, the more centrally organized political parties on the nationalist side, including Sinn Fein, marshaled broad support for the agreement in spite of misgivings among some of the rank and file.

While a united nationalist vote in favor of the Good Friday Agreement guaranteed a numerical majority in support of the new arrangements, the structure of the agreement itself was so complex that it will remain vulnerable to significant shifts in opinion within unionism and nationalism. It is rather easy to imagine a majority vote in favor of the agreement in Northern Ireland as a whole that cannot be operationalized because opposition to the system is concentrated in one community or the other. While the agreement therefore represents a triumph of diplomatic politics, the task of building a secure basis of support for its institutions remains to be fully accomplished.

Notes

1. Frank Wright, *Two Lands on One Soil* (Dublin: Macmillan, 1996). Also see David Miller, *Queen's Rebels* (London: Macmillan, 1985).

2. A modern excursion into this territory is found in Fionnuala O'Connor, *In Search of a State: Catholics in Northern Ireland* (Belfast: Blackstaff, 1995).

3. This is best summed up by a well-known story in Northern Ireland concerning the British home secretary in 1970, Reginald Maudling, who, on the return from his first visit to Northern Ireland, is reputed to have remarked: "What a bloody awful country. Get me a whisky."

4. Roel Kaptein, "Ethnocentrism in Northern Ireland: Its Escalation into Terrorism," paper delivered to the Colloquium on Religion and Violence, Stanford University, Stanford, Calif., 1992.

5. The notion of a postmodern Ireland is developed by Richard Kearney, *Postmodern Ireland* (London: Faber and Faber, 1996).

6. See Adrian Guelke, *Northern Ireland: An International Perspective.* (London: Gill and Macmillan, 1988); and Frank Wright, *Northern Ireland: A Comparative Analysis* (Dublin: Macmillan, 1987).

7. See Paul Doherty, "The Numbers Game: The Demographic Context of Politics," in Arthur Aughey and Duncan Morrow, eds., *Northern Ireland Politics* (New York: Longman, 1996), pp. 199–210.

8. Brendan Murtagh, *Life on a Rural Interface* (Belfast: Community Relations Council, 1997).

9. Karen Eybin, Duncan Morrow, and Derick Wilson, *A Worthwhile Venture? Equity, Diversity, and Interdependence in Northern Ireland* (Belfast: University of Ulster Press, 1997).

10. An exception to this rule is the proposals of the loyalist Ulster Defence Association New Ulster Political Research Group, which proposed an independent Ulster in their *Common Sense* document of 1979. Most nationalists regard delivery into the hands of an Ulster Protestant majority without any outside guarantees as untenable, and many Protestants are unhappy about losing the British link.

11. A blunt recent restatement of this was made by the staunchly unionist Cadogan Group of academics in a pamphlet entitled "Squaring Circles," published in 1996.

12. Even the New Ireland Forum, a constitutional nationalist think tank, in 1984 named a unitary Ireland as its "preferred" outcome.

13. The classic statement of this view of Anglo-Irish maneuverings is Arthur Aughey's *Under Siege* (London: Hurst, 1989).

14. See Paul Dixon, "Civil Society to the Rescue," *Democratization* (winter 1997).

15. Some of these ideas are explored in Duncan Morrow, "Violence and the Sacred in Northern Ireland," *Contagion* 2 (spring 1995): 145–164.

16. Joseph Schumpeter, *Capitalism, Socialism, and Democracy* (London: Allen and Unwin, 1942); and Giovanni Sartori, *The Theory of Democracy Revisited* (London: Chatham House, 1987).

17. Alexis de Tocqueville, *Democracy in America* (New York: Vintage Books, 1990).

18. See Mike Tomlinson, "Can Britain Leave Ireland? The Political Economy of War and Peace," *Race and Class* 37, no. 1 (July–September 1995): 1–22.

19. One of the best books on this period is Paul Bew and Henry Patterson's *The British State and the Ulster Crisis* (London: Verso, 1985), although it is completely wrong on the Anglo-Irish Agreement.

20. The best book on the hunger strikes is probably Padraig O'Malley's *Biting at the Grave: The Irish Hunger Strikes and the Politics of Despair* (Belfast: Blackstaff, 1990).

21. The republican press, such as *An Phoblacht* and the *Andersonstown News,* is full of events opposing the agreement during 1986.

22. *Irish Times,* October 28, 1993.

23. *Observer,* November 28, 1993.

24. *Irish News,* September 1, 1994.

25. *Belfast Newsletter,* September 1, 1994.

26. *Belfast Telegraph,* September 16, 1994.

27. *Observer,* September 18, 1994.

28. *Belfast Telegraph,* September 18, 1994.

29. *Sunday Tribune,* April 23, 1995. See also Paul Bew and Gordon Gillespie, *The Northern Ireland Peace Process, 1993–1996: A Chronology* (London: Serif, 1996), p. 97.

30. *Hansard,* January 24, 1996, pp. 353–354.

6

Bosnia After Dayton: Transforming a Compromise into a State

Susan L. Woodward

Third-party intervention to end civil wars succeeds, it is commonly accepted, when there is what I. William Zartman calls a "hurting stalemate."[1] Parties are ready to shift from fighting to negotiating, with outside help, because they think they can gain more by the shift. Conversely, parties will not begin to negotiate seriously, or will fail to implement a settlement, if they believe that more can still be gained by war or by holding out the prospect of a return to war. The Dayton Accords of November 21, 1995, established a "general framework for peace" to end the Bosnian war (1992–1995) through the intervention of negotiators from the United States, with backing from major European powers and their prior agreement to join forces in an international coalition and military deployment to help implement the accords. Of the three parties at war in Bosnia and Herzegovina (Bosnian Muslims, Bosnian Serbs, and Bosnian Croats), however, only one could be said to have reached that hurting stalemate.

That party, the Bosnian Serbs, had been ready to settle for more than two years, in hopes of consolidating politically the gains they had made militarily early on in the war. The terms of their preferred settlement, however, were not acceptable to the second party, the Bosnian Muslim–dominated[2] Bosnian government, or their international supporters, primarily the United States. Bosnian Croats, fully in control of their minimum conditions and with unassailed backing from neighboring patron Croatia, were in a position throughout the war to accept a cease-fire or hold out for more. During the summer of 1995, a change occurred in the position of the one external party with influence over the warring parties—the United States. Bill Clinton's administration in Washington, D.C., facing a form of hurting stalemate of its own with its European allies over the fate of the

North Atlantic Treaty Organization (NATO) and with the president's political party over the fate of elections in 1996, decided the time had come
for a negotiated peace, rather than a military victory, with the Bosnian
Serbs; it thus began to seek a political settlement it could accept.

Engaging in coercive diplomacy, the United States led a brief but devastating bombing campaign with its NATO allies to destroy Bosnian Serb
communication lines, ammunition dumps, antiaircraft installations, and
military headquarters and to give cover to the other two Bosnian parties—
temporarily aligned by Washington for this purpose since March 1994—
to overrun Bosnian Serb towns in western and northern Bosnia. The goals
of this military campaign were to get Bosnian Serb compliance with a *territorial division* of Bosnia—49 percent to them and 51 percent to a Bosnian Muslim and Bosnian Croat federation—by creating such a fait accompli on the ground and then to deny the Bosnian Serbs' wartime goal
of separate statehood by gaining their agreement to hand over negotiating
authority to their patron in neighboring Serbia, President Slobodan Milosevic, in U.S.-led talks aimed at a peace agreement.[3]

The effect of the combined land and air campaign, however, was to reduce the incentives of the other two parties to abandon the battlefield for
talk. The alliance (called a federation), which U.S. negotiators had forged
between them in March 1994, had been aimed at defeating Bosnian Serbs.
Now the Bosnian Croat and Bosnian Muslim armies were in a contest
themselves over relative territorial control, as was clear from the fact that
their ground operations to take territory from Bosnian Serbs in August–
September 1995 ran in parallel but were in no place joint operations. Bosnian Croats, moreover, were fighting as units of an invading Croatian army,
on a juggernaut to expel Serbs on both sides of the Croatian/Bosnian border beginning the previous May.[4] And to prevent another Serb exodus of
hundreds of thousands from the main Bosnian Serb city, Banja Luka, and a
fight between the two allies—Muslims and Croats—over control of that
city, NATO threatened air strikes against them as well to stop their advance.

The Political Compromise

Until the Socialist Federal Republic of Yugoslavia dissolved in the summer
of 1991, the three warring parties in Bosnia had been coalition partners
elected in November 1990 (the first multiparty elections in forty-three
years) to govern the republic. Each claimed to speak for the national interests of their voters, in accordance with the equal constitutional rights to
self-determination in Yugoslavia of the three nations of Bosnia (Muslims,
Serbs, Croats), but they were not able to agree on the political future of a

post-Yugoslav Bosnia. Each sought a different state: Serbs to remain in a smaller Yugoslavia with other Serbs, Croats to leave Yugoslavia and join neighboring Croatia, and Muslims (and many non-Muslim supporters) to create an independent Bosnia and Herzegovina. Despite European-sponsored negotiations over such an agreement, impending international recognition of Bosnian independence interrupted these talks, and the conflict over their competing visions of the right to national sovereignty became a war for land. Skirmishes throughout the fall of 1991 escalated by April 1992 into full-fledged war, in which territorial control became a precondition for political control and bargaining leverage. At the same time, ruling parties in the two neighboring federal republics of Croatia and Serbia (the former now a recognized state) had their own nationalist visions for independent statehood after Yugoslavia. These visions included new international borders that together incorporated most or all of Bosnia and found expression in military support for Bosnian Croats and Bosnian Serbs, respectively.

The international community had been unwilling to do what was necessary to prevent a Bosnian war: to use coercive diplomacy in the service of a series of proposed peace plans during the fighting that would have stopped the war in midcourse when the level of ethnic parceling, destruction, and population displacement was more easily reversible and, least of all, to enter the war directly to defeat one or more of the parties. But it had also been unwilling to allow Serb military victories in 1992–1993 to dictate a peace or Muslim victories over Croats in 1993 to run their course. Humanitarian assistance to the civilian population, limits on the instruments of war (with an arms embargo, a no-fly zone, and economic sanctions), and diplomatic interference in the course of the war were aimed solely at containment—reducing the flow of refugees to Western Europe and a possible spread of war to the southern Balkans. Nevertheless, the peace negotiators declared in the fall of 1995 that Bosnia and Herzegovina would remain one sovereign country, within the internationally recognized borders of those it had as a federal unit of former Yugoslavia. Acceptable interlocutors were also identified: the leaders of Croatia (Franjo Tudjman) and Serbia (Milosevic) were to negotiate for their clients in Bosnia, apparently to commit Croatia and Serbia to Bosnian sovereignty, while the Bosnian Muslim leader (Alija Izetbegovic) was to represent Bosnia. On the basis of the coerced truce of September 1995 and its two-way territorial division, the United States and its allies began to construct a political compromise to be negotiated.

Within those borders, Bosnian Serbs (about 33 percent of the population before the war) would be allowed a republic (Republika Srpska) as one of two constitutional entities of a Bosnian state but not their war aims to secede and join the new Federal Republic of Yugoslavia (composed of two remaining republics, Serbia and Montenegro). Bosnian Croats (about 17 percent before the war) received recognition of their right to self-determination in constitutional documents and power-sharing agreements within the other entity, a federation with Bosnian Muslims, but they were also denied the choice of separation, to join Croatia, as they wished, and, unlike the Serbs, were not permitted a separate republic (their de facto Herzeg-Bosnia) within the new Bosnian state. Bosnian Muslims (about 44 percent before the war) won the sovereign Bosnia that they sought, but they had to share power in the federation entity with Croats, dismantle the central republican government, over which they had achieved total control during the war, and accept Muslim majority control in only 27 percent of the territory.

This compromise was institutionalized with a constitutional balancing act, combining a single country with substantial decentralization. By requiring the Bosnian Muslims to abandon the central government of the former Bosnian state in favor of substantial devolution of power and jurisdictions to the two entities, Bosnian Serbs and Bosnian Croats were to gain protection against the dominance they said they feared from the more numerous Bosnian Muslims. Bosnian Serbs and Croats, in turn, had to stay in Bosnia. The Bosnian state designed by the constitution in the Dayton Accords resembles more the European Union (EU) than most modern states. It has a common market and a central bank operated by a director from the International Monetary Fund (IMF) as a currency board for six years; a parliament of delegates representing the three nations (in two entities); a shared, large-scale infrastructure; and a bureaucracy to staff these foreign and macroeconomic functions, financed by means of equal contributions from the three communities. The primary jurisdiction of its umbrella government (Serbs preferred calling it a "thin roof") was foreign policy, including foreign economic relations—but not defense. All the normal functions of government, from the collection of taxes and customs duties to defense, and from education to property rights and the judiciary in between, were devolved to the two entities.

The political system was designed on the principle of power sharing among the three national communities, which meant that representation and decisionmaking in the all-Bosnian institutions and in the two entity institutions were based on national identity and ethnic subdivisions. Thus, the president is a committee of three members, one Muslim, one Serb, and one Croat. The upper house of the parliament has fifteen delegates, each community sending five. While representation to the lower house does not specify national qualifications for election, its forty-two members are elected proportionally "within their respective entity"—thus, in practice, one-third from each of the three nations. Citizens can freely register to vote in any part of Bosnia, based either on their 1991 residence or their choice of postwar residence, but they can be elected to office only in the territory of "their" nation. An individual in the "wrong place"—a Croat in Muslim territory, a Serb in Croat territory, a Muslim in Serb territory, a Jew, Romi, Turk, Vlach, Bulgarian, or other minority or person of mixed background anywhere, and so on—is discriminated against on the basis of ethnicity, no matter how free and fair the election. Although reflecting the prewar Yugoslav system that guaranteed the right of self-determination to each recognized ("constituent") nation through the proportional distribution of offices and decisionmaking rights, this constitution in fact divided Bosnia in a non-Yugoslav way: Serbs no longer had a right as constituent nation in the federation (although they had comprised 17 percent of its prewar population, equal to the proportion of the Croatian population in all of prewar Bosnia), and the Republika Srpska was a Serb entity in which non-Serbs who asserted their right to return home (established by the Dayton Accords) would also be treated as minorities, rather than as constituent nations.

The comparison of the Dayton constitution to the European Union provides an important warning for Bosnia's future. This highly decentralized country—more like a confederation of three national communities—is likely to suffer the same "democracy deficit" as Brussels and Strasbourg and similar obstacles to political integration from jealously guarded national sovereignties. No powers or functions were granted to the common government that might inspire loyalty or identity among all Bosnian citizens—with the possible exception of the Commission on Human Rights—or that would tie politicians elected to the central government to domestic issues and constituents. The accords built in few rewards for power, status, or wealth in joint activities at the center or in common institutions that might nurture centripetal over centrifugal forces. They provided no means to instill a sense of protection for people who wished to choose nonethnic or mixed-ethnic identities (against pressures from their own group to conform), except the ombudspersons for human rights, which were also subordinated to ethnically defined authority in the entities.

There is even some doubt whether the power-sharing arrangements institutionalized by the Dayton constitution would be able to function at all or would necessarily be subject to constant stalemate. As a result of the national guarantees in the constitution, the parliament could only take decisions by qualified majority. If leaders of any one of the three constituent nations chose to define an issue as in its vital interests, they could block proceedings by abstention and turn to their provincial (entity) assembly for a vote. In cases of such "vital interests," votes in parliament would be tallied according to entity (and by each nation in the federal entity), and legislation would require a majority of each nation—and two-thirds within each entity if a decision of the presidency was at issue. Even if few issues are classed as vital, this provision encourages parliamentary delegates to caucus by nation on most issues, discourages voting on interests that do not align by nation, and places nonnationalist parties in permanent opposition.

Implementation

Although the three parties at war had different incentives to comply with the peace agreement, and none behaved as if they had reached a "hurting stalemate," there is a separate literature regarding the success or failure of settlements to civil wars after they have been negotiated and signed and are ready for implementation. In this case, the determining factor is the willingness of outsiders to assist in their implementation.[5] The question in November 1995 when the Dayton Accords were signed was, thus, whether external powers would be willing to do what was necessary to make this compromise work.

The results of the first two years of Dayton's internationally supervised implementation did little to change the situation at the time of its signing—the political system being shaped reflected the mixed compromises of the Dayton constitution, and the parties continued to withhold commitment with provisions they considered to be against their national goals and interests. Primary attention in the first eight months was focused on consolidating the cease-fire by implementing Annex 1A (the military aspects of the accords), and the process went very well. But in supervising the military separation of forces and cantonment of weapons and soldiers, the NATO-led Implementation Force (IFOR), by the very nature of its task, reinforced the lines of separation drawn by battle. Civilian tasks took a backseat to consolidation of the truce, and because those in charge of civilian tasks had no authority other than the commitment of the parties to peace implied by their signatures on the accords (the Bosnian Muslims and the proxies in Croatia and Serbia of the Bosnian Croats and Bosnian Serbs) and because military authorities insisted on a strict separation between military and civilian aspects of implementation, the diplomats overseeing civilian tasks depended on the cooperation of the three nationalist leaderships, issuing exhortations of their moral responsibility to implement what they had agreed. To legitimate the authority of Bosnians over the peace process, and thus to hasten implementation of the political settlement, in fact, elections for new Bosnian governments (common, entity, and, in the federation, cantonal) were rushed—held ten months to the day after the accords were formally signed at Paris. But this pace gave insufficient time for opponents to the three warring nationalist leaderships to organize party members, mobilize funds and independent media, or reach voters. Moreover, in making appointments to the official commissions, such as on elections, displaced persons and refugees, human rights, national monuments, transportation, and public corporations, which the peace agreement designated for the transition from war to peace, international administrators reached automatically for "one Bosniac, one Croat, and one Serb," thus giving the three *official* parties control by default over personnel choices and the policies that would result.

The Bosnian parties themselves interpreted all aspects of the implementation process and their responsibilities, including the election process and the issue of refugee returns, as opportunities to consolidate or increase their control over territory—as if the accords were only a new stage in the war over political control. Negotiations over foreign aid and technical assistance dragged on and on while the parties fought over who had authority to sign for the country. The formation of governments and ministries after the elections was further delayed by fights over who would gain which governmental portfolios and jurisdiction and the patronage and funds that they bring. The three ruling parties thus took up their prewar practice where they had left off, during the one year and three months when they governed in coalition—namely, to collaborate on a division-of-spoils principle, competing over party control of specific ministries and jurisdictions and over the distribution of benefits going to each national territory and party while locking competitors out.

The negotiators' idea, in other words, that a single but decentralized country was a compromise through which each party would gain something did not appear to settle the conflict. Bosnian Muslims refused to dismantle the republican government they controlled, until pressured in early 1997 to acknowledge the results of elections and the accords, and then they showed no interest in signaling to others that they did not wish to dominate. A primary example illustrating this fact is that they insisted on majoritarian rules wherever they had a numerical majority, including rejection after many months of extensive efforts by the deputy high representative, German diplomat Michael Steiner, to create a special regime for Sarajevo as a model for the capital of a multiethnic Bosnia, and obstruction into 1998 of the return home of non-Muslims. The idea that the Dayton Accords were restoring a multiethnic Bosnia, and that this was the wartime goal of the Muslim leadership, got no support from that leadership itself. Taking advantage of the right of people to return to their prewar homes, it also orchestrated a campaign of returns by Muslim refugees and displaced persons to places in the Republika Srpska that were strategically located villages and towns, as if the right to return (and later municipal elections) was simply another means to continue the war for territory and it had no intention of accepting the legitimacy or finality of a separate Serb entity. The Muslim leaders took every advantage of the insistence by international donors that there can be only one representative of the Bosnian state, with its seat and occupant in Sarajevo.

The Bosnian Serb leaders, for their part, acted to protect all measure of sovereignty within their republic, to the point of such minimal cooperation with the aspects of the Dayton Accords that mattered to the international actors that they received no international assistance (1.3 percent of the total disbursed) in the first two years of peace. For example, they refused to accept the requirement from international financial institutions that they sign contracts with the wartime Muslim prime minister Hasan Muratovic; they delayed for almost two months participating in the common governmental institutions elected in September 1996 and obstructed the formation of the central bank and common currency into late 1997; and they did almost nothing to allow non-Serbs to return to their prewar homes, as the Dayton Accords guaranteed, or to cooperate with the International Tribunal for War Crimes in Former Yugoslavia by handing over indicted war criminals to The Hague.[6]

Bosnian Croats, finally, made no moves, as required by the peace accords, to abandon their separate military and governmental apparatus (which they called the "Croatian Republic of Herzeg-Bosnia," but which was not recognized by the Dayton Accords) and merge into a single federation with Bosnian Muslims. They also insisted on either parity or separation wherever they shared territory or offices with Muslims. Throughout 1996 and 1997, they refused to participate in the federation parliament until legislation was placed on the agenda (and adopted) to redraw administrative boundaries of the remaining mixed (Bosnian Muslim–Bosnian Croat) towns to divide them into separate administrative units along the model of the divided city of Mostar, which they had stubbornly resisted reunifying against constant international pressure since March 1994. In autumn 1997, they added a campaign, endorsed by the federation's minister of education, to create separate elementary schools in the federation for Croat and Muslim children, offering each group of young people the right to study in their own language (even though the language was the same) so that separate textbooks could inculcate a different curriculum and separate sense of political community.[7]

The first stage of the Dayton peace, therefore, revealed that it had stopped the war before any of the three warring parties had achieved its political goals and that this mattered to the extent of its implementation. The primacy of national identity and nationalist goals over reintegrative identities and political forces was given official recognition, and the map drawn at Dayton, which required a few transfers of territory between the two entities and allowed other transfers if mutually agreed, completed the aim of the war: to change the geographical distribution of the population so that separate national control over territory was irreversible. The one remaining significant exception to this manufactured homogeneity at the time of the truce—five Serb suburbs of Sarajevo—was lost, despite contrary international intentions and protest, in the massive exodus and expulsion of Serbs in February 1996 (with both Bosnian Muslims and Bosnian Serbs playing their part). At the same time, the accords did not affirm the irreducible element for peace of each of the three—*external* recognition of their *national right* to self-governance—nor did it choose among their conflicting political views of a Bosnian state. The Dayton peace agreement is not a political settlement. The ruling parties used their truce to continue the war by peaceful means.

The Peace Strategy Behind the Accords

Beneath the explicit tasks assigned the warring parties by the Dayton Accords and international officials were four implicit strategies to get around willful obstacles by the parties and create a peace process to transform this truce into a sustainable peace and its political compromise into a state.

The first, and most important to the U.S. negotiators, was a strategy of military balance. In the view of the Clinton administration, the war had been the result of a military imbalance to the advantage of the Bosnian Serbs, which allowed them to overrun 70 percent of Bosnian territory and to murder or expel all non-Serbs (primarily Muslims) from it within nine months of the start of the war. This aggression was made possible by the assistance of the Yugoslav federal army (itself in dissolution into an army dominated by Serbs for a new rump Yugoslavia), which had left them weapons, officers, and supplies in their forced retreat from Bosnia and gave logistical support and material thereafter. The only way to end the war and prevent its resumption, in the U.S. view, was to create a military balance between the Serbs and the allied Bosnian Muslims and Bosnian Croats, equipping and training the latter to deter further Serb aggression and to make them decisive on the battlefield should they need to defend themselves again. This "train-and-equip" program for a federation-entity army was not, in fact, a part of the peace accords, but among side agreements between the U.S. negotiators and the Bosnian Muslims made known to U.S. allies only later in the process of obtaining President Izetbegovic's signature on the accords and congressional support for sending U.S. troops. The program also contained the prior condition that there be a federation army; namely, that the two armies—the Croatian Defense Councils, which were actually units of the Croatian army, and the Bosnian government army (*Armija*)—unite into one under joint command. Within the peace accords, however, there was also a provision for arms control (Annex 1B) according to the venerable tradition of peace agreements and recent European experience in ending the Cold War on the European continent: that arms reductions and limitations are the means to prevent renewed war. An arms control agreement negotiated at Vienna within six months of the accords incorporated all three countries—Bosnia, Croatia, and Yugoslavia—and a process of arms reductions by October 31, 1997, of Serb holdings. The task of overseeing the military stabilization annex and its obligatory reductions was handed to the NATO-led IFOR.

The second implicit strategy was justice. There had to be a way to stop the cycles of revenge and unavenged historical grievances, which many outsiders viewed as the cause of the war, from renewing the violence after international troops departed. For the U.S. negotiators, this had two aspects: giving each Bosnian family a right to return to their prewar home if they wished (and to receive compensation for their property if they chose not to return), and taking international responsibility for the indictment, prosecution, and punishment of persons responsible for war crimes so that the average Bosnian felt that "justice" had been done and would be spared from taking it into his or her own hands. Many also argued that if people were able—through the right to return, an internationally supervised environment of security, and freedom of movement throughout the former country—to reconnect with former neighbors, friends, schoolmates, or work colleagues, then the process of forgiveness and reconciliation viewed necessary to peace could begin.

The third strategy was economic reconstruction. Under the initial leadership of the World Bank, a massive program of economic reconstruction and assistance to Bosnia and Herzegovina was drawn up for donors on the widespread recognition that if the economy did not begin to revive and the majority of the population remained without jobs for some time, and especially if demobilized soldiers found no work, then there would be renewed popular support for politicians and generals willing to wage a new war. A concept of reconstruction and myriad projects were designed even before the Dayton negotiations began,[8] and donors' conferences were held several times during the first year alone to obtain pledges, eventually of $5.5 billion over three to four years. While the World Bank mission continued to take the lead in implementing this program, it joined forces early on with the European Commission and the European Bank for Reconstruction and Development (the EBRD was established to assist former socialist countries in Eastern Europe in making the transition of macroeconomic stabilization, liberalization, and privatization to market economies). Governmental aid agencies followed their troops on the ground, providing bilateral humanitarian and developmental assistance to localities; the United Nations Development Programme took up residence; the Netherlands financed Bosnia's debt arrears to the IMF so it could gain membership immediately; and hundreds of nongovernmental organizations expanded from relief to conflict resolution, human rights, democratization, and development work. Although the World Bank staff was preoccupied the first year with large-scale infrastructural projects, it began the second year by insisting on economic reform and policies for cost recovery. The peace would not be self-sustaining, it argued, if Bosnia was unable to make the transition to a market economy from its socialist past and if it did not develop policies and governmental capacity to become economically viable but remained instead a ward of the international community and plagued with debt.

The fourth strategy was political institutionalization. While the Dayton constitution laid out the principles of a sovereign Bosnian state, the implementation process had to create the offices, ministries, and fundamental legislation of an entirely new political system. And because much of the peace process depended on a functioning government, the international administrators in the Office of the High Representative—the civilian coordinating field staff for the Dayton process—drew up a list of the essential offices and legislation that would need to be adopted as soon as the first elections were over (the list was even called the "Quick Start Package") and then took the lead in pushing their adoption rapidly. As with the early elections and a program of police reform, the goal was to leave the Bosnians to their own devices as soon as possible, equipped with Western institutions.

In fact, all four strategies aimed at a quick retreat of the international community. The Dayton Accords were the result of impatience among the major powers—with four years of war and refugees, a humanitarian operation (the United Nations Protection Force), and a succession of peace negotiations—that had led them in 1995 to force a negotiated end to the war. The driving force of the peace process was also impatience. To gain congressional approval for U.S. troop participation in an international implementation force considered essential to a successful peace, President Clinton offered to deploy troops for only twelve months. This temporal limitation set the pace for peace. Deadlines were incorporated into the accords, and success was measured by the timeliness of task completion.

Nonetheless, it soon became apparent that a twelve-month limit was foolish, that the international community also did not have a ready-made capacity for implementing its responsibilities, and that the parties had no intention of cooperating quickly with provisions that they viewed as undermining their wartime goals. As soon as President Clinton was reelected, in November 1996, he announced a new troop deployment of eighteen months. By its midway point, moreover, sharp debate ensued within Washington and between Washington and its main European troop-contributing allies over whether yet another deployment would be necessary (after June 1998) to sustain the gains of the cease-fire and prevent war from resuming because those gains were not yet self-sustaining.

While the unexpected delays in the departure of international troops was due in part to the fact that the parties were using the implementation process to continue the war, causing frequent delays due to explicit obstructions or constant haggling over the terms of the accords and of power sharing, there were also delays as a result of contradictions among the four implicit strategies of the peace agreement itself. The war termination element was internally contradictory. The train-and-equip program for the federation army discouraged Bosnian Serbs from implementing the arms control agreements rapidly or from reducing by half the size of its police force, as the civilian policing reform by the UN's International Police Task Force demanded. With their army disintegrating, their equipment in an extreme state of wear and disrepair, and discouraging signals from the Yugoslav army about future support, the Bosnian Serbs saw the train-and-equip program as building an offensive capacity for a new Muslim-initiated war and thus a vital threat against which they had to build a defense, such as in the police, where the accords allowed.[9] The United States had billed the train-and-equip program as the best method to end the war definitively and as the means to an early exit of troops because a local self-defense capacity would be in place, but by mid-1997, the program was instead becoming the primary reason to prolong the international troop deployment, including U.S. units. European allies and U.S. military critics of the program began to insist that the influx of new arms and training to the one party that felt itself most aggrieved territorially (Bosnian Muslims) had become a new source of war, against which the only deterrent was a continued international military presence.

The goal of the Dayton compromise, to assure all three communities their claimed right to self-determination within a single Bosnia, was also in conflict with the two elements of the strategy for justice because the indictment of war criminals and the return of refugees to prewar homes were perceived by the two minority groups—Bosnian Serbs and Bosnian Croats—as weapons in a new war to reverse their territorial gains and thus their right to self-determination. The Hague tribunal indicted only a handful of low-level Bosnian Muslims for war crimes, while it indicted more than fifty Bosnian Serbs, including their top political and military leaders, Radovan Karadzic and Ratko Mladic, and more than a dozen Bosnian Croats, some quite prominent in the war. Bosnian Serbs, in particular, thus viewed the tribunal as a political instrument against them, profoundly biased, and they refused to cooperate in handing over indictees. Bosnian Croats also delayed cooperating for two years and then began to question as well why it was that no Bosnian Muslims had been indicted for crimes against Croats. In addition, for all three leaderships, the obligation to implement the Dayton commitment to the right of return was perceived as *reducing* their security, since territorial control was seen as necessary to national rights, and that control was insecure if the local ethnic balance did not favor their side. Resistance to allowing persons whom they had expelled to return was strongest among Bosnian Serbs and Bosnian Croats, but Bosnian Muslims also began to create homogeneous communities (beginning with the capital city, Sarajevo, in February 1996) and to make minorities feel unwelcome in their areas, despite their continuing insistence on the right of Muslim returns as the sine qua non of the Dayton Accords.

In addition to these contradictions in the design of the peace accords, the process of implementing it also encountered conflicts among tasks and goals that tended to produce vicious circles, whereby achieving one goal would reduce the chance of achieving another and efforts to intensify implementation of some aspects would cause a slowdown in others. For example, because the Bosnian Muslim leadership viewed the right of Muslims to return home as critical to compensating for its political control in only 27 percent of Bosnia and for its loss of a central government it controlled, it also began to feel more insecure when Muslims were not being allowed to return, and thus to seek other sources of control and to demand international action. These actions, in turn, made the Bosnian Croats and Bosnian Serbs resist all the more. Within months of the start of implementation, refugee organizations and aid workers abandoned programs for minority returns and directed their resources to returning home people who would be going where their ethnic group was in the majority. At the same time, diplomats in the Contact Group and the Peace Implementation Council (PIC)—the two international committees overseeing the peace process—began to seek more robust but noncoercive means of securing compliance on indicted war criminals and the provisions for return. Resorting to political conditionality of all economic assistance as the primary instrument of leverage over the parties' compliance, they threatened to withhold assistance to any community (local or national) that was not cooperating with the tribunal on the right of return. But because the housing shortage, and thus the gridlock of displaced persons in other peoples' homes, was a genuine reason for some communities to resist returning refugees (where would they put their own displaced when previous residents moved back?), the lack of economic assistance, including funds for new housing, became an additional reason—or excuse—for obstructing returns.

Political conditionality for economic assistance, as an instrument for gaining compliance, also conflicted with the economic-reconstruction strategy of peace building. The more Bosnian Serbs were perceived to be obstructing the accords, the more economic punishment was used against them. The economic reconstruction perceived to be a critical element of peace building, to provide jobs and give a peace dividend in improved lives that would win adherents to peace among the population, did not occur in the Bosnian Serb entity until 1998. Two years after Dayton, the federation had received 98.3 percent of all assistance, and the Republika Srpska, 1.7 percent. While unemployment in the federation had been reduced in the second year of peace from 90 to 50 percent, it remained at 90 percent in the Republika Srpska, which did little to improve Serbs' commitment to Bosnia and the accords.

This operational economic element of the peace strategy was also in conflict with the fourth strategy, political institutionalization. Because aid was no longer humanitarian and would have to be repaid, it could not be given until there were legitimate authorities to be accountable for the implementation of projects and repayment of loans. Both within the federation and between the two entities, economic reconstruction depended on contracts and agreements that the parties were not yet ready to make with one another; the disbursal of monies depended on the formation of governmental institutions, such as a central bank, customs authorities, and tax systems, which were taking substantial time to create and reform. And because these political disagreements and the lack of progress on reintegration began to suggest that the Dayton Accords were not a compromise but a stalemate, international actors grew increasingly impatient.

International Impatience

Because the international commitment to the Bosnian peace process was governed by the willingness of NATO powers, and thus the United States, to deploy troops, the debate over that deployment in major foreign capitals, above all Washington, began to take on a life of its own. During 1997, and during the second military deployment (of what is called the Stabilization Force [SFOR]), outsiders debated whether the accords had ensured Bosnia's survival as a single, multiethnic state or had, in fact, recognized its partition. This debate between the partitionists and the Daytonists was expressed as an argument about time: Should the military deployment end in June 1998 by accepting a fait accompli of partition so that troops could leave, or did the Dayton Accords need patience to be fully implemented? Pressured by the announcement in February 1997 by the new U.S. secretary of defense, William S. Cohen, that U.S. troops would withdraw definitively at the end of the second deployment, in June 1998, a new U.S. foreign policy team under a new U.S. secretary of state, Madeleine Albright, attempted to pick up the pace of implementation during the spring. The goal was to demonstrate progress by June 1998 in implementing key provisions of the accords to an opposing U.S. Congress—in case it decided that yet another troop deployment was necessary.

To hasten the pace, U.S. diplomats became far more assertive in imposing certain provisions of the accords. This soon became manifest in U.S. pressure, for the first time, on Croatia to cooperate and to get Bosnian Croats to cooperate in handing over indicted war criminals and allowing refugee returns. Expressions of frustration with Bosnian Serbs also grew louder and motivated action. The lack of visible progress toward a reintegrated Bosnia was explained by the recalcitrance of Bosnian Serb leaders toward some provisions of the accords and, in particular, by the continuing presence of the aforementioned indicted war criminal and wartime political leader Radovan Karadzic, who was accused of remaining politically active, despite his formal removal from official positions as required by Dayton, and of presenting the primary obstacle to the accords. The PIC met at Sintra, Portugal, in May and vowed to use all measures possible, including intensified political conditionality of aid, to get results, thus winning the battle within the international operation against those who argued that economic recovery was essential to the process of peace and should not be an instrument of other goals. During the summer of 1997, new leadership in NATO (in the form of a new supreme allied commander for Europe, General Wesley Clark) and in the British foreign office (when British parliamentary elections brought the Labour Party to power and a new foreign minister, Robin Cook) reversed the reluctance until then of NATO commanders and the Pentagon to use force for any other aspects of the accords than their strictly military obligations under Annex 1A and Annex 1B. Their concern had been that to do so would be to abandon the impartiality that they viewed as necessary to performing their military obligations under the Dayton Accords and to the low risk of casualties needed to continue support at home for their deployment. Now NATO troops arrested some indicted war criminals and began actively to support, with the use of force, a U.S. policy to transform Brčko, the strategically vital town linking the two halves of the Serb entity, into a multiethnic core of a future Bosnia, including military support for the efforts of Muslim refugees to return to their homes there. By July, they were using force to intervene in a quarrel within the Bosnian Serb leadership in support of an alternative power center around the elected president of the Republika Srpska, Biljana Plavsic, and her efforts to purge and reform the police (including forceful change of personnel in police stations), to wrest monopoly control over the media from leaders in Pale by creating an alternative official media (which SFOR troops aided by taking physical control of TV transmitters), and to shift political power and revenues away from the leadership in Pale to her and the northern city of Banja Luka.

By October 1997, the tide was beginning to turn in the Washington debate over troop deployment in favor of the Daytonists, who opposed premature withdrawal from Bosnia and who feared failure through a resumption of war. In contrast to the wait in 1996 for a decision on whether there would be a follow-on force the second year, both the Clinton administration and NATO leaders began to make it clear that there would be a continued military deployment after June 1998. The announcement came in

late November, and the deadlines for implementing the accords were replaced with "benchmarks" toward a "self-sustaining peace" that had no
specific time limits attached.

The Partition Debate

At the same time that the Daytonists won on the issue of time, however,
the partitionists were beginning to win the wider debate regarding perceptions about the conflict itself and the substance of a peace process. Basing
their policy recommendations on a primordialist view of the causes of war
in Bosnia, the partitionists went beyond a realist position about spending
resources in line with interests, which they believed to be low in the case
of Bosnia, to a philosophical position that war based on ethnic conflict and
historical hatreds would never yield to a stable solution through a multiethnic political system.[10] This hatred, they argued, had been magnified by
the atrocities of the war such that reconciliation was not possible. There
were only two choices: partition or renewed war. By this logic, the Dayton
Accords were increasingly seen as idealistic and in need of adjustment because they aimed to transform a war-torn, demolished society and a territory divided by three nationalist parties, separate areas of control, and ethnically homogenized villages and towns into a multiethnic, integrated,
sovereign state.

Moreover, according to this unfolding school of thought, Bosnia was
now an example of post–Cold War conflict in general: ideological wars of
the Cold War period had, it argued, given way to ethnic conflicts, which
had different characteristics and were best addressed by population transfers and territorial partition if the goal was to minimize loss of life. The
Dayton implementation process was becoming a test of mechanisms for
regulating international order, not of a hypothesis about "ripeness" for negotiating an end to war or of explanations of the success or failure in implementing those negotiated settlements.

The difficulty with the primordialist and partitionist views of Bosnians
and their war is empirical: they are contradicted by a large body of evidence. Key to all of that evidence is the abstraction and selection, by these
outside partitionists, of one particular political identity they believe characterizes the Bosnian conflict and Bosnians over many alternative identities or combinations of identity. Bosnians, for example, whatever their ethnic or national identity, share a common political culture, *as Bosnians,* that
distinguishes them from other persons of the same national community in
neighboring parts of the former Yugoslavia. The claim of each of the three
communities for total political power, privilege, and protection so as to
avoid becoming a cultural or political minority in a state governed by

majoritarian rules need not lead necessarily to separate states. Moreover, the origins of the conflict in former Yugoslavia occurred in a society where ethnic (national) identity was not the single most important core of people's private or public identity, not to speak of the 40 percent of the population living in mixed marriages, the large number who themselves were the product of mixed unions, many generations over, and their children. Choices forced by war into one of the three communities were not really choices. These choices simply ignore the many people in Bosnia who did not belong to any of the three national communities but to one of many other minority ethnic groups. Nor are the three national communities internally homogeneous. Differentiation within each community is as great as or greater than the differences among the three—differences born of the many characteristics that matter more to individuals and households than their national identity, such as political views, religious practice, local loyalties, regional identities, class interests and professional identities, and even peace tactics. And even if these facts were not true, why would one assume that transforming substate nationalities into state nationalities necessarily creates stability, rather than instead opening up further causes of instability? The partitionists have no answer to this. In the Bosnian case, ethnic homogeneity of local communities—the result of the war—is not the same as whole territories washed of others that can be separated by defensible state boundaries and become three viable, independent states.

Even if the three Bosnian communities are territorially separable in a way that might facilitate a true partition into separate states, the current post-Dayton situation does not reflect the basic requirements, beginning with the Bosnian Croat and Muslim divided municipalities that abut each other. To begin with, an entirely new set of borders would have to be drawn—by a new Dayton-style conference or by a new war—and many more hundreds of thousands of people moved. Even then, none of the three can survive without cooperating economically. A simple look at the map, communication lines, trading routes, and economic specializations will show that trade among sovereign entities will not be enough to make each viable economically. Finally, the partitionist argument presumes the creation of pure nation-states out of the former Yugoslavia—a Greater Croatia, a Greater Serbia, a Bosniac Bosnia (the borders of which might include areas of contemporary Serbia and Montenegro), and presumably a greater Albania, combining Albania, Kosovo, parts of Montenegro, and parts of western Macedonia. Partitionists do not propose how these new borders would be drawn throughout the region, when they could not be drawn in 1991, and they have not tested the other half of their partition equation: that Bosnian Serbs or Bosnian Croats and the territory each controls in Bosnia would be welcomed by their national homelands—the Federal Republic of Yugoslavia (Serbia and Montenegro) and Croatia. Much anecdotal and public opinion survey data reveals strong opposition to annexation of their co-nationals; the majority in both neighboring states appear to prefer that their Bosnian cousins remain in Bosnia.

Dealing with the Causes of a Conflict

The partitionist argument does not, in fact, deal with the causes of conflict, arguing instead that once a conflict becomes defined ethnically, then population movements and separation are the only stable solution.[11] They do not address how ethnically defined communities would be better suited, after separation, to manage the original causes of the conflict than ones that are mixed (particularly as in the Bosnian case, where mixed identities were the rule). Moreover, the term "ethnic conflict" is a misnomer. The conflict in Bosnia is *national,* not ethnic; it is about states' rights and about the right to and content of citizenship. But it is also about a transitional moment, when the characteristics of the conflict are defined by the *previous* system, not by aspirations for the *future*.

The starting point of any peace process is to recognize the causes of war—in this case, the effort by Yugoslav politicians to redefine the basis of citizenship and its political rights during the 1980s, when the socialist system and its concept of citizenship were losing both political legitimacy and the budgetary resources necessary to that concept. Of the two alternative concepts of citizenship then possible within the Yugoslav system, communitarianism in Bosnia began to win out over the civic alternative during 1990, when the political system was taking a dramatic shift from one-party rule to multiparty elections.[12] Under conditions of economic crisis, political power becomes more clientelistic. When the ruling Communist Party collapsed at the end of January 1990 and the two northwestern republics became assertively secessionist, new political parties in Bosnia—legal only from early 1990—sought to imitate the ruling Communist Party through appeals that would maximize their following and their control over the levers of state power through maximum control over people's loyalties and livelihoods. Appeals to communal loyalties and collusive tactics among nationalist politicians not to disturb one another's political space were an easy route to monopoly power, within national communities, within the republic. The socialist conception of the state as providing material protection was replaced with the concept of the nation as the protector and refuge for members of a single national community, to the exclusion of others—first in terms of economic rights and privileges, then in cultural expression, and finally in purely physical terms of survival. People were persuaded by political rhetoric, distorted information, economic crisis, and actual discrimination to fear becoming a member of a minority, despite decades of legal (and in a wide sense, substantive) equality, while politicians claimed power and authority by defining human rights in group (national) terms. These claims were made above all in terms of economic assets; namely, political power remained a means to control money, jobs and patronage, and the property that was becoming available through privatization.

Instead of a brief, transitional form of political competition on the road to democratization and a market economy, nationalism and nationally based competition in Bosnia were institutionalized by the war. The economy and society of Bosnia were transformed into three separate political communities linked primarily by criminal networks and petty traders. But this war economy and war psychology were not stable either. As a result of war, the peace-building process faced three immediate issues before a stable future could be constructed. The war and politicians' rhetoric had together created an internal security dilemma, by which Bosnians of one national community perceived members of the other communities with fear and defensiveness, making it difficult to disarm psychologically and militarily so that one overarching community could start to regenerate once the cease-fire held. Individuals were not ready for reconciliation. And the fuzziness of the political arrangements created by the compromises of the Dayton Accords prolonged and even increased uncertainty about both the internal character and the external relations of the future independent Bosnian state and citizens' rights.

Whereas partition might provide a short-term solution to the second issue, by declaring the question of reconciliation across ethnic communities irrelevant, that would not deal with reconciliation between citizens and the leaders who had led them to war and produced little else. The first issue, the security dilemma, might be transferred from the individual level to state relations, but it would still have to be resolved at the level of border relations. The third issue of the nature of a postsocialist state and political society, the one that was the immediate cause of war, would remain. If at least two out of the three immediate issues of peace building would not be solved by partition, it would seem to make more sense to address them directly.

An Internal Security Dilemma

Fear of cohabitation in one state with the numerically stronger and internationally supported Bosnian Muslims has been so well ingrained in the Bosnian Serb and Bosnian Croat populations, as has fear for the Bosnian Muslims of becoming a minority or even ceasing to exist altogether in a Bosnia divided between its neighbors, that any process of reconciliation requires time and consistent reassurances directly aimed at counteracting these fears. Moreover, while the international military presence to monitor the cease-fire and demobilization should have removed the real basis of such apprehensions born of wartime experiences, the role of nationalist political propaganda and fear-mongering in the mass media actually intensified after the peace agreement was signed. Multiple projects were initiated by international donors to establish independent media, and in September 1997, the international operatives actually used force to shut down transmissions from official Bosnian Serb media, on the grounds that the venom and falsehoods of their reporting posed a direct threat to the international troops. But in Sarajevo, the political leadership of the Bosnian Muslims claimed sovereign rights against interference by those wanting to establish an independent TV station, while in Herzegovina, the absence of any political opposition to the ruling Bosnian Croat party meant there were few, if any, groups wanting to provide alternative messages for the international community to assist.

In this atmosphere, a forced pace of reintegration across the three communities and of refugee returns to homes where one would be in a minority is bound to fail. Instead, an international commitment (including a military presence) to the Dayton goal of one state and to no change of borders for a minimum of five years would seem to be essential to any peaceful outcome. As analysis of decades of experience with third-party negotiated settlements to civil wars suggests, the success of the Dayton Accords as a definitive end to the Bosnian war has only a fifty-fifty chance, and that depends on the extent to which international assistance helps overcome the obstacles to cooperation that lie in this continuing fear, sense of vulnerability, and lack of trust among the parties.[13] The primary determinant of success, in other words, does not lie with the agreement itself—for agreements are always compromises and general principles—but in the role of outsiders during the fragile period after a settlement is signed when parties need help to get beyond their fears of being at risk from former enemies and thus can cease thinking and acting solely in terms of their own protection. If they do not, the defensive psychology of each group only perpetuates the defenses of the others and the mentality of war.

Such a role requires those outsiders to be religiously impartial. The effect of the U.S.-sponsored train-and-equip program, however, is to recognize the fears of only one group. Bosnian Croats fear subordination in the federation to the more numerous Bosnian Muslims, even though they are also beneficiaries of this program. Bosnian Serbs, as the target of this military buildup, while being condemned for not being more willing to allow Muslim refugees to return to homes in the Republika Srpska, were kept in a defensive posture, fearful that the Dayton Accords were only a lull in a war being prepared under the patronage of a more activist U.S. policy toward Dayton implementation in mid-1997, which Serbs perceived as explicitly pro-Muslim. By abandoning impartiality, even if they viewed Muslims as needing and deserving greater support, the United States intensified the fears among Bosnian Serbs and Bosnian Croats that led them to prefer separation and to cooperate as little as possible in re-creating Bosnia. The logic behind the program, that peace required a self-defense capacity for Bosnian Muslims, even hinted that the primary patron of peace, the United States, did not believe in the political goal of the peace accord, that a common state for the three communities could be re-created, and that the fears of the minority groups were justified. It was as if they were preparing for partition.

Readiness for Reconciliation

The fear of becoming a minority in a state dominated by another nationality occupied most Bosnians in all three communities and was the primary source of popular support for nationalist leaders.[14] As long as the accords or their implementation did little to allay these fears, efforts at individual forgiveness and reconciliation would not go very far. Even the heads of the four religious communities of Bosnia (Muslim, Catholic, Orthodox, and Jewish), brought together during 1997 in an internationally sponsored Inter-Religious Council to provide moral leadership for peace and reconciliation, appeared to be more concerned with consolidating singular control over their flocks and designing mutual pacts against proselytizing than with ecumenism.[15]

Advances could be made, however, by working first for change within each community where the risk of being a minority—as a political minority—and the issue of minority rights could be faced without the complicating national element. All three communities shared the need to develop legal guarantees, political channels for redress of grievances, and checks against clientelistic and one-party dominant politics. If each developed effective mechanisms for policing their own against intolerance, discrimination, and violations of human rights, then processes of cooperation across communities and even multiethnic reintegration would be likely to occur more naturally and faster.

The lack of political institutions to provide assurances was made worse, moreover, by the staging of the economic assistance program. Public opinion surveys repeatedly identified the same top priority for Bosnians of all three communities of finding employment and the income, status, and security associated with a job. By giving priority to large infrastructure and to building the financial institutions for a market economy and for cost recovery, the program inevitably was slow to develop new jobs other than those tied directly to the international presence. Economic insecurity, particularly in the Republika Srpska with its 90 percent unemployment, and the continuing dependence of most Bosnians on officials (and thus party politicians) for access to jobs, housing, and relief were not likely to foster generosity and sharing with persons one had only recently fought. Because the bureaucratic rules of the EU, IMF, and the World Bank—the lead agencies in economic reconstruction—require these donors to work with counterparts who can provide guarantees, moreover, the aid program reinforced the political position of the three ruling nationalist parties whose interests were in consolidating national power, not in reconciliation.

The Lack of Clarity in the Dayton-Prescribed State and Its External Relations

Peace and stability in Bosnia depend on its capacity to survive and function as a country. The viability of small states depends on two conditions: first, openness to global communications and trade and, therefore, effective relations with neighbors and the international community, including a macroeconomic capacity to regulate these external relations and open borders; and second, a government that can function. The fuzziness of the Dayton concept for a Bosnian political system raised institutional questions about that second aspect of viability, and it would be some time before those doubts would be answered. After elections required the formation of a government, for example, the special relations between the Bosnian Muslim leadership in Sarajevo and the donor community had to give way to more complex bargaining about who represented whom, or who represented Bosnia. Even more complex were the property issues, where the privatization process had first to resolve who had ownership rights over companies and activities that the Dayton map had divided among municipalities or entities. Yet the speed of both under pressure from outsiders gave advantages to persons who had waged the war and were able to leverage wartime power into peacetime election and control over the privatization process to perpetuate personal and party gain.

External relations were equally confusing. The U.S. negotiators insisted on three negotiating partners at Dayton: the leader of the Bosnian Muslim party, Bosnian President Izetbegovic, and the presidents of neighboring Croatia and Serbia. This was ostensibly to get the two presidents' public commitment to Bosnian sovereignty and their leverage over Bosnian Croats and Bosnian Serbs to comply with the terms of the agreement. Furthermore, whenever the cooperation of either of these two was considered a problem, such as the refusal of Karadzic to cease political activity in the run-up to national elections in September 1996, U.S. diplomats flew to the neighboring capitals of Belgrade or Zagreb to demand compliance from Bosnian parties. The effect, along with the Dayton provisions for special relationships between the Republika Srpska and Yugoslavia and between the federation and Croatia, was instead to continue to raise doubts about Bosnian sovereignty, particularly in the minds of Bosnian Muslims. Croatia even granted Bosnian Croats dual citizenship, with rights not only to vote in Croatian elections, but also to be represented with special seats in the Croatian parliament. The Bosnian Croat political party was a branch of the ruling party in Croatia. Many of the Bosnian Serb political parties were branches of parties in Serbia and engaged in frequent consultations. In fact, all three Bosnian parties continued to have external patrons and sources of support (for the Bosnian Muslims, these were the United States and a number of Islamic states in the Middle East and Asia, including Iran, Malaysia, Saudi Arabia, Pakistan, and Turkey) that protected each from having to make the real political compromises necessary to one country and to working together. As for open borders, Croatia continued to keep its border with the Republika Srpska closed, preventing economic revival in the Banja Luka area, which depended on normalization of trade, although this was critical to the shift in U.S. policy during 1997 to speed implementation of Dayton by supporting a new Bosnian Serb leadership in the Banja Luka area as an alternative to hard-liners in Pale. At the same time, U.S. policy toward Serbia—maintaining an outer wall of economic sanctions until the separate problem of Kosovo and Albanian rights was solved, and insistence that political conditionality over economic aid did work to influence Bosnian Serbs—also imposed restraints on trade and produced a criminalization of border exchanges that did not contribute to Bosnian viability.

Conclusion: The Political Economy of Reconciliation

There should be no reason why a Bosnia partitioned into three areas could not remain one country, evolving over time from three nationally controlled parastates to three regions of a democracy with open borders. A single Bosnia composed of three national units is a compromise for all three parties that only awaits the emergence of political forces who want to make it one country. Such an evolutionary process would be composed of stages, beginning with an end to the uncertainty about Bosnia's political future and its citizens' rights of self-determination, a stage that the process of implementation has been prolonging unnecessarily. The first two years of peace building—the Dayton phase—could be seen as setting the stage for a new political contract for Bosnia, or for separation. Reassurances to those citizens who feel, even after two years of cease-fire, that the only protection is with their own national community and who fear that they will be forced to live in a minority position would have to be firmer. But by removing this uncertainty, radical nationalists would also lose influence, and nonpolitical processes of integration could begin.

Even more threatening to a sustainable peace than the electoral acclamation of nationalists responsible for the war that occurred in the September 1996 elections, and more or less in the municipal elections one year
later, would be the consolidation of one-party states in each of the three
areas. The idea that the greatest threat to individuals comes from members
of other national groups is simply wrong. Keeping that threat alive keeps
everyone on a war footing. The most important issues for citizens since the
settlement are local, within their own community, over jobs, rights to
housing, relations between original residents and the newcomers displaced
by the war who wish to remain where they are (particularly the rural population now in the cities), and tensions between persons who stayed during
the war and refugees returning from safe havens abroad. Greater focus on
these issues would reorient the population and their leaders to the rigors of
peace, and if the three national areas of Bosnia and Herzegovina are internally democratic and respect individual rights, then cross-unit political alliances, economic relations, and personal contacts can form and soften the
internal borders.

From the point of view of international assistance in this process,
however, the primary problem of peace in Bosnia appears to be that what
needed to be done was not likely to happen. As Alvaro de Soto and Graciana del Castillo write on the basis of the El Salvador peace process, the
question is, "Who will pay for the peace?"[16]

Of the various types of intervention and assistance, countries are most
reluctant to send troops and risk lives to prevent wars. But once they intervene, ironically, they are most willing (and able) to pay for military de-
ployments and aid, not for civilian tasks. Although the difficult stage of
peace building follows the military separation of forces, when matters of
internal security take prominence, countries are less willing to spare and
finance police forces or to create an international gendarmerie that could
be armed and replace costly soldiers.[17] National interests remain strong in
the giving of aid. Thus, for example, the U.S. energy behind the train-and-
equip program for the Bosnian federation came increasingly from its own
views of Iran, wanting to prevent Iran from gaining a toehold in Europe by
substituting U.S. patronage of Bosnian Muslims. The most immediate delivery of tangible assistance came from bilateral aid (such as from the U.S.
Agency for International Development, the British Overseas Development
Agency, or the Swedish International Development Authority) that was
available to communities located where that country's troops were stationed, which led to duplication in some cases and unnecessary neglect in
others. Donors pay for projects that are visible, to gain political credit and
foster national objectives, and that domestic legislatures will support, not
necessarily what is needed to consolidate the peace. Members of the U.S.

Congress were adamant that refugees were not being allowed to return home fast enough at the same time that they refused to fund housing construction for their own homeless citizens. The Organization for Security and Cooperation in Europe developed impressive programs for human rights to follow its work supervising elections, but the European Commission saw no reason to fund them. The phases of economic revival are determined not by the human stages of reconciliation, but by the programs for financial-sector reform and for cost recovery of banks that want (and need) to be repaid.

Opinion surveys of Bosnian citizens from all three communities during the first two years revealed overwhelming preferences for a job above everything else, and secondly for resolution of property issues for their apartment or house.[18] Experience with other peace-building efforts emphasizes the necessity of disarmament and demobilization, although this experience also demonstrates that neither is possible until the main political issues have been resolved,[19] and it emphasizes the need for time. The Bosnian peace process instead put strict deadlines on international commitment (renewing that commitment a year at a time), put assistance into economic stabilization and structural reform more than into local employment, and emphasized the transfer of indicted war criminals to The Hague and the vetting of police forces for accused war criminals, but it ignored the development of local judiciaries and criminal justice systems and sent in additional arms. While outsiders debated whether Bosnia was headed for multiethnic reintegration or for partition, they were not examining the role that they were contributing to this outcome and whether a different approach might be better.

If its first years of peace implementation demonstrate anything about the wider literature on peace settlements, then it is not a hurting stalemate among local parties but the ripeness of international patrons and powers that matters most in the decision to seek a negotiated peace. The necessity of partition after ethnically defined conflict is difficult to assess when the activities of the international negotiators, military forces, and civilian officials aiding the implementation of a peace agreement all reinforce the ethnic divisions of the population, the political system, and the distribution of jobs, housing, and other economic benefits. The peace process in Bosnia is being driven by the decisions of donors about what they are willing to finance, when, and how. Whether that includes activities that can lead to reconciliation and a sustainable peace was not clear in the first three years of peace, although comparison with what Bosnians say they need and with the experience in other cases of peace building after civil war suggest a major divide:[20] between the needs of peace and the goals of international actors in the process.

Notes

1. See I. William Zartman, *Ripe for Resolution: Conflict and Intervention in Africa* (New York: Oxford University Press, 1989); and Stephen John Stedman, "Conflict and Conflict Resolution in Africa: A Conceptual Framework," in Frances M. Deng and I. William Zartman, eds., *Conflict Resolution in Africa* (Washington, D.C.: Brookings Institution, 1991).

2. During the war, the leadership of the largest Bosnian Muslim political party, the Party of Democratic Action (SDA), decided to change the political name of its community from Muslim to Bosniac (*Bošnjak*). Many had resisted this for some time because its historical legacy was that of a pre–World War II party of the landed aristocracy and a post-1990 liberal, secular wing of the SDA that bolted to form a separate party. In changing to Bosniac, the SDA leadership hoped to provide a new identity for its constituency that was more closely associated with Bosnia and left open the political and religious connotations of being Muslim for postindependence debate. In this chapter, I choose for reasons of clarity, and of not prejudging political outcomes, to remain with the older designation, that Yugoslav constitutional identity of Muslim, and apologize for any offense given as a result.

3. Reflecting what was to become the dominant U.S. view, chief Dayton negotiator Richard Holbrooke writes in his memoirs of the Croatian (and later joint Croatian-Bosniac) offensives during the summer of 1995 that their success "was a classic illustration of the fact that the shape of the diplomatic landscape will usually reflect the balance of forces on the ground. In concrete terms, this meant that as diplomats we could not expect the Serbs to be conciliatory at the negotiating table as long as they had experienced nothing but success on the battlefield" (*To End a War* [New York: Random House, 1998], p. 73).

4. Critical to this change in strategic balance were military events in neighboring Croatia in May and August, when the Croatian army overran the three (of four) United Nations protected areas in Croatia that bordered Bosnia and were populated by Croatian Serbs allied with Bosnian Serbs. The expulsion and flight of these Croatian Serbs deprived Serb towns in northern and western Bosnia of defensive protection and left them fully exposed to the Croatian juggernaut in September. The United States had facilitated this "assist" from Croatia, including a defense agreement signed in Split in July 1995 between the Bosnian president and leader of the SDA, Alija Izetbegovic, and the president of Croatia, Franjo Tudjman, to legitimize the invasion, apparently viewing as of secondary concern the known Croatian ambitions to annex large parts of Bosnia as legitimate Croat territory.

5. See Barbara F. Walter, "The Critical Barrier to Civil War Settlement," *International Organization* 51, no. 3 (summer 1997).

6. For the sake of accuracy, however, it is worth noting that in 1996–1997, all three communities obstructed the right of refugees and displaced persons to return to their homes, and until October 1997, the Bosnian Croats also refused to turn over their indicted war criminals to the tribunal. Thus, in practice, the denial of economic aid to the Bosnian Serbs on the grounds that they were not cooperating seemed motivated more by the prevailing emotion that Serbs were the most egregious offenders during the war.

7. It must be noted, however, that all federation ministries were headed by one Muslim and one Croat, with each ministry differing only in the nation holding its senior position. Thus, a Muslim deputy minister had to sign off on this education agreement.

8. See "Bosnia and Herzegovina: Economic Issues and Priorities," discussion paper of the Central Europe Department of the World Bank, September 29, 1995, and its companion piece, "Rebuilding Bosnia and Herzegovina: Priorities for Recovery and Growth," both of which were prepared on the basis of meetings in Warsaw during the week of May 22, 1995, by representatives of the World Bank and of the wartime government. The first post-Dayton program, "Bosnia and Herzegovina: Priorities for Recovery and Growth," was issued jointly by the World Bank, the European Commission, and the European Bank for Reconstruction and Development on December 8, 1995, for the first donors' conference, held in Brussels.

9. This was so until summer 1997, when a new U.S. policy of more assertive implementation of the accords, focused primarily on changing the leadership of the Bosnian Serbs toward politicians willing to cooperate with their implementation, declared military units of police to be covered by Annex 1A and in violation of the accords.

10. See Chaim Kaufman, "Possible and Impossible Solutions to Ethnic Civil Wars," *International Security* 20, no. 4 (spring 1996): 136–175; John J. Mearsheimer and Robert A. Pape, "The Answer: A Three-Way Partition Plan for Bosnia and How the U.S. Can Enforce It," *New Republic*, June 14, 1993, pp. 22–28; John J. Mearsheimer and Stephen W. Van Evera, "When Peace Means War," *New Republic*, December 18, 1995, pp. 16–21; and Robert Hayden, "Schindler's Fate: Genocide, Ethnic Cleansing, and Population Transfers," *Slavic Review* 55, no. 4 (winter 1996): 727–748.

11. Kaufman ("Possible and Impossible Solutions") is clearest on this.

12. See Xavier Bougarel, "Bosnia and Hercegovina: State and Communitarianism," in David A. Dyker and Ivan Vejvoda, eds., *Yugoslavia and After: A Study in Fragmentation, Despair, and Rebirth* (London: Longman, 1996), pp. 98–99.

13. Barbara Walter, "The Resolution of Civil Wars: Why Negotiations Fail," Ph.D. diss., University of Chicago, December 1994, and "The Critical Barrier to Civil War Settlement," *International Organization* 51, no. 3 (summer 1997).

14. On the "rationality" of these fears, however unrealistic they may be, see Rui deFigueiredo and Barry R. Weingast, "The Rationality of Fear: Political Opportunism and Ethnic Conflict," in Jack Snyder and Robert Jervis, eds., *Civil War and the Security Dilemma* (New York: Columbia University Press, 1999), chap. 8.

15. This observation is based on visits of the four leaders to the United States, including presentations at the Catholic Bishop's Conference, Washington, D.C., May 21, 1998. The Inter-Religious Council was established in Sarajevo on June 9, 1997, "to promote inter-faith cooperation in the region" and as a "forum for issues affecting intercommunal relations"; the four leaders were Mustafa Ceric, the *reis-ul-ulema* of Bosnia and Herzegovina; Jacob Finci, president of the Jewish community; Vinko Cardinal Puljic, archbishop of Sarajevo; and a representative of Serbian Patriarch Pavle.

16. Alvaro de Soto and Graciana del Castillo, "Obstacles to Peacebuilding," *Foreign Policy* 94 (spring 1994): 87–102.

17. The need for such an international gendarmerie to assist in the Dayton implementation and fill the "security gap" between international military forces and the local police was recognized early, in large part by military commanders who did not want to take on civilian policing tasks, but it took another two years for the idea to be adopted by the PIC and NATO. Then, the difficulty of finding and funding this special unit, which would be assigned to the SFOR commander, delayed it further, so that six months after its creation, it had still not been deployed.

18. See the regular issues of *Opinion Analysis* from the United States Information Agency, Office of Research and Media Reaction, which are based on surveys commissioned from reputable Bosnian, Croatian, and Serbian polling firms.

19. Mats R. Berdal, *Disarmament and Demobilisation After Civil Wars: Arms, Soldiers, and the Termination of Armed Conflicts,* Adelphi Paper No. 303 (London: Oxford University Press, August 1996).

20. See, for example, Fen Osler Hampson, *Nurturing Peace: Why Peace Settlements Succeed or Fail* (Washington, D.C.: United States Institute of Peace Press, 1996).

7

Reflections on a
Schizophrenic Peace

Dusko Doder

Where there is no vision, the people perish.

—*Book of Proverbs*

I have cried twice on assignment. Once in Beijing during the 1989 Tiananmen revolt when, in order to cover the story properly, my wife (also a journalist) and I sent our four-month-old son with a friend on a flight to Hong Kong to the safety of his grandparents' home. The second time was in the summer of 1996 in Bosnia as we interviewed Muslim women whose men had disappeared from Srebrenica a year earlier during the greatest bloodbath of the Yugoslav wars.

The second experience was more wrenching. How do you respond to a three-year-old girl still waiting for her father and brother to return, saving them daily scraps of food and dreaming of a magic wand to turn herself into a bird "so I could fly over the woods and find them"? The eyes of this girl's mother, Djeva, stared crazed from a gaunt face as she recalled the last moments—it was a scorching July 1995 day—before her husband and son were taken away by Bosnian Serb soldiers. "I know my son is alive," she declared. "A mother just knows."

The emotions of the Srebrenica survivors were tweaked each time—at first every few weeks, then months—some man turned up from hiding in mountain caves and thick forests, prolonging their deluded hopes. One survivor, Suljo Halilovic, thirty-six years old, arrived in Muslim-held Tuzla seven months after his wife had received word he was killed at Srebrenica. Their sixteen-year-old son, Amir, was still missing. Suljo, I suspect, was reconciled to the loss: separated from Amir in a Serb ambush, he had spent days turning over hundreds of corpses in the woods looking for him. His wife was still hoping.

These personal snapshots of Srebrenica illuminated for me the wrenching tragedy of Bosnia. Forty-two thousand people—mostly Muslim refugees from neighboring villages—spent months encircled by Serb forces in Srebrenica, a one-road town wedged in a deep valley. The town was a so-called UN safe area, protected by a 700-strong Dutch force. But they proved helpless when Bosnian Serb commander Ratko Mladic made his move. His men entered, handing chocolate to children and separating out men and boys as young as fifteen. More than 23,000 women, children, and old people were deported. Several thousand Muslim fighters escaped. More than 6,000 men—according to International Red Cross statistics—disappeared. There is little mystery about what happened to them. A soldier in the Bosnian Serb army testified that he helped execute around 1,000 men who surrendered. Two Muslim survivors described how they played dead under the bodies of hundreds of others similarly executed.

Srebrenica symbolizes the war. The inhumanity. And the betrayal. Its people were betrayed by everybody—the United Nations, the international community, the Muslim government in Sarajevo, the Dutch peacekeepers who were supposed to protect them—and ultimately by their executioner, General Mladic, who promised them that "nothing would happen" if they surrendered.

The UN role was always murky. Flamboyant UN commander French General Philippe Morrilon made an unauthorized visit to the besieged enclave in early 1993. "You are under the protection of the United Nations!" he declared. "I will never abandon you!" But he had tried to sneak out the first night (leaving on foot to meet a transport vehicle; the Muslims spotted him and took him virtual hostage on orders from the Sarajevo government). His words captured the world's imagination and panicked UN headquarters. The Security Council adopted a resolution declaring "Srebrenica and its surroundings" a UN safe area.

The people of Srebrenica had a chance to escape, but the Sarajevo government would not allow them to move to safety. Srebrenica was a key military pressure point against the Serbs. Between the outbreak of the Bosnian war in April 1992 and January 1993, the Muslim warlord of Srebrenica and his troops attacked and burned down scores of villages in the area, killing about 3,000 Serb villagers in raids notorious for their brutality. Muslim forays into the Serb-held areas continued after the town was declared a UN safe area and was supposedly demilitarized. When Mladic's troops took their revenge, however, the Muslim fighters were long gone. The UN soldiers proved weak and inept, in contrast to the fighting words of politicians.

In a larger sense, Srebrenica is a metaphor for the Bosnian war. The prevarications of various generals and international bureaucrats—described, perhaps unjustly, as men with feet of clay, hearts of stone, and heads of wood—merely obscured the fact that key political leaders in the United States and Western Europe had simply chosen to ignore Bosnia. Ultimately, it was the horror of Srebrenica that exposed as threadbare the rhetorical fabric that held together a cascade of Western policies and promises, and this horror practically forced Western leaders to react forcefully. The town would never have been seized and thousands of its residents slaughtered had the United States and other members of the Security Council displayed readiness to send their own troops.

The full scope of the tragedy was apparent by July 17, when President Bill Clinton attended a meeting of his Bosnia crisis group (which included a handful of the senior officials). The *Washington Post* on the previous day carried on its front page the photograph of a woman—described as one of some 10,000 refugees from Srebrenica—who had committed suicide by hanging herself from a tree. Vice President Al Gore confronted the president with a personal story. "My twenty-one-year-old daughter asked me about that picture. What am I supposed to tell her? Why is this happening and we're not doing anything? My daughter is surprised the world has allowed this to happen. I am too."

Within the next few months, the United States managed to bring an end to the fighting in Bosnia. A political settlement, however, has yet to be reached. The Balkans had failed to produce someone with Nelson Mandela's political wisdom and generosity of spirit who could generate compromise and end the vicious cycle of violence (nor were there any F. W. de Klerks around). Leaders in former Yugoslavia are provincial warlords steeped in blood who masquerade as politicians, narrow-minded men filled with hate who—to borrow Mandela's description of them—think "through their blood, not through their brains." With such men still in power, Bosnia remains a great, unfinished drama.

At humbler levels, however, the situation is somewhat different. Even among those who have suffered most, I encountered amazing magnanimity. I have mentioned Suljo Halilovic, still mourning for his son. When I told Suljo I was going to Srebrenica, which is now occupied by Serbs, and offered to attempt to bring some mementoes from his home back to him, he asked me instead to call on a Serb official in the nearby town of Bratunac to whom he owed his life. Suljo launched into a story explaining how it all happened, then said: "Please tell him I'm alive and that I am grateful to him for saving my life."

I should first of all confess a personal interest in the fate of Bosnia. I was born in Sarajevo, its capital, where I spent a rather unhappy childhood during World War II. My first, strongest, and most enduring image of the war was a glimpse I caught when I was about five. My mother had spread bedsheets over the windows and in a hushed voice ordered me not to remove them. I disobeyed her, naturally, and peeked out as soon as grown-ups stepped out. It was a frigid winter morning. The street was empty, except for a few patrolling Nazi soldiers. Then I noticed a man hanging from the lamppost in front of the house and human figures hanging from each tree along the boulevard, turning into swinging pendulums by swirling winds.

I survived the war and moved to a new home in the United States, with nothing scarred about my person and the sights of repetitive bombardments, killings, and privations forgotten. I was, as this is now conventionally described, in denial: Bosnia for me became a place to forget. I was in love with the United States and desperately wanted to become a genuine part of it.

Years later, when I was preparing my dissertation on the role of ethnic violence in the Balkans that lubricated much of Europe's diplomacy leading up to the 1878 Congress of Berlin, I began to understand something about Balkan violence. What came to be viewed as a temperamental predisposition toward violence was, in reality, a form of social action by a people subjected to the rule of foreign masters.[1]

There was another aspect of Bosnia's historical legacy that I understood only later, when I was sent to Yugoslavia in 1973 as chief of the *Washington Post's* East European bureau. It was the general attitude of the people toward authority: deep down, they feel that public life is a fraud, regardless of who is in power, and that men seek power and influence to get rich. Time and again I confronted the complex web of rituals (involving graft and corruption) that I had to learn to navigate through within the bureaucratic maze of the Balkans. I spent three years on this assignment, and I often wondered what would have happened to me had I remained in Sarajevo. Would I still be me?

This became my recurring fancy when I returned to Belgrade in the summer of 1990—after long assignments in Moscow, Washington, D.C., and Beijing—to witness Yugoslavia's disintegration. I was now coming face-to-face with a different country. Before the outbreak of hostilities, the once jovial and hospitable people had turned militant, nationalist, and surly. Later, watching them succumbing to ethnic fanaticism or coping stoically with wartime privations, they seemed depleted of life. I was at a loss to understand Sarajevo. If there ever was a place where the multinational Yugoslav idea of kindred peoples living in harmony had a chance of succeeding, that place was Sarajevo.

Tragedy triggers an introspective search for meaning. Whose army would I have fought in had I remained in Sarajevo? Which side would I have taken? Neutrality was not an option. (Complicating matters still further, my parents were not Sarajevans and came from widely divergent backgrounds: Slav on my father's side, non-Slav on my mother's.) Given the tenuous relations between a man's intention and the consequences of his acts, these thoughts were disturbing indeed. Perhaps the multicultural- ism was always a sham, at least in the eyes of sizable sections of the pop- ulation; Yugoslavia was never a multinational state, but merely a doomed country comprising many nations.

After the guns fell silent following the Dayton Accords, I went to check out my boyhood home. These were strange, moody moments. Here, along the banks of the river, was the front line. The nearby bridge stood half destroyed, unusable. The charred shell of the detached, one-family house where I had spent the first five years of my life was a total wreck, its two chimneys protruding at an angle suggesting imminent collapse. Roadblocks and barbed-wire barricades were still there, shabby obscenities straggling across the face of the city. But I was appalled most by the sight of burned old trees that once provided green lushness and deep shade along Woodrow Wilson Boulevard. What had unleashed such gruesome savagery in Europe half a century after Adolf Hitler?

The ethnic and religious divisions of Yugoslavia were not unique but had always been seen as more complex and intractable than anywhere else. Its people have no common vision. In my 1978 book, I wrote that

> the Yugoslavs have a hazy notion of their common purpose and . . . there is in fact no such thing as a Yugoslav. There were Serbs, Croats, Slovenes, Macedonians and others, who in some respects seem as unlike each other as people from different countries. Although of a common South (Yugo) Slav origin, they speak different languages, use different scripts, and had never lived within a common state prior to the creation of Yugoslavia in 1918.[2]

Yugoslav harmony was not grounded in ethnic tolerance and respect but, rather, in a defensive joint aspiration against foreign enemies—especially the Soviet Union and Soviet-style communism.

In a certain sense, this was a common vision but a negative one. Mar- shal Tito certainly made the most of it. In a world in which the threat of communism was indivisible and the obligation to resist that threat unlim- ited, a defector from what was then seen as a homogeneous Sino-Soviet bloc—particularly as resourceful a heretic as Tito—was to find a welcom- ing embrace in the West.

Most observers feared that Yugoslavia would not survive his death and that his successors—lacking his authority, his native wit, his balancing skills—would be unable to perpetuate the old illusions. But everybody wanted Yugoslavia to survive: the United States was committed to support its "independence, territorial integrity and nonalignment."[3] The desire over- came critical scholarship. To quote the 1974 edition of the *Encyclopedia Britannica:* "The Yugoslav system is so deeply rooted, and the survival of a strong, independent, nonaligned Yugoslavia is so vital to the maintenance of European stability, that the country will undoubtedly survive the shock of Tito's departure."

Western strategists in particular tended to ignore portents of things to come. Since public expressions of nationalism were taboo in Communist Yugoslavia, sporting events provided an outlet for such feelings. The Adriatic port city of Split became famous for such outbursts of violent nationalism. I visited it after one crucial soccer match in 1975 between top Serb and Croat teams, when a riot broke out in which hundreds of persons were injured and a train carrying fans was demolished. The army eventually quelled the brawl but not before jubilant Croat fans celebrated the victory by tossing hundreds of cars bearing Serbian license plates into the sea.

But such incidents were carefully shielded from reaching foreign eyes and ears by a well-oiled propaganda machinery humming the mantra of "brotherhood and unity" for domestic and foreign consumption. Apart from the strategic considerations, it was easy to admire Tito's experiment. Tito himself was more humane and less bloodthirsty than contemporary dictators. If measured by Soviet bloc standards, Yugoslavia had made real strides toward democratization. Tito had recognized new nations—the Montenegrins and Macedonians in 1945 and the Bosnian Muslims in 1971—and had advanced cultural and political rights of non-Slav minorities more than anyone else in Eastern Europe. He granted the people a long-coveted freedom of movement and opened the country's borders. But all along, Yugoslavia remained an oppressive Communist state, and Tito remained an orthodox Marxist, but our kind of Marxist. As C. L. Sulzberger put it, "Sure Tito is a Marxist, but his dogma was written by Groucho, not Karl."[4]

Yet, for all his activism and magic, the old illusionist had neglected the most intractable problem of all: the Serb-Croat relationship. And what was subsequently shown to be a brilliant balancing act was also a trap Tito had built for his country. In reality, Tito's vision worked only in the context of East-West competition; the disintegration of the Soviet empire sounded its death knell, and the first free elections in 1990 meant a revival of tribalism and an inevitable implosion. The primary responsibility for this lies squarely on the shoulders of Tito and his Communist Party.

War came in 1991. It was fought between Croats and Serbs and was brutal, brief, and confined to border areas with mixed Serb-Croat populations. The Roman Catholic Croats fought against "hegemonism" by the Eastern Orthodox Serbs, whom they regarded as an inferior, Eastern culture. Serbia, militarily stronger and in control of the remnants of the Yugoslav army, masked its expansionist designs by insisting it was seeking to protect its minority (which accounted for 13 percent of Croatia's population) from a reemerging Croatian fascism. Both sides expressed a strain of fanatic idealism; nationalists fought side by side with Communists; and, for the most part, it was warfare in the shadows—ambush, murder, and torture, leaving in its wake a trail of destroyed towns, burned villages, and wrecked families.

But the flames of war stopped at Bosnia's borders. Everybody knew that Bosnia was a powder keg, but everybody hoped Bosnia's languid harmony could be preserved—first and foremost, Bosnians themselves. But if the multinational Yugoslav federation was doomed and Serbs and Croats were shooting at each other, what future could Bosnia have, being, as it was, the microcosm of Yugoslavia?

Bosnia, a triangle-shaped territory that was literally and metaphorically the heart of Yugoslavia, was the real bone of contention between Serbia and Croatia, however. By 1991, Bosnia's ethnic composition had changed: it was 31 percent Serb, 17 percent Croat, and 41 percent Muslim. How could Bosnia be subdivided along ethnic lines when 27 percent of marriages were mixed?

The Muslims had no interest in the breakup of Yugoslavia and sought to preserve it by proposing a new federal or confederal state. But Serbia's Slobodan Milosevic would not even consider the idea. Milosevic was the most powerful politician on the scene and he was disinterested in reasoned exchange. This unpleasantly arrogant man was a perfect expression of communism's failure to nurture new generations of good officials. He was a sycophant of the bullying sort, but one far more ambitious and far less capable than men from the older Communist generation. His first nationalist catchphrase was an order to police against restraining the crowd at a rally. "No one will beat you again!" he barked to the crowd, which complained that the cops had used their truncheons on them. This was hardly a new vision of Serb nationalism, but it was good enough because it legitimized the venting of anti-Communist grievances and inarticulate anger against the prospect of economic decline. He became a vastly popular figure by simply siding with Serb nationalists against the Albanian majority in Kosovo.

Milosevic's strength was his consummate capacity for lying and intrigue. He worked covertly through his secret police and Serb proxies to foment internal unrest, first in Croatia, then in Bosnia, using uniformed or secret armies until the whole process descended into a long Bosnia bloodbath. Television was his primary tool; its blatant chauvinism had inflamed public opinion and helped him assume absolute authority. His was a new type of dictatorship—a television dictatorship backed up by police.

The Serbian people, as a whole, overcompensated for their inherent anarchical tendencies by bowing willingly to despotism on the strict understanding that their subservience served a larger cause and that they would be rewarded for it. "All Serbs in one country" seemed to reflect the legitimate aspiration of a people intermingling with other nations and races. "No one will beat you again!" plausibly signaled the end of dictatorship. So Milosevic's dictatorship was not a blight imposed on the Serbian people by outside forces; it was a response to a popular demand. This is not to say that the people later liked what they had asked for. People of talent or substance realized early on that he was leading the whole of Yugoslavia into a disaster. A few attempted to warn the people of an impending catastrophe, but they were promptly silenced.

Milosevic found a worthy partner in Croatia's Franjo Tudjman, a former Communist general, who channeled the emotions of Croat nationalism unto himself and used them without scruples to establish his power. The two men met twice before the outbreak of hostilities to plan "ethnic cleansing and an expansion of their respective borders" at Bosnia's expense. Neither believed the Muslims could be a separate nation. Tudjman contended they were all Croats; Milosevic insisted they were Serbs.[5] Such claims were far from irresistible; they were based on murky medieval legends, false linguistic arguments, and the time-honored Balkan justification of appropriating territory for a higher national cause.

It was difficult for Muslim politicians to imagine the Muslim future in such a state, yet they were immobilized and seemingly resigned. Like the heroes of the old Greek tragedies, they seemed condemned to an ineluctable fate from which there was no escape. There was none on the scene strong enough to put the brakes on; Milosevic had the army on his side. The secret understandings reached by Milosevic and Tudjman suggested that a partition of Bosnia was inevitable.

The Muslims rightly regarded any division of Bosnia as an intolerable threat to their security and interests, and they were determined to resist. Being militarily weak, there was only one avenue open to them: to exploit the Serb-Croat conflict by entering into an alliance with one of the predators. The choice between Milosevic and Tudjman was hardly a choice (it was, in Alija Izetbegovic's famous quip, "like choosing between leukemia and a brain tumor"), but it had to be made.[6]

At that point, the leadership of the Muslim national party split into two over different visions of their future. The smaller one, led by Adil Zulfikarpasic, a wealthy businessman just returned to Bosnia after four decades in Switzerland, favored a "democratic, European party" and liberal values. It was supported by Muslim intellectual and cultural elites. The larger, led by Izetbegovic, embraced Islamism; it excluded non-Muslims.[7]

Both factions had the same goal: to prevent partition of Bosnia. By stressing liberal democracy, Zulfikarpasic never stood a chance against the man who championed Muslim national interest, who emphasized Muslim identity, and who had spent years in jail for organizing Muslim groups and was the author of the "Islamic Declaration" calling on Muslims everywhere to rediscover Islam and take their destiny into their own hands.

There was another point of contention. The minority favored an alliance with Serbia; the majority opted for Croatia. It was said later that Izetbegovic's decision to enter into an alliance with the Bosnian Croats (the latter controlled by Tudjman) had disrupted the three-way harmony and slowly forced the issue to a showdown. But that is a moot point. Facing predators from Belgrade and Zagreb, the Muslims were making a defensive, rather than an aggressive, maneuver; they desperately sought to avoid violence (they had no weapons to challenge the heavily armed Serbs who had seized control over the remnants of the Yugoslav army). Given the secret Milosevic-Tudjman deal, anything the Muslims did was bound to provoke conflict. Harmony in Bosnia depends not on amalgamating its nations (or creating alliances) but, rather, on balancing them—Tito had this principle enshrined in the Bosnian constitution.

Social disintegration was so rapid in the weeks that preceded the outbreak of hostilities that there was almost a palpable conflict between the values of a disintegrating order and the absence of clearly emerging values of a new order to come. The fragmentation was strictly along ethnic lines.

The main source of hatred and fear-mongering was Milosevic's Belgrade television: its chauvinist crudities took on the aspect of a quasi-religious movement with overtones of hysteria, preaching an apocalyptic confrontation between Christianity and Islamic fundamentalists. Zagreb media urged patriotic Croats to volunteer to fight for their brothers in Bosnia.

Behind the scenes, according to Tudjman's onetime second in command, Stipe Mesic, Serbia and Croatia were working out details on population movement (a euphemism for "ethnic cleansing") and new maps; a series of meetings between then Croatian Prime Minister Hrvoje Sarinic and Milosevic's counselor, Smilja Avramov, was required to divide the spoils.

In the end, nothing could stop the outsiders from starting war on April 6, 1992. The governments of Serbia and Croatia have to bear the blame for the atrocities of a rash of pogroms, above all for ethnic cleansing in eastern Bosnia and western Herzegovina, in which thousands of persons—a vast majority of them Muslim—were massacred over several weeks. These murderous actions by paramilitary gangs were led by such persons as Zeljko Raznjatovic (Arkan of Belgrade), who was under direct control of Milosevic, and Vojislav Seslj, Milosevic's political ally. (Dobroslav Paraga of Zagreb, whose gangs carried out murderous cleansing in the Neretva River valley, was controlled by Tudjman's government. Ditto for Dario Kordic, who held the rank of general in the Croatian army.)

Within weeks, Sarajevo was under daily Serb bombardment, thousands of Muslims were dead, and tens of thousands displaced. This, in turn, touched off the gangsterlike atrocities of Muslim paramilitaries. But since the Muslims were clearly the victims of the war—and since the war was imposed on them—such actions were at first dismissed as an understandable response of a David fighting a Goliath. The Muslims, indeed, had to be accorded an extra measure of compassion for waging a military and propaganda war against the militarily stronger Serbs, on the one hand, and Croat chauvinists masquerading as Muslim allies, on the other. Later, after the West came firmly down on the Muslim side, Muslim infractions and atrocities were simply ignored.

By the summer, the whole of Bosnia had exploded into savage war; the Serbs had quickly seized more than 70 percent of Bosnia's territory. War, ironically, provided a sense of relief for the souls subjected to incessant propaganda barrages and fear-mongering. It put everything into context—everybody was fighting for their tribal lands.

On July 30, 1992, David Owen, former British foreign secretary, urged the West to launch air strikes against the Bosnian Serbs. "We are witnessing real outrageous racial intolerance which we haven't seen since the Nazis," he said in a BBC radio interview. "If we allow this to happen then the world is in a very perilous stage."

Six weeks later, in Sarajevo for the first time as a European Community peace negotiator, Owen was outraged that his arrival coincided with Serb bombardment of Sarajevo's Kosevo Hospital. The attack was shown on Sarajevo TV as another act of Serb savagery, and Owen promptly denounced it as such. Within hours, Owen recalled later, he learned that the incident was provoked by the Muslims and that General Philippe Morillon had protested privately to Izetbegovic.[8] Owen said,

> The UN monitors actually saw the Muslim troops enter the hospital and, from the hospital grounds, firing at Serb positions. Then the mortar was packed up and removed [as] the television crew showed up. A few minutes later a retaliatory fire of course landed in or near the hospital and all was filmed for television. I asked Morillon why didn't he make this public, and he shrugged his shoulders in the typical Gallic way and quipped, "We have to live here."

Owen made the incident public more than three years later while promoting his book about the Yugoslav crisis.

Before moving forward, it is necessary to move back a bit to understand the point at which the Bosnian society finds itself at the end of the twentieth century. A distinguishing feature of Bosnia's history during the past two centuries—when compared with all other Balkan states—was the virtually total absence of any constructive interplay between the rulers and their subjects. There is an element of latent rebellion in the makeup of Bosnian peoples; history has left them without a clear concept of consensus building, or what we call the "democratic procedure." Whatever Bosnia's social and cultural development prior to the Turkish conquest in the fiftieth century, its people were plunged deep into darkness and

Oriental inertness that the Ottomans imposed on the world they conquered. An English traveler described it this way: "Scarcely a ray of light and progress brightened the intellectual, social and industrial stagnation that settled (in 1463) upon their people until 1875, when, exasperated by extortion, taxation, rape, murder and religious persecution, they rose in rebellion."[9]

This was true as far as it went, but it did not go far enough. The Ottoman rule was harsh and brutal indeed; but it was not an uninterrupted orgy of rape, murder, and religious persecution lasting four centuries. While not a model of religious freedom, Turkey did allow non-Muslims to maintain their churches and synagogues and in fact showed more religious tolerance than the Muslims would be accorded later by Christian governments. Moreover, Bosnia's internal developments were peculiar and unique even within the Ottoman Empire; no other Ottoman Slav province developed such a formidable native ruling elite that, by the time Ottoman decadence turned into slow disintegration, were perpetually challenging the imperial authority.

In fact, the 1875 Serbian rebellion capped more than two decades of turmoil directed not against the Ottoman regime in Istanbul but, rather, against the Bosnian Muslim elite. The rebellion quickly deteriorated into an intercommunal war between Serbs and Muslims. Money from private subscription began pouring into Bosnia and, with the money, a trickle of volunteers from Serbia and Montenegro. Ardent Pan-Slavists in Russia encouraged Serbia and Montenegro to go to war against Turkey; the Serbs were to provide an excuse for Russia, the self-appointed "protector" of afflicted Orthodox Christians under Muslim rule, to seize the Straits from Turkey. Soon, Russian armies marched toward their manifest destiny on the Bosporus.

The question of the Dardanelles was at the time still important on the level of realpolitik, as well as for sentimental reasons: Dardanelles was "the key to the house"—Russia's house. By January 20, 1878, Russian armies swept all the way to Adrianople. Istanbul lay wide open. Turkey was prostrate.

It was at this point, when the European power balance was disturbed, that the Western powers, led by Great Britain, forced Russia to stop its advance and push for a peace treaty. (The British sent their navy through the Straits into the Black Sea.) At San Stefano, only seven miles from Istanbul, the Russians forced a treaty to bring Russian power into the heart of the Balkans by creating a very large new state of Bulgaria, which owed its existence to it. After screaming for a holy war on behalf of Slavdom, the Russians quickly abandoned Bosnia, even though that meant abandoning their afflicted Serb brothers. As a result, the Serbs were accused of being already tainted with Western ideas, whereas the reliable Bulgars were pure and wide open to Russian influence.

Within months, the Treaty of San Stefano was dismantled by the Congress of Berlin, which reversed much of Russia's thrust into the Balkans. It was here that Russia's diplomatic and military activities appeared most clearly to impinge on the vital interests of the Western powers. The Berlin gathering gave Bosnia to the Hapsburgs and broke up Bulgaria into three parts, two of which were returned to Turkey while the third—a smaller Bulgaria—was accorded independence. The outcome planted seeds of future conflicts by bringing Russia and Austria face-to-face with each other directly in the Balkans.

The abrupt end of Turkey's rule left the Muslim community in a state of shock. The Muslims found themselves facing an uncertain future, demoted and, for the first time, under the rule of a Christian government. It was a new, difficult, ambiguous, and exposed position. Psychologically, this was initially assuaged by the fact that Bosnia, at least formally, remained under the Sultan's sovereignty until the outright annexation in 1908.

As a way of life, Islam over three centuries had established a strong Muslim society. Although ethnic Slavs, they had no interest in becoming a part of any new Christian Slavic state; they assumed the superiority of their faith, and they were divided on the question of whether the Holy Quran allows them to live under, and cooperate with, the new Christian rulers. How deep this feeling was would very soon show. For it was the religion, Islam, that defined the Bosnian Muslims, rather than ethnicity. Islam also defined their collective memory. In fact, they had no national image, nor did they have a historical state to look back on. (Medieval Bosnia, like its ancestors, was Christian.)

The substitution of religion for national identity was of crucial importance to Bosnia's political development; in the view of some experts, this "may have been a factor making for more intense and less conciliatory national positions" taken subsequently by the three major groups.[10]

Intense national frictions were subsequently exacerbated by Austria's colonial rule and, after World War I, by Serbia's chauvinistic policies. When Austria assumed control of Bosnia, the Roman Catholic Croats gained in status and privilege because they shared the same religion with the new rulers. But they were the smallest group. The Austrians had no experience in dealing with large Muslim and Orthodox groups, who accounted for 80 percent of the backward province's population (the first Austrian census, in 1879, showed the Muslims at 38 percent; Orthodox Serbs, 42 percent; Roman Catholic Croats, 18 percent; and Jews, 0.25 percent). The majority lacked the basic understanding that there was a link between Austria-Hungary's material advancement and the rule of law and the moral development of Western Christendom.

This was the source of confusion in Vienna as to how to integrate the new province.[11] Obsessed by Russia's support for an expansionist Serbia, the Austrians were actively concerned to limit Serbia's influence in the province, in which, it was furiously believed in Vienna, Serbian and Russian agents constantly schemed and intrigued for the Hapsburgs' undoing.

At first, Austria offered the Bosnians a joint vision of the future. It created an official Bosnian nationality to which all three religious groups would belong—the term "Boshniak" was used for this purpose in contrast to "Bosnian," which denotes a person belonging to a region (like a New Yorker). The local language was named Bosnian.[12]

But these misbegotten, clumsy administrative measures never took hold. Having recognized the failure, the Austrians sought to co-opt the Muslims and thus gain the loyalty of more than 50 percent of the population. The first such move was to detach their new Muslim subjects from the religious authorities in Istanbul; to this effect, Vienna created the position of a *reis-ul-ulema,* the local supreme religious authority, backed up by a four-member religious council, the *mejlis al-ulema.* It was a fateful decision with long-term consequences.

The Austrians also created a local assembly, and the three religious communities eventually formed their ethnic parties. This assembly showed itself from the beginning not so much as a debating chamber as an aggressively uncompromising agent of the imperial administration. The Muslims quickly learned the power of their swing votes on a variety of divisive issues; the Austrians, on the other hand, were all too eager to extend to the Muslim elite the privileged status they had enjoyed before, provided they collaborated with the Austrian authorities. This gained momentum after Austria annexed Bosnia in 1908 in direct violation of the Treaty of Berlin; by 1910, the Muslims swore allegiance to the Hapsburg Empire.

This sequence of events, however, aroused in Belgrade the profoundest misgivings. By that time, the advocates of the Yugoslav idea offered a vision that found resonance among the Serbs in general and a considerable portion of Croats as well. On the eve of World War I, Bosnia was again buzzing with rebellious energy. The writer Ivo Andric, whose novels focus on the oscillations of history in Bosnia up to the war, captures the romantic idealism of Yugoslav nationalists in his book *The Bridge on the Drina.*

The year is 1913. The setting is an ancient Ottoman bridge over the Drina River. Two friends are talking about the future: Toma, whose father is Croat and whose mother is Serb, and Fehim, who is Muslim:

> "You'll see"—says Toma—"you'll see. We shall create a state which will make the contribution to the most progress of humanity, in which every effort will be blessed, every sacrifice holy, every thought original and expressed in our own words, and every deed marked with the stamp of our name. We are destined to realize all that the generations before us have aspired to: a state, born in freedom and founded on justice, like a part of God's thought realized here on earth."[13]

Toma's vision is evidently not shared by his resigned friend, who seems unable to imagine a Muslim future in such a state and who therefore keeps silent. As they walk back to town—Andric here compresses his skepticism into an image—the impassive eyes of the author follow a glowing cigarette stub one of the two youths had tossed over the parapet, falling "like a shooting star in a great curve from the bridge into the Drina."

Here we are not concerned with literature as such; but any social study of Bosnia in the early twentieth century is difficult to imagine without taking into account the work of this writer of genius, whose oeuvre and career reflect the mood of the times. Born in Travnik, Bosnia, in 1892 of Croat parents, he attended high school in Sarajevo, where he was infected with revolutionary Yugoslav idealism and suffered a three-year spell in an Austrian jail. He graduated from an Austrian university—his dissertation was on Bosnia under the Ottomans—and joined the Yugoslav diplomatic service, ending up as ambassador to Berlin at the time of the outbreak of World War II. He was photographed with Hitler four days before the latter ordered the destruction of Yugoslavia.

Andric withdrew from public life in 1941 and settled down in Belgrade, where he seemed a misfit who belonged neither to the old world nor to the new one created by Tito, standing proudly aloof among the new intelligentsia as the author of some poetry and prose of the highest quality; in fact, *The Bridge on the Drina* was the first great Yugoslav novel to win the Nobel Prize for literature. After its appearance in 1947, he dominated the Yugoslav literary scene absolutely, infecting it with social consciousness and a certain clinical empathy.

In contrast to his youthful idealism, Andric as a mature novelist was not optimistic about the multicultural experiment:

> Our people's lives pass bitter and empty, among malicious, vengeful thoughts and periodic revolts. . . . To anything else they are insensitive and inaccessible. One sometimes wonders whether the spirit of the majority of the Balkan people has not been forever poisoned and that perhaps they will never again be able to do anything other than suffer violence, or inflict it.[14]

He was particularly skeptical about Bosnia, which he had thoroughly explored and which was his natural habitat. Toma's idealism of 1913 was followed by an anti-Serb pogrom of 1914, shortly after the assassination of Archduke Ferdinand that touched off World War I. Andric is impassive and matter-of-fact, reproducing screaming headlines that aroused fanaticism and, directed by regime agents, flared up into violent chauvinism:

> Followers of three different faiths—Muslim, Roman Catholic and Orthodox—they hated one another from the day of their birth to their death,

deeply and blindly, transmitting this hatred even to those who were no longer alive. . . . They were born, they grew up and died in this hate.[15]

After the war, however, the victorious Serbs claimed revenge with a vengeance. Bosnia was a part of the Yugoslav kingdom created in 1918. But the new country was far from the one Toma yearned for in 1913—a state "founded on justice, like a part of God's thought realized here on earth." Yugoslavia was ruled by the authoritarian Serbian king, his army, and his police. The grand Yugoslav vision was betrayed. Bosnia itself remained a land of intolerance and hate, lacking a vision acceptable to all its people; and again the novelist records all details, overlooking nothing, hinting with lightning speed at the likely consequences and side effects of all actions.

The year is 1920. The setting is a railway station in northern Bosnia, where Andric is waiting for an eastbound train. He encounters a high school friend whom he has not seen in almost a decade: Max Levenfeld is a doctor and a doctor's son, member of an established Sarajevo Jewish family.

Max is horrified by the fear, mean-spirited intrigue, and hysterical hatred he has experienced during the past few years. He wants to emigrate to France or South America. He would never come back, he says, even though he knows that "all my life long I'll be struggling with the memory of Bosnia, as if with some Bosnian disease."[16] The normally impassive author chides his friend for running away from his homeland, finding his cold detachment almost embarrassing. Levenfeld's response is interrupted by the arrival of his train.

Three weeks later, Andric receives a letter from Levenfeld (written in German; both had their college education in Austria). He was not running away from Bosnia, a resigned Levenfeld writes:

> There's one thing that the people of Bosnia, at least people of your kind, must realize and never lose sight of—Bosnia is a country of hatred and fear. . . . And instinctively you recoil and protest when you hear the word [hatred]—I saw it that night at the station—just as everyone of you refuses to hear, grasp and understand it. . . . The fatal characteristic of this hatred is that the Bosnian man is unaware of the hate that lives in him, shrinks from analysing it and hates everyone who tries to do so. And yet it is a fact that in Bosnia and Hercegovina there are more people ready, in fits of this subconscious hatred, to kill and be killed, for different reasons and under different pretexts, than in other much bigger Slav and non-Slav lands.[17]

Levenfeld argues that hatred in Bosnia is "not limited just to a moment in the course of social change, or an inevitable part of the historical process; rather it is hatred acting as an independent force [and] as an end in itself." There are admirable sides to Bosnia: firm beliefs, strength of character, loving passion, loyalty, unshakable devotion, and a thirst for justice.

But "perhaps your greatest misfortune is precisely that you do not suspect just how much hatred there is in your loves and passions, traditions and pieties." Bosnian urban life is marked by counterfeit courtesies, resounding statements, and stylized ceremonies, yet "the rifts between the different faiths are so deep that hatred alone can sometimes succeed in crossing them."

This is what Max saw living and working as a doctor in Bosnia and what kept him awake at night. He decided to emigrate in the middle of a sleepless night, shortly before he met Andric at the railway station:

> Whoever lies awake at night in Sarajevo hears the voices of the Sarajevo night. The clock on the Catholic Cathedral strikes the hour with weighty confidence: 2 a.m. More than a minute passes (to be exact 75 seconds—I counted) and only then with a rather weaker but piercing sound does the Orthodox church announce the hour, and chime its own 2 a.m. A moment after it the tower clock on the Bey's mosque strikes the hour in a hoarse, far away voice, and that strikes 11, the ghostly Turkish hour, by the strange calculation of distant and alien parts of the world. The Jews have no clock to sound their hour, so God knows what time it is for them by the Sephardic reckoning or the Ashkenazy. Thus at night, while everybody is sleeping, division keeps vigil on the counting of the small hours, and separates these sleeping people who, awake, rejoice and mourn, feast and fast by four different and antagonistic calendars, and send all their prayers and wishes to one heaven in four ecclesiastical languages. And this difference, sometimes visible and open, sometimes invisible and hidden, is always similar to hatred, and often completely identical with it.[18]

Andric much respects these lucid observations, perhaps because they are genuine and honestly presented. But he is categorical in his rejection of Levenfeld's conclusion. Andric is writing this autobiographical story in the 1940s, after having witnessed evil stalking Europe. If demagogues could inflame the country of Ludwig van Beethoven and Johann Wolfgang von Goethe, what is one to expect from the wretched Bosnia? Imagine a land existing for centuries without *any articulate force* offering opposition to a despotic will; that was Bosnia. In his novel *The Woman from Sarajevo*, Andric notes the emergence of a new society in the first decade of the century, in which people from "good family"—decent professional people, businesspeople, the educated class in all four religious communities—were capable of maintaining civilized relations under normal conditions. This trend continued in the Yugoslavia of Alexander I. Indeed, the first decades of the twentieth century were a springtime of mind and spirit in Yugoslavia (and in Bosnia), which showed promise of great possibilities. But summer never came.

Hate, Andric says, is not a special Bosnian disease but, rather, part of the human condition. His friend Levenfeld says he wants to stay in Bosnia, take over his father's practice, and even make a social contribution—to investigate hatred as a disease. But he cannot accept living with hate and therefore migrates to France.

Andric ends the story by noting that his friend had established a lucrative practice just outside Paris and was widely respected in the Yugoslav community for his generosity. In 1938, Levenfeld decided to join the Spanish Republic Army as a volunteer. A year later, in a village in Aragon, Francisco Franco's planes bombed the hospital, killing everybody, including Levenfeld. Andric condenses his wisdom in his last sentence: "Thus died the man who tried to escape from hate."

I have been dwelling on Andric because Yugoslavia's scholarship had never achieved the capacity to fairly confront the past, perhaps because anyone attempting to do so was regarded by authorities as subversive. The nature of Bosnia's multiethnic culture is to regard as foolish, naive, and downright irresponsible any attempt to concede that one's ethnic group has committed crimes, let alone to publicly examine these crimes.

The gruesome and deeply troubling crimes committed during World War II are still unexamined; partisan public debates on this issue inflamed Serb-Croat relations in 1991. Judge Richard Goldstone, chief prosecutor at the International Tribunal for War Crimes in Former Yugoslavia (The Hague tribunal) said he believes that one of the reasons for the atrocities of the 1990s was that the atrocities of the 1940s remain unresolved.[19]

Recent historical assessments all too often have been twisted, turned, and carried to a ludicrous point in various debates to advance tactical plans of all warring parties. The leader of the Bosnian Serbs, Radovan Karadzic, a moody egomaniac whose compelling personality was harnessed to an exceptional talent for intrigue and lying, had repeatedly invoked "ancient hatreds" to justify anti-Muslim pogroms, rape, and pillage. This notion has been used by others, including political observers and high officials, to justify inaction before the ghastly spectacle of violence and barbarity that claimed more than 200,000 lives and forced more than a million others to flee their homes.

Liberated from the responsibility of nonfiction, Andric records events through the ages, retells old legends, reports everyday conversations, and draws on the dispatches of French and Austrian diplomats stationed in this remote part of the Ottoman Empire. The empathy with Muslim characters makes the novelist show an extra measure of compassion for their stoicism in the face of the retreat of Ottoman power from Europe and the sudden onslaught of European modernity.

It is not simply that we are reading a vivid commentary on Bosnia at the turn of the century. The novelist makes it clear that, in the profoundest sense, the history of modern Bosnia, from 1878 to the present, has been the product of an interplay between authoritarian rule and religion(s) harnessed to nationalist causes in the competition for economic and political power. Bosnia's politics and culture are completely subordinated to distant capitals. Kings and dictators manipulate the ethnic balance to their advantage.

At times of great calamity, when the established order is shaken and law and reason suspended, the venal demagoguery of extreme nationalists can easily incite the impoverished classes to the vilest passions and appetites. It has happened in World War I, again in World War II, and again in the 1992 Bosnian war.

The international community—and the U.S. public—has since fallen into disenchantment with post-Dayton Bosnia and its squabbling peoples. The U.S. establishment is divided. The "realists" have come to believe that Bosnia is an impossible, false creation stitched together by violence and that it does not merit sustained attention and support. In contrast, the "moralists" are given to paroxysms of righteous indignation directed against Western governments' practical sloth and moral torpor.

Lost in the unfolding debates on what to do about Bosnia is the extraordinary fact that Dayton has given Bosnia—for the first time in its history—a genuine opportunity to turn itself into a viable country. It has internationally recognized borders; it enjoys support from the international community. Bosnia's society, changed dramatically due to the secularism enforced by the Communists, could be helped to join the twenty-first century. The essential point is that Bosnia's statehood must be built upon Tito's legacy.

With the collapse of communism, it's become fashionable to denigrate Tito, portray communism as an accidental thing, and paint Tito's wartime effort against Germany and Italy as a cynical struggle for power. For all its divisive past, Bosnia did enjoy four decades of relative harmony in Tito's Yugoslavia. The point is that Bosnian society had started changing during the four decades of Austrian occupation—particularly with regard to educated classes, businesspeople, and professionals. It was obvious that, as time went on, this upper stratum of the population became for all practical purposes an estate within the Yugoslav kingdom in which people of decency and goodwill from the three religious communities were in some degree united with aggressive leftist revolutionaries who detested the very idea of royal dictatorship and who sought reforms.

They combined two sets of ardent reformers who found guidance in very different sources: on the one hand, in the Marxist promise of antinationalism; on the other hand, in the example of Western Europe and its cultural and material achievements (the inherent conflict between the two was fuzzy at the time, thus allowing for a joint front against the authoritarian regime). Many people from "good family"—from all ethnic backgrounds—became closet Marxists; once the country was dismembered by Hitler and quisling regimes installed, the Communists were the only party to appeal to all the ethnic groups.

This, more than anything else, accounts for Tito's success in mobilizing public support and gaining power. The interplay of cause and effect was complex in the extreme to provide a clear answer. The Communists had declared King Alexander's Serb-dominated Yugoslavia a "prison of nations" and vowed to create a new Yugoslavia of equal nations. This was done in the middle of the war, by a constitutional assembly meeting in the Bosnian town of Jajce on November 29, 1943. One of its crucial decisions was to make Bosnia-Herzegovina a separate republic equal to the other five republics in the federation.

Under Tito's rule—for all its shortcomings and inherent coercion—the traditional ethnic hostilities in Bosnia had become so muted that the three ethnic groups had been able to forge agreements and share power, to consult together, and to combine in opposition to the domination of Yugoslavia by other, stronger republics. More than that. This understanding survived the initial stages of the Yugoslav disintegration when the leaders of Bosnian Serbs and Bosnian Croats refused to heed the siren songs of nationalism.[20] It survived the Croatian war, when Serbs and Croats fell to slaughtering each other with great ferocity. It succumbed only to direct acts of subversion and terrorism from the outside, mainly organized by Milosevic, that injected fear and revived old hostilities among sections of the have-nots whom Andric calls the "ragtag and bobtail."

What Bosnia lacks is a political image of itself. Dayton is the point of departure. It provides for joint institutions, as well as home rule for each tribe. Beyond that, the international community led by the United States can help Bosnians create uniform rules and regulations throughout the country and, in effect, help reestablish civilized coexistence. A new TV station—initially under the control of an international board—must be introduced to set standards of fairness and decency, as well as to provide a clearinghouse for ideas and a forum accessible to all groups. A new election law can be devised—something akin to Lebanon's—to allow the electorate to break loose from the straitjacket of sectarianism, regionalism, and tribalism; even though the parties may be on a confessional basis, political candidates would have to court voters from all communities to win elections. This would eliminate current leaders on all sides whose policies are grounded in nationalist instincts and confrontation.

Finally, the Bosnian parties must be helped to establish an independent European country that is the homeland of all its citizens; the objective is not an enforced homogenization but, rather, a confederal state in which each party can maintain its unique identity. From such a hybrid culture—which already is in existence—Bosnia can gain a new image based on practical reality, rather than on counterfeit notions that are currently advanced by all three sides. And it is the Muslims, the victims of the last war and the one before it, who must provide imaginative and generous bases for a broad reconciliation.

At this point, the Bosnians are incapable of accomplishing this by themselves and need outside help, first and foremost from the United States. But such outside intervention must include a sensitive understanding of Bosnia's divided society at the end of the twentieth century. It must also involve an understanding that Dayton, although the point of departure, contains serious shortcomings. These must be remedied. Above all, it must involve a real commitment to get the job done.

If the real potentials are ignored, Bosnia will remain a boiling and angry source of perpetual conflicts in the south of Europe. But if approached in a forceful and comprehensive way, Bosnia may become an example for the post–Cold War environment in which tangled ethnic and religious problems—as opposed to ideology—pose the main threat to international order.

This presents a unique challenge for the United States currently. It comes at a time when the United States has no rivals for global reach and can do pretty much what it pleases in world affairs. Hence, the challenge does not involve taking into account what other superpowers' reactions to U.S. moves may be; instead, it is the question of what the United States wants to do (or what foreign policy goals it ought to set for itself). Given the complexity of Bosnia, it is difficult to imagine a subject less suited for a meaningful public debate about the fundamental principles of U.S. foreign policy in the post–Cold War era.

The fact is that the Bosnia conflict cannot be wished away. It is America's and Western Europe's most significant project in the post-Soviet era; it is also the only action undertaken by the North Atlantic Treaty Organization, the proposed enlargement of which forms the centerpiece of Washington's foreign policy.

U.S. citizens, it can be said, are bored with small, distant countries that somehow appear unworthy of the sustained interest of intelligent minds; such lands remain below the U.S. radar screen, except during periodic outbursts of violence and turmoil that expose meager traditions of stability or continuity. Although Bosnia may not be a land obviously meriting the full attention of a great power, a violent ethnic conflict within Europe's borders is a matter that could not be ignored. Dayton had brought the fighting to an end in 1995 and had pushed Bosnia off TV evening news and out of the public mind. The public disinterest apparently drove Defense Secretary William S. Cohen, a former Republican senator, to the gloomy conclusion that U.S. troops would be withdrawn from Bosnia by June 1998 even if that meant a humanitarian catastrophe. If the warring parties "go back to slaughtering each other," he said, this is "going to be up to them."[21]

There are several questions and a couple of problems with this proposition. One, the president and his top aides are publicly on record as rejecting the idea of a permanent division of Bosnia. And two, would this serve U.S. national interests? Madeleine Albright, before she became secretary of state, came closest to an answer when she said: "We are in Bosnia because we don't have a choice. Let's not pretend we have a choice."[22]

In retrospect, it is conspicuously obvious that the United States at Dayton had no strategic clarity as to what sort of political settlement has to be achieved. The accords were not only misconceived politically. They were also misconceived technically. By design, as U.S. officials now say, the military and political aspects of the policy were not placed in balance—an arrangement lacking coherence at the top.[23]

The result is a schizophrenic treaty that seems tailor-made for dodging responsibility. What is conspicuously missing is an integrated political-military command, which is critical for the success of the mission. Since the mission's political purpose and objectives are unclear, the absence of an agent of coordination makes the mission an end in itself. Cynics say the administration's only objective was to stop the war and get Bosnia off television screens before the 1996 U.S. elections—hence the twelve-month deadline set for the U.S. troop presence in Bosnia. (Everybody knew this was not going to work, but that was the price the president had to pay.)

The core of the Dayton Accords contains a fundamental contradiction. While they could be interpreted as providing for a unitary state, the accords recognize two distinct political entities with effective sovereignty and exclusive political authority on their respective territories. Equally important, and perhaps more troublesome, is that Dayton provides for the predators who plotted the division of Bosnia (Milosevic and Tudjman) to act as the chief guarantors of the agreement and relies chiefly on Izetbegovic to build a multiethnic state.

In retrospect, Bosnian Muslim intellectuals had publicly argued since 1993 that Izetbegovic was against a modern, multicultural Bosnian state and that his "hidden agenda" includes the partition of Bosnia and the creation of a purely Muslim state in Europe. If this is indeed the case—and there is some evidence to this effect apart from the argument of Izetbegovic's Muslim critics—the U.S. political strategy must be reexamined.

Secretary of State Albright has started a new initiative marked by toughness of intention and care that leaves all sides a face-saving way out. This could bear fruit if it is accompanied by an imaginative political program and the muscle to put it into effect. Carl Bildt, who recently ended his eighteen-month term as the international community's top political representative in Bosnia, believes that Europe remains incapable of dealing with the Bosnian problem and that only the United States has the power to act effectively in the Balkans. This may well be the case, but the Europeans must be prepared to share the financial and military burden.

Readers may well ask whether the goal of Dayton, a multiethnic Bosnia, remains a viable objective the United States ought to pursue. But many U.S. officials believe that we have a stake in the future of Bosnia and that failing to defend that stake would abdicate leadership in Europe, betray our responsibilities, and ignore the lessons of the twentieth century.

Notes

1. I discovered in the process that virtually all works in major languages dealt with Bosnia in terms of diplomatic maneuverings of the great powers and, to a lesser extent, of the smaller Balkan states. Apart from a few works in Serbian, historians hardly gave any attention to Bosnia's internal developments. This remains a problem today.

2. Dusko Doder, *The Yugoslavs* (New York: Random House, 1978), p. 126.

3. Quoted in ibid., p. xii.

4. C. L. Salzberger, quoted in ibid., p. 126.

5. From testimony of the last president of the Socialist Federal Republic of Yugoslavia, Stipe Mesic, before The Hague's International Tribunal for War Crimes, Vijesnik, June 1997. A comprehensive account is provided by Warren Zimmermann, *Origins of a Catastrophe* (New York: Random House, 1996), p. 996.

6. It is significant to note that Izetbegovic had appealed to the European Union and the international community not to recognize the independence of secessionist republics before a political settlement was reached for the entire Yugoslav area.

7. As stated by Izetbegovic: "For now, unfortunately, our Party must be sectional [sectarian]. The parties that try to represent everyone are small and weak. . . . Until now, Muslims have had no political leaders. We need a big party, then we need political power" (quoted in Mark Thompson, *A Paper House* [New York: Pantheon, 1992], p. 121).

8. In a letter to Izetbegovic, Morillon said: "I now have concrete evidence from witnesses of this cowardly and disreputable act and I must point out the harm such blatant disregard for the Geneva Convention does to your cause."

9. William E. Curtis, *The Turk and His Lost Provinces* (Chicago: F. H. Revell, 1903), pp. 273–274.

10. Mark Pinson, *The Muslims of Bosnia-Herzegovina* (Cambridge, Mass.: Harvard University Press, 1994), p. 91.

11. The Imperial Ministry of Finance was given supreme authority over Bosnia.

12. Izetbegovic's government had revived these ideas, but it had appropriated the term "Boshniak" only for the Muslims.

13. Ivo Andric, *The Bridge on the Drina* (Chicago: University of Chicago Press, 1977), p. 245.

14. Ivo Andric, *House of Cards,* quoted in Thompson, *A Paper House,* p. 121.

15. Ivo Andric, *The Woman from Sarajevo* (Belgrade: Svjetlost, 1955), pp. 92–93.

16. Ivo Andric, *The Damned World,* trans. by Celia Hawksworth (Boston: Forest, 1965), p. 107.

17. Ibid., p. 110.

18. Ibid., p. 120.

19. Croatia's President Tudjman has spent considerable time researching gruesome statistics linked to the infamous Croatian death camp Jasenovac, where tens of thousands of Serbs and Jews were exterminated. Serb historians have vehemently insisted that 700,000 Serbs were murdered at Jasenovac; Tudjman and other Croat historians insist the figure is less than 100,000.

20. It is worth noting that it was a Serb, Bogic Bogicevic, representing Bosnia in the federal Yugoslav presidency, who cast the decisive vote against the imposition

of martial law in 1991—thus thwarting Milosevic's planned coup by the Serb-dominated Yugoslav army. Bogicevic was not an isolated figure appearing out of the blue; I encountered scores of urban Bosnian Serbs before the outbreak of the war the next year, and the vast majority of them remained unswayed by Milosevic's propaganda.

21. William S. Cohen, quoted in *Washington Post,* June 12, 1998, p. 6.

22. Madeleine Albright, *Washington Post,* March 7, 1995, p. 10.

23. The United States did not want any non-American to have control over the U.S. troops stationed in Bosnia. As one senior U.S. official put it, "We did not want a strong political figure and dual key. So we have Carl Bildt as top political figure who cannot order anyone to do anything. Also we did not like Bildt" as relayed to author in a private conversation.

Part 2

Strengthening a Fragile Peace

8

Transforming the Relationship Between Former Enemies: A Social-Psychological Analysis

Herbert C. Kelman

In this chapter, I examine the process of reconciliation within the framework of interactive problem solving, an approach to conflict resolution anchored in social-psychological principles.[1] Interactive problem solving is a form of unofficial diplomacy, derived from the work of John Burton and epitomized by the microprocess of problem-solving workshops.[2] These workshops are unofficial, private, confidential meetings between politically influential members of conflicting parties, designed to develop new insights into their conflict and new ideas for resolving it, which can then be infused into the political process within each community. My work in this genre has focused primarily on the Israeli-Palestinian conflict,[3] but the approach can be—and has been—applied to other protracted conflicts between identity groups.

The concept of interactive problem solving can also be used as a metaphor for the macroprocess of negotiation and peacemaking, for both descriptive and prescriptive purposes.[4] What happens—or ought to happen—in negotiation can be captured by the three words that make up the term. First, negotiation treats the conflict as a problem shared by the parties—in essence, a problem in their relationship: the relationship has become wholly competitive and mutually destructive, such that each party's pursuit of its own needs and interests undermines or threatens the needs and interests of the other. Second, negotiation explores ways of solving this problem, not by eliminating all conflict and potential conflict between the parties, but by addressing the underlying causes of the conflict and reversing the escalatory dynamics of the conflict relationship. And, third, negotiation is an interactive process, capable of producing ideas for solution of the problem that are responsive to the parties' fundamental concerns and to which they are committed. This process itself contributes to building a new relationship between the parties.

Transforming the Relationship as the Goal of Negotiation

Within an interactive problem-solving framework, the ultimate goal of negotiation is to transform the relationship between the parties. Negotiations are designed not merely to produce a minimally acceptable political agreement, but to provide the basis for a stable, long-term peace and a cooperative, mutually enhancing relationship that contributes to the welfare and development of both societies.

Transforming the relationship becomes increasingly important the more intense and destructive the conflict is and the more interdependent the parties are. The ethnic conflicts that have dominated the world scene in the 1990s—such as the conflicts within and between the states of the former Yugoslavia and the former Soviet Union, or in Rwanda and Burundi, or in Northern Ireland, or between Israelis and Palestinians—are high on both of these dimensions. They are protracted conflicts, marked by a recent history of massive violence, at times involving genocide and other gross violations of human rights, and they raise profound concerns in the embattled communities about national and personal survival. In such conflicts, there is no substitute for an agreement that addresses the parties' grievances and existential fears and transforms the relationship between them, since they must continue to live together in the same limited space.

Conflicts among parties that are less interdependent may not require an equally thoroughgoing transformation of their relationship. Still, the degree of global and certainly regional interdependence among states in such domains as security, economic affairs, natural resources, environment, health, and migration requires an approach to conflict resolution that addresses the long-term relationship between the parties. The desired relationship is not one devoid of conflict, but one in which mechanisms of communication and problem solving are readily available so that conflicts can be resolved before escalating and becoming mutually destructive.

If the ultimate goal of negotiation is to transform (or restore) the relationship between the parties, what kind of outcome must the negotiations seek? The sine qua non, in my view, of a solution that can provide the foundation of a new relationship is that it addresses the fundamental needs and fears of both parties. Conflict is caused and escalated to a considerable degree by unfulfilled needs—not only material needs, but also such psychological needs as security, identity, recognition, autonomy, and a sense of justice. Parties in conflict, in pursuit of their own security and identity and related needs and interests, undermine and threaten the security and identity of the other. To resolve the conflict and begin to build a new relationship requires an agreement that satisfies the fundamental needs of both parties and reassures them that their fundamental fears are no longer warranted. In the Israeli-Palestinian case, for example, an agreement that meets these criteria must be based on mutual recognition of the other's national identity and on arrangements that assure each side's political independence, security, and survival.

The microprocess of interactive problem solving in workshop settings is specifically geared to exploring the overall shape of a solution that would meet such criteria. It is helped by the fact that such psychological needs as identity and security—in contrast to more material interests like territory and resources—are not inherently zero sum in nature.[5] Although identity and security are often perceived in zero-sum terms in intense, protracted conflicts, it is often the case that each party's own security and identity are actually enhanced by agreements that meet the other's needs in these domains. Only integrative solutions of this kind enable the parties to move from a relationship in which each sees the other as blocking the fulfillment of its own needs to one in which they actively work toward promoting the fulfillment of both sets of needs.

An outcome that addresses the fundamental needs and fears of both parties will almost certainly be imperfect from each party's point of view. Neither party is likely to feel that all of its interests have been fully met or that the agreement has given it everything it justly deserves. Insofar as the agreement entails division of territory and apportionment of resources claimed by both sides, or curtailment of rights claimed by one side or the other (such as the right of return of refugees, the right to settle in the other's territory, and the right to exercise full sovereignty in military or foreign affairs), it will inevitably require a compromise shaped in heavy distributive bargaining. And the outcome of such bargaining is likely to reflect the conditions on the ground and the relative power of the two parties. Granting the inevitability of compromise, however, it is essential that the negotiated agreement not require either party to sacrifice its fundamental needs—the needs that it considers nonnegotiable—or to jeopardize its national existence.

Does the outcome described here meet the criteria for a just solution to the conflict? One of the hallmarks of the practice of interactive problem solving at the microlevel is the nonadversarial character of the approach. Without implying moral equivalence in the positions and actions of the two parties, interaction proceeds on the basis of the "no-fault" principle. No attempt is made to establish who is right and who is wrong in terms of legal or historical criteria (although participants are not discouraged from discussing their perceptions of legal and historical rights as part of the process of sharing their differing perspectives with each other). The presumption is that such a process will not yield ideas for a mutually satisfactory resolution of the conflict. While eschewing a juridical and historical approach to determining a just solution, interactive problem solving is not oblivious to the issue of justice. The search for a solution that addresses the fundamental needs and fears of both parties can be viewed as the operationalization of the quest for justice in this approach. To the extent that the solution is responsive to these needs and fears, it does justice to each party.

From an interactive problem-solving perspective, there is another way in which considerations of justice enter into negotiations. To provide a basis for changing the relationship between the two societies, an agreement must have wide support within each population so that a national consensus in favor of the new relationship can evolve.[6] Public support depends heavily on the perception that the negotiated agreement is just and fair. Insofar as the agreement addresses fundamental needs and fears, it is likely to be perceived as just. Indeed, in a protracted and bitter conflict, people's sense of justice—the feeling that at least minimal justice has been achieved—is itself one of the fundamental needs that the agreement must satisfy. Perception of justice also depends, however, on people's conviction that the process whereby the agreement was achieved was fair: that their side's concerns were seriously considered; that the other side did not take advantage of their leaders' weak bargaining position in order to impose an unacceptable agreement; that third parties did not interfere in the negotiations to their disadvantage. In other words, procedural justice interacts with substantive justice in people's satisfaction with the negotiated outcome. People judge the fairness of the process on the basis of both what they know about the process itself and what they infer from the outcome.

Two important criteria in assessing fairness are equality and reciprocity. In the microprocess of problem-solving workshops, these are two principles governing the interaction between the parties. Within the workshop context, the parties are equal in the sense that both parties' needs and fears are addressed and given equal weight in the deliberations, regardless of whatever asymmetries of power or of moral standing may characterize their relationship at the macrolevel. Similarly, both in the discussions and in formulations of possible solutions, there is an emphasis on reciprocity in the sense that each party is urged to give to the other what it demands for itself—whether it is reassurance about its security, acknowledgment of its identity, or understanding of its political constraints.

At the macrolevel, the negotiated agreement—though it is bound to be characterized by inequalities in outcome (in the Israeli-Palestinian case, for example, in the size of the territory or of the military force granted to the two parties)—can and ought to reflect a process incorporating the principles of equality and reciprocity. Equality is conveyed by indications that the needs and fears of both parties have been given serious and thoughtful consideration. Reciprocity—perhaps the most powerful foundation of a new relationship—is conveyed most clearly by the terms of the agreement itself: each party extends to the other the same kind of recognition, respect, and reassurance that it receives from the other.

Conditions for Transforming the Relationship

I have argued that negotiation of a protracted conflict must aim toward transforming the relationship between the parties if it is to yield an agreement conducive to a stable and durable peace that allows the former enemies to coexist and cooperate to the benefit of their respective societies. Peace manifests itself not only in the diplomatic agreements and strategic arrangements signed by governments, but also in the relationships established between societies and peoples. Moreover, peace goes beyond ending belligerency to creating a new state of affairs that can be defined in positive terms. A positive peace in the relationship between nations or communities with a long history of conflict and war has four essential components:

1. Mutual acceptance and reconciliation
2. A sense of security and dignity for each nation or community
3. A pattern of cooperative interaction between the nations or communities
4. Institutionalization of a dynamic process of problem solving

Transforming the relationship between former enemies toward such a peace is of necessity a gradual process, one that is not confined to the peace treaty hammered out at the negotiating table. What happens at the negotiating table and the nature of the agreement that emerges from the negotiations have significant effects on the future relationship, as discussed in the preceding section of this chapter: transformation of the relationship is more likely if the agreement addresses both sides' fundamental needs and fears; if it is perceived as just; and if it emerges from a process that is perceived as fair and consistent with the principles of equality and reciprocity. But negotiations are most likely to produce such an outcome if the process of building a new relationship begins at the prenegotiation stage and continues in unofficial interactions—at the elite and grassroots levels—alongside of the official negotiations. Moreover, the nature of the new relationship that evolves after the signing of a peace agreement depends on the way the agreement is implemented, on the way it is communicated to the two populations, and on subsequent activities in the public and private sectors. The period on which the present volume focuses—that is, the period following the signing of an incomplete agreement that does not yet establish a firm peace—is particularly crucial for the transformation of the relationship. What happens at that stage may well determine whether the conditions for building a new relationship consistent with peaceful coexistence are put in place.

Some of the conditions for transforming the relationship between former enemies can be identified by examining each of the four components of a positive peace that were distinguished above.

Mutual acceptance and reconciliation. To establish a state of peace between communities that have been engaged in a protracted, bitter, destructive conflict over many years presupposes a process of reconciliation, whereby the former belligerents come to accept each other not only diplomatically, but also psychologically. What are some of the conditions required for mutual acceptance and reconciliation between former enemies in a protracted identity conflict?

First, the peace agreement itself must entail a solution that satisfies the fundamental needs and fulfills the national aspirations of both parties, rather than one that is experienced as defeat and subjugation by one of the parties. A humiliating defeat is never a good basis for reconciliation, but in conflicts that are clearly interstate in character—such as that between France and Germany or between the United States and Japan during World War II—reconciliation could be achieved in the wake of a total defeat. By contrast, in protracted identity conflicts—such as those in Israel/Palestine, Bosnia, and Northern Ireland, in which both sides' national existence is at stake and in which they must find a way to live together in the same small space—it seems virtually impossible to build reconciliation on the defeat of one of the parties. Total defeat in such conflicts is tantamount to destruction of the losers' national community and deprives them of the hope to give political expression to their national identity. The resulting demoralization and resentment are not likely to leave an opening for reconciliation. An agreement conducive to reconciliation must leave each party with the sense that its basic needs have been met and that it owns a share of the contested land in which it can express its national identity.

Second, reconciliation requires the parties' mutual acceptance of each other's national identity. The history of the Israeli-Palestinian conflict has been particularly marked by systematic attempts on each side to deny the other's identity. The parties have tended to view their dispute as a zero-sum conflict with respect to national identity and national existence.[7] In other protracted conflicts as well, the parties seek to delegitimize each other and to redefine significant elements of the other's identity in ways that suit their own narratives and strengthen their own claims. Mutual acceptance of each other's national identity therefore requires a process of negotiating identity, based on separating out the different components of the images of self and other. The objective is to come up with language and actions that would allow each party to acknowledge the other's identity in ways that are meaningful to the other without thereby negating their own narrative and threatening their own identity.[8] Acceptance of the other's identity means acknowledging the authenticity of the other's self-image—for example, acknowledging the other as a nation with historical links to the land. To gain such acceptance from the other, each party may have to give up those elements of its identity that negate the other—such as the view of itself as the sole owner of the land. Negotiating identity along such lines may, in some respects, be easier than negotiating over land or water, because identity is socially constructed and can therefore be deconstructed into its component elements and reconstructed in ways that do not threaten the other.

The third prerequisite of reconciliation is basic human acceptance of the other and respect for the other's life, welfare, and dignity. Protracted identity conflicts are characterized by dehumanization of the other, withdrawal of empathy from the other, and exclusion of the other from one's own moral community. Clearly, reconciliation presupposes the rejection of extreme acts of dehumanization, including indiscriminate killing (whether by planting bombs or dropping them), torture, rape, expulsion, and other forms of ethnic cleansing. Beyond the rejection of such extreme forms of denying the other's humanity, reconciliation requires the development and propagation of new attitudes, marked by inclusion, empathy, and respect. These attitudes must be expressed in symbolic gestures and public statements that acknowledge the other's suffering, victimization, and shared humanity and that convey commitment to the other's security, well-being, and human rights. One of the casualties of protracted conflict is the ability to see the other as a victim and empathize with their suffering, since each side is possessed by its own grievances and sense of victimization. Reconciliation becomes possible when the two sides—without evading their own responsibility—come to recognize that they are both victims of their conflict.

Sense of security and dignity for each nation or community. A transformed relationship between former enemies that can be characterized as positive peace must provide a sense of security and dignity to both communities. I deliberately join these two desiderata together because there is often a state of tension between them. Security for one side may be ensured at the expense of dignity for the other. Moreover, within each community, security arrangements may conflict with a life of dignity. The challenge is to achieve each of these goals without sacrificing the other.

The sense of security depends on the kinds of security arrangements that are put into place, such as demilitarized zones, early warning systems, international observation posts, or joint patrols. But there are also some perhaps less obvious psychological conditions for ensuring that security arrangements are consistent with the dignity of both sides.

First, security arrangements must be based on recognition that security is a matter of mutual concern. It is in the nature of intense, protracted conflicts that each side feels threatened by the other, even where there is considerable disparity in the two sides' military capabilities. Although the fears may at times seem exaggerated, they have a realistic basis in the history of violence that characterizes such conflicts. Whether or not the other side's fears are (or appear to be) warranted, each side must recognize that these fears exist and must respect the other's security concerns. President Anwar Sadat's acknowledgment of the depth of Israel's security concerns when he visited Jerusalem in 1977 had a powerful impact on the Israeli public, who had felt dehumanized by Arab dismissal of Israeli fears. Today, Palestinians feel dehumanized by Israeli policies that give primacy to Israeli security without regard to the security, well-being, and dignity of Palestinians. Security is inconsistent with dignity if either side ignores or dismisses the other's security concerns or claims a monopoly on security needs.

Second, careful distinction must be made between genuine security requirements and the use of security as a cover or justification for other policies or practices, such as expansion, control, or punishment. Arrangements that are designed to meet specific security purposes can be worked out between the parties and accepted much more readily if they are clearly defined and separated from other considerations. It is interesting in this connection that the Israeli Labor government and the Palestinian National Authority were quite successful, by and large, in establishing cooperation between their respective security forces. Such cooperation, when addressed to specific, joint security concerns, can become a vehicle for building trust and transforming the relationship between the two sides. However, when the term "security" is used broadly and loosely—as it has been used, for example, by Israeli authorities, to justify the confiscation of Palestinian lands or imposition of collective punishment—it becomes a competitive commodity that erodes the peace-building effort.

Third, to be consistent with the dignity of both sides, security arrangements must be based on the recognition that security ultimately depends on mutual trust. Military and strategic capacities may contribute to security by deterring attack and ensuring each party that it is able to defend itself if deterrence fails. They cannot, however, substitute for the development of trust, which provides assurance that the other has no intention to mount an attack and no interest in doing so. The search for military and strategic advantage may have the paradoxical effect of damaging long-run security by undermining trust and, in fact, setting an escalatory process into motion. Positive peace requires an active effort to search for security arrangements that help to build trust, rather than destroy it. Such efforts are exemplified by cooperative security arrangements and by confidence-building measures designed to promote a de-escalatory process—along the lines, perhaps, of C. E. Osgood's GRIT (Graduated and Reciprocated Initiatives in Tension Reduction) strategy.[9]

In sum, insofar as security is sought in a context of reciprocity and mutual respect, it can enhance dignity, rather than detract from it. An overarching condition for such congruence between security and dignity is mutual reassurance through actions, gestures, and acknowledgments that address the existential fears of each party and persuade each that the other is genuinely committed to peace. Belief in the sincerity of the other's commitment to peaceful coexistence, based on its own interests, is an essential condition for the development of the working trust on which a sense of long-term security must ultimately rest.

Pattern of cooperative interaction. A third component of positive peace in the relationship between former enemies is the development of a pattern of cooperative interaction between the two nations or communities. Promotion of functional relations between the parties can in no way be viewed as a substitute for the political and diplomatic processes required for achieving peace. However, in the wake of a political agreement—particularly one that has not yet solidified—cooperative activities in the economic sphere, as well as in such domains as public health, environmental protection, communication, education, science, and culture, can make significant contributions. By establishing crosscutting ties, common interests, and personal relations, they can help stabilize and cement a new peaceful relationship and create commitments, habits, and expectations consistent with maintaining and perpetuating peaceful coexistence.

What are some of the conditions that cooperative activities must meet if they are to contribute effectively to a transformation of the relationship between the two communities?

First, the emphasis must be on interactions that have a genuine functional value in meeting the real, interdependent needs of the two societies. The political and symbolic value of cooperation among former enemies should not be minimized, but activities that are selected purely on that basis are not likely to be rewarding to the participants and sustained over time. The political and symbolic impact is greatest when it emerges as a by-product of activities that are inherently meaningful. It is the inherent value of cooperative projects to both of the parties that creates the crosscutting ties and the mutual trust that help transform their relationship.

Second, the interaction must be based on a dynamic conception of each other's society, rather than essentialist (or dispositional) assumptions that view the other as fixed by its culture, national character, religion, or ideology. Cooperative activities are conducive to a new relationship if they reflect a mutual effort to understand the other society's evolving needs and an appreciation of the other's changing character in response to changing realities—including the evolving peace. Interactions based on stereotyped conceptions of the other are likely to confirm old attitudes and inhibit the development of a new relationship. Moreover, they are unlikely to foster the mutual responsiveness to the other's needs and appreciation of the other's reality on which a new relationship must be built.

Third, the interaction must be based on an awareness of the sensitivities and anxieties that the other brings to the relationship and a commitment to cooperation on the basis of equality and reciprocity. Cooperative ventures are particularly problematic when the parties are characterized by asymmetries in power and level of development. The sensitivities that arise in any asymmetric relationship are exacerbated by a history of conflict. The less powerful party is especially inclined to be afraid of domination and exploitation by the more powerful one, to react to signs of arrogance and paternalism on the other's part, and to be sensitive to any implications that it is being treated as inferior. The more powerful party is confronted with the often contradictory requirement of providing assistance without establishing a pattern of dominance, dependency, and interference in the affairs of the other society. There is inevitably an element of ambivalence in the relationship: the less powerful party expects and feels entitled to assistance but, at the same time, resents it and experiences it as a threat to self-esteem. In developing cooperative activities, therefore, both parties must work to make sure that the cooperation builds toward a relationship based on equality and reciprocity. This requires genuine respect—on the part of both parties—for the other's perspective and experience, as well as genuine interest in what the other has to contribute. A one-sided relationship, in which one party does all the giving and the other all the taking, is not conducive to positive peace. More generally, the way in which the interaction is conducted and the kinds of attitudes that are conveyed in the course of it—attitudes of respect for the other's integrity, sensitivity to their concerns, and responsiveness to their needs—significantly affect the potential of cooperative activities for transforming the relationship between the parties.

Efforts to establish cooperative ventures between former enemies that meet these conditions confront major obstacles, as the Israeli-Palestinian case clearly illustrates. The history of a relationship between occupier and occupied creates structural impediments to cooperation on a basis of equality and reciprocity. In the economic sphere, for example, access to jobs in Israel is vital to the Palestinian economy, yet the reliance on these jobs reinforces the dependence of the Palestinian economy on the Israeli economy that resulted from the occupation. These difficulties demonstrate why functional relations cannot be meaningfully pursued apart from the political process. In the context of political movement, however, cooperative ventures can gradually overcome the structural obstacles as long as the participants have genuine mutual respect for each other.

Institutionalization of a dynamic process of problem solving. Interactive problem solving, briefly described at the beginning of this chapter, is an approach to the resolution of protracted identity conflicts. Variants of this approach may also play a significant role in the peace-building process after an agreement has been concluded, as both a vehicle for transforming the relationship between the parties and a component of the new relationship. The institutionalization of an ongoing mechanism for conflict resolution through joint problem solving can be seen as a building block of a new civil society formed across the old conflict lines and as an indicator of positive peace.

The assumption here is that peace is not just a state of affairs created by a diplomatic agreement and by the political and legal structures that it puts into place. Rather, peace is a dynamic process; and a significant part of that process calls for institutionalized mechanisms to resolve the problems that are bound to arise in the relationship between any two nations, particularly nations emerging from a history of protracted conflict. An ongoing process of conflict resolution through joint problem solving is especially vital in the wake of a weak, incomplete agreement. The mechanisms for engaging in such a process can be seen as a type of insurance policy against the inevitable setbacks in the implementation and completion of the agreement. They can help the parties anticipate such setbacks and deal with them when they arise. Availability of this resource makes it easier for the parties to regain the sense of possibility when the peace process is on the verge of breaking down and to reestablish the relationship when it has been ruptured.

The institutionalization of a process of problem solving must meet several conditions if it is to contribute effectively to transforming the relationship between the former enemies and help lay the basis for positive peace.

First, the process must be based on a dynamic view of the relationship between the parties. It must take account of the occurrence of change within each society and in the relationship between them, of the possibilities for future change, of the capacity of each party to encourage change in the other through its own positive actions, and of the ways in which new situations create their own dynamics for further change. As long as the parties fail to recognize the dynamic character of their relationship, the problems that are bound to crop up along the way are likely to rearouse the images and habits rooted in their long-standing conflict. As a result, they would miss opportunities for discovering creative and mutually beneficial solutions to these problems. Above all, a dynamic view of the relationship alerts the parties to ways of influencing the other by being responsive to the other's needs.

Second, a central feature of the ongoing problem-solving process must be a readiness to engage in exploratory communication. Conflict resolution is hampered when each party enters into it with a strong commitment to a specific outcome, which narrows the range of possible accommodations that they are likely to consider. This effect is magnified when the parties make public pronouncements or take unilateral actions that make it difficult for them to retreat from their demands. What is needed, instead, is a commitment to a process that keeps the options open, allows the parties to explore each other's concerns and priorities, and enables them to reframe the issues. This kind of communication broadens the range of mutual accommodations that can be considered in negotiating a suitable solution. Institutionalizing a dynamic process of problem solving requires a venue in which exploratory communication can take place before the parties bind themselves into rigid positions.

Third, the conflict-resolution mechanisms to be institutionalized must follow a nonadversarial model. They must approach conflicts within a no-fault framework, treating them as shared problems that require cooperative efforts in order to arrive at mutually satisfactory solutions. The aim of negotiation in this approach is to find integrative solutions in which both parties win, rather than strictly distributive solutions in which one party's gain represents the other party's loss.

This last condition for institutionalizing a dynamic process of problem solving in the wake of a political agreement refers specifically to negotiating style, but it reflects the general attitude toward each other that former enemies must evolve as their relationship is transformed. It brings us back full circle to the first condition for mutual acceptance and reconciliation as a component of positive peace: the peace agreement itself must entail a solution that satisfies the fundamental needs and fulfills the national aspirations of both parties, rather than one that is experienced as defeat and subjugation by one of the parties. The negotiation of a final agreement inevitably requires distributive bargaining over specific issues, trade-offs between issues, and painful compromises. But the overall agreement must be based on certain basic principles shared by both sides. Only an outcome that both sides see as fair and just and that leaves them better off than they were before can pave the way to reconciliation.

Notes

1. H. C. Kelman, "Informal Mediation by the Scholar/Practitioner," in J. Bercovitch and J. Rubin, eds., *Mediation in International Relations: Multiple*

Approaches to Conflict Management (New York: St. Martin's, 1992), pp. 64–95; H. C. Kelman, "The Interactive Problem-Solving Approach," in C. A. Crocker and F. O. Hampson, eds., *Managing Global Chaos: Sources of and Responses to International Conflict* (Washington, D.C.: United States Institute of Peace Press, 1996), pp. 501–519; and R. J. Fisher, *Interactive Conflict Resolution* (Syracuse, N.Y.: Syracuse University Press, 1997).

2. J. W. Burton, *Conflict and Communication: The Use of Controlled Communication in International Relations* (London: Macmillan, 1969); J. W. Burton, *Global Conflict* (Brighton, United Kingdom: Wheatsheaf, 1984); and H. C. Kelman, "The Problem-Solving Workshop in Conflict Resolution," in R. L. Merritt, ed., *Communication in International Politics* (Urbana: University of Illinois Press, 1972), pp. 168–204.

3. H. C. Kelman, "Contributions of an Unofficial Conflict Resolution Effort to the Israeli-Palestinian Breakthrough," *Negotiation Journal* 11 (1995): 19–27.

4. H. C. Kelman, "Negotiation as Interactive Problem Solving," *International Negotiation* 1, no. 1 (1996): 99–123.

5. J. W. Burton, "Conflict Resolution as a Function of Human Needs," in R. A. Coate and J. A. Rosati, eds., *The Power of Human Needs* (Boulder, Colo.: Lynne Rienner, 1988), p. 198.

6. H. C. Kelman, "Coalitions Across Conflict Lines: The Interplay of Conflicts Within and Between the Israeli and Palestinian Communities," in S. Worchel and J. Simpson, eds., *Conflict Between People and Groups* (Chicago: Nelson-Hall, 1993), pp. 236–258.

7. H. C. Kelman, "The Political Psychology of the Israeli-Palestinian Conflict," *Political Psychology* 8 (1987): 347–363.

8. H. C. Kelman, "Acknowledging the Other's Nationhood: How to Create a Momentum for the Israeli-Palestinian Negotations," *Journal of Palestine Studies* 22, no. 1 (1992): 18–38.

9. C. E. Osgood, *An Alternative to War or Surrender* (Urbana: University of Illinois Press, 1962).

The Long Road to Reconciliation: Some Moral Stepping-Stones

Donald W. Shriver Jr.

How can societies deal with the debris of suffering that hangs heavy over all their formal attempts to "settle" violent past conflict?

As I attempt to contribute some moral perspectives to our deliberation around this great question, I feel bound to offer a diffident apology. We who write our scholarly reflections on other people's agonies are not necessarily useless for the prevention of repetitions of such agonies; but we have an obligation to make clear from the first that we have no right to peer over the boundary between our comfort and their pain without first admitting our *un*expert first-order qualifications to speak about the matter. Here, the wisdom and respect of the three men who came to Job's blistered side seem altogether the right model for all outsiders who look on at the pain of others: "They raised their voices and wept aloud." But then, "They sat with him on the ground seven days and seven nights, and no one spoke a word to him, for they saw that his suffering was very great."[1]

Tears are seldom at home in academic gatherings, and silence almost never is. But we do well to make room for both gestures, lest we add to the unjust pejorative popular reputation of the word "academic." Hannah Arendt said that to "describe the concentration camps *sine ira* [without outrage] is not to be 'objective' but to condone them."[2] My subject is what peoples may have to do if they are to recover from the atrocities that have afflicted their past relations with one another. Without dwelling on horror stories, I mean to reckon with the victims' momentous rightful resistance to the superficial advice, "Let bygones be bygones." If your grandfather's bones turned to ashes at Auschwitz, if you threw your child into the river for a better death than one at the edge of a Hutu machete, if your mother was raped on orders from a Serbian officer, if your brother hobbles on crutches to this day from the effects of an Irish Republican Army (IRA) bomb, if . . . if . . . if. Was there ever a human century that turned so many ifs into grim reality?

That diffidence tendered, I would like to explore some moral ingredients of "transitional justice," or postsettlement peacemaking, in the context of a model of forgiveness that is at the center of my recent book, *An Ethic for Enemies: Forgiveness in Politics*.[3] There I identify four elements in a collective act of forgiveness: moral judgment, forbearance from revenge, empathy for the humanity of the enemy, and the intent to construct a civic relation that might eventually deserve the name "reconciliation." These elements coexist and are mutually implicated in one another; they are not seriatim stages of social interaction, but circular, interactive, and iteratively reinforced. Each is an element in a social process of possible long duration. Each implies and calls for a counteraction from the "enemy": confession, acknowledgment that revenge might be justified, empathy for the victims, and a matching intention to "knit up the ravel'd sleeve" of a broken civic relationship.[4]

If I regard these four as indispensable, moral stepping-stones to real restoration of a broken civil society, I do not assume that the moral and the practical-empirical sides of a polity are related in some Kantian dualistic way. A noted social psychologist once said that nothing is as practical as a good theory,[5] and I would simply add that bad theories too are practical. In turn, what any person or culture assumes to be practical is likely to have some moral force behind it. The conflicting parties in Bosnia, Ireland, and Rwanda all have moral and even religious justifications for what they have done to their adversaries. Those very justifications have helped fuel the conflict. Rather than argue at length over in what sense moral beliefs are "real," however, I want to explore the empirical practicality and the empirical difficulties of each of my four elements of forgiveness. This will involve some attention to what other scholars have stated about the Middle East, Bosnia, and Ireland, plus some extra illustrations from South Africa, Burundi, and Latin America. In all the cases, I want to ask: (1) What is morally and politically urgent about this dimension of forgiveness in dealing with the debris of anguished past atrocity? And (2) what are some of the difficulties that any party to these postsettlement negotiations is likely to encounter in effecting these dimensions?

Judgment: Justice as Public Truth-Telling

Sociologist Nicholas Tavuchis remarks that there is something mysterious about the power of a mere "speech act" to transform human relationships.[6] Two factors make for this transformation: the power of truth and the power of ascertained responsibility. There is an indispensable connection of the two: an action confessed without moral blame fails to touch the resentments of the victims; and unattached to specifics of actual history, blame is superficial. The moral and political problem of most amnesties consists of the absence of one or both of these elements. Paz Rojas Baeza, a psychiatrist who has worked with many victims of torture in Chile, is sure that blanket amnesties, and the promise of impunity for the official crimes of the past, are ultimately destructive of peace in deeply damaged persons and societies. Indeed, they are the destruction of ethics.

> With impunity, the whole structure of civil responsibility has collapsed beyond repair, producing a *dissociated communal life in society: knowing yet concealing; being informed but keeping quiet; wanting to forget but remembering; seeking good but doing wrong; wanting to be conciliating and rebelling.*[7]

In recent years, political leaders and their constituencies have devoted unprecedented attention to the thirst of victims of politically enacted atrocity for *public rehearsal* of the facts of that atrocity. One remarkable illustration was the 1990 "Final Report" of the Chilean Truth and Reconciliation Commission (TRC), publicized on television by then President Patricio Aylwin, who apologized to the Chilean people, on behalf of the state, for the crimes of Augusto Pinochet's dictatorship. Such official confession, says Charles Villa-Vicencio, in the context of his current work with the similar commission in South Africa, "has to do with what the Chileans called *reconvivencia*—a period of getting used to living with each other again. For this to happen, there has to be a diagnosis of *what* transpired, *why* it transpired and ultimately *who* was responsible."[8] The jury is still out on the long-range effect of the work of truth commissions, of course. Supposedly democratic assemblies in Chile and El Salvador, for example, have effectively nullified their respective commission reports by granting blanket amnesty to virtually all the "official criminals" in the reports.

Western social scientists and philosophers are notoriously nervous about the concept "truth," especially substantive moral truth susceptible to intercultural consensus. The Universal Declaration of Human Rights to the contrary, the United Nations officially refused to call the Rwandan massacres "genocide" because, under UN rules, the international agency would then have to intervene to try to stop the killing. Instead, says William O'Neill, the Western world has taken little notice of "the systematic inequities visited upon Tutsis since their disenfranchisement in 1959."[9] The excuse, of course, was that these were local matters belonging to the standards of local government and local cultures—a view that fits nicely with the Western intellectual architects of so-called postmodernism. But victims and survivors of murder, either single murder or massive murder, make poor postmodernists. They think that they have a right to life, that it is wrong to kill a neighbor, and that the smallest conceivable *political* neighborhood exists on a foundation of respect for the life of the human person. In our time, authoritarian architects of genocide have propounded explicit, complex theories of why some groups of people do not deserve to live. Whether practiced with the aid of gas ovens or machetes, theirs has been a grimly practical theory, which should send us all scrambling for a solid reason to affirm the value of our own, as well as our neighbors', existence. Is there a universal "we" to whom we can ascribe nonnegotiable dignity? O'Neill answers "yes," but not on grounds of liberal cultural relativism. Protest against murder requires in the protester "an antecedent prejudice of respect." He concurs with an African scholar from Benin in making a stab at a universal moral-empirical datum: "in no society is awareness of dignity truly absent, perhaps because in no society, alas, has this dignity ever been fully respected."[10]

The millions of postsettlement victim cries for the publication of the facts of their suffering are in consensus on the point: "Our dignity was grossly violated, and we seek a modicum of restoration—public rehearsal of our indignities at the hand of official power." Michael Lapsley, having scarcely survived an assassination attempt in South Africa in 1990, spoke for all victims when he said: "In the name of reconciliation, some ask that we sacrifice truth. The burden of truth will not disappear. We demand to know. This much is not negotiable."[11]

It may be a slim version of "justice," but the TRC of Nelson Mandela's government believes that it is essential to the daunting task of building a new political culture in South Africa. Ernst Renan is credited with the surmise that nations found themselves initially by getting their history wrong.[12] Getting it right, getting it more truthful, is a step in the building of new nations.

But the observation is at best half right. A first problem with truth-telling in a peace process is that the truths of personal and collective experience are various indeed. There is a black South African truth of Sharpeville, and there is an Afrikaner truth of the Great Trek. So the process of building a new political culture involves what Alan Falconer and his Irish colleagues have called "the reconciliation of memories."[13] Or as Villa-Vicencio puts it in a quotation from H. Richard Niebuhr, "where common memory is lacking, where [people] do not share in the same past, there can be no real community, and where community is to be formed common memory must be created. . . . [T]he measure of our unity is the extent of our common memory."[14] The accent is on "common": once one party to a conflict internalizes the memories of another party, they may be on their way to creating a "collective story" larger than any that one party could have constructed on its own. The truth commission in El Salvador determined that 5 percent of the atrocities in the long civil war were committed by the insurgents, the Farabundo Martí National Liberation Front, and the other 95 percent by agents of the government.[15] Both the 5 percent and the 95 percent are important. The public telling of all sorts of stories, including the most painful and embarrassing ones from all sides, signals the hope for an inclusive body politic, in which no one's suffering is invisible in the public record, the history books, the mass media, and the celebratory occasions of religion and government. As Robert Rothstein puts the same point: "Stable peace may thus require a concerted effort to revise the historical canon, to begin teaching a new version of history, and to marginalize and contain the extremists who reject this effort." Basic to this new history is acknowledgment of the atrocities on one side that the other has often found it convenient to forget.[16] The slogan here cannot be merely: "Forgiveness for the past and accountability for the future." It has to be: "Accountability for the past as a step toward forgiving it."

That there are problems in this side of a peace process should surprise no one. Never does the course of victims' truth-telling run smooth. In the face of awful truth, the relation of perpetrators and victims may in fact worsen, especially from the side of those victims who yearn not only for the truth to be known, but also for punishment of the guilty. The cry of families for a judicial trial of the murderers strikes an old chord in the legal tradition of punitive justice. Public embarrassment is a sort of punishment, but does it fit the crime? The most critical political-legal challenge of all may be the simultaneous combining of the "carrot" of amnesty with the "stick" of judicial trials—a risky combination not only for the rule of consistency, but also for reforming a judicial system still staffed by appointees of the old regime. Finally there is the problem of whether truth-telling, rather than sheer punishment, is likely to become a factor in the reform and civic restoration of the perpetrators themselves. Is an honest confession good for the political soul? For new constructive behavior of perpetrators? Or does mere truth-telling permit them to retire smugly into their own uncivil ghetto? The question deserves research.

The most important question of ethical theory in all of this, however, is the definition of "justice." Proponents of truth's relation to reconciliation stress that the justice most worth seeking is the healing of sick, atrocity-fractured persons and bodies politic. For that cause, abstract punitive justice may be of limited use. *Restorative* justice is the concept that persons and societies may most sorely need. Such justice is compounded, not only of public truth-telling, but also of two other dimensions of forgiveness: the retreat from vengeance, which we may call "forbearance," and the retreat from mutual dehumanization called the "renewal of empathy."

Forbearance: Breaking Cycles of Revenge

Long ago, the Greek dramatists displayed the impulse to vengeance as the great enemy of coherent civic life. To establish courts of justice was to take the right to vengeance out of the hands of victims and to allocate it to the state.

Even longer ago, the myths of the Hebrew people named murder as the primeval crime but established, in God's protective "mark" on the face of Cain, the principle that ultimate vengeance "is mine, says the Lord."[17] It is remarkable that in this familiar tale, so few modern Jews and Christians have not perceived a question mark over the institution of capital punishment.

When murder is massive, as in state-sponsored violence, the case against revenge hinges on strategies for the rescue of civil society. Nothing eats away at the "glue" of civic order so surely as cycles of escalating revenge and counterrevenge. The question often is: Which side will take a first step to interrupt the cycle? In a recent paper on economic incentives for changing hostile relations into positive ones, David Cortright and George Lopez speak of "the power of positive reciprocity." One side of violent conflict makes a tentative offer of help to the other without for the moment demanding an offer in return but in the hope "that this will prevent a renewal of bloodshed, or encourage a process of dialogue and negotiation." Such offers, they say, "are central to the art of diplomatic persuasion."[18] As Moshe Ma'oz says succinctly, "To be generous is to be rewarded."[19]

In early-twentieth-century history, the difference between the Treaty of Versailles and the Marshall Plan is a classic case in point. Nearer at hand are those instances in midcentury Soviet-U.S. arms negotiations when, in seven out of eight instances, a conciliatory offer from the West prompted some counterconcession from the Soviets. The George Bush–Mikhail Gorbachev nuclear demobilizations of 1991 were an even more dramatic example, constituting, say these authors, "the largest single act of denuclearization in history."[20]

Forbearance from strict vengeful reciprocity can be the authentic beginning of any reconciling process worth the name of "forgiveness."[21] South Africa, again, is the most stunning contemporary national example of the politics of positive reciprocity. No one doubts that, had Mandela wanted the civil war that, some estimate, would have killed three million people, he could have had that war during or after his twenty-seven-year imprisonment. The interests in avoiding that war were large on all sides in South Africa, but in politics, as in other organized human life, interests have a way of escaping the bounds of rationality, as when dying for the emperor became for many Japanese soldiers in World War II an end in itself. One might also observe that the mass executions following some revolutions, the Soviet in particular, build up "wrath to come" in the memories of those who survive with deep cynicism about the pretensions of the new government to be more just than the old.

The certainty is: *vengeance kills politics,* if by "politics" we mean those negotiations between groups that permit them to realize their mutual vital interests without destroying those very interests in acts of violence. Somewhere in the progress of combatants toward war-weariness, somebody cuts the nerve of revenge in deference to a vision of a return to a civil society. If the vicious cycle of revenge begins with "what they first did," the cycle of forbearance begins with "what we can first do." Realists in politics, from Thucydides to Mahatma Gandhi and Martin Luther King Jr., know that an eye for an eye makes the whole world blind, that vengeance does not *work* as an establisher of justice. Some forms of judicial punishment may work, but not tit-for-tat vengeance.

The practical-theoretical problem is what forms of punishment, short of revenge, do help to establish justice and to stabilize relations between victims and perpetrators. Here, philosophies of criminal justice and peacemaking have to engage each other at length. An elementary feel for justice compels most humans to resist letting their persecutors "off the hook" of some retribution for their evil deeds.[22] But here again, for the mending of political communities, the primacy of restorative over punitive justice has a claim to practical priority, especially if the aim of restorative procedures is to reintegrate both victims *and* perpetrators into some approximate positive civic relationship. I will deal further with this moral ingredient of political forgiveness later in connection with a discussion of reparations.

Empathy for Perpetrators and Victims: Rehumanizing the Dehumanized

In his work on the racism that infected the conduct of World War II, historian John W. Dower deals extensively with the dehumanizing stereotypes used by both sides as propaganda weapons. For example, an upcoming generation of Americans may find it difficult to identify the time, place, and occasion of the following quotation:

> [They are] utterly lacking in any ability to understand the principles of humanity. Whatever may be the state of their material civilization, they are nothing but lawless savages in spirit who are ruled by fiendish passions and unrestrained lust for blood. Against such enemies of decency and humanity, the civilized world must rise in protest and back up protest with punitive force. Only through the complete chastisement of such barbarians can the world be made safe for civilization.

The words would serve any side in most wars. In fact they were published in the *Nippon Times* of Tokyo on March 29, 1945, in the wake of the March 10–11 firebombing of Tokyo that killed some 100,000 people.[23] Illustrations from Bosnia, Rwanda, Ireland, and the Middle East tumble in for making the point: both for the persuasions that leaders invoke for leading a people to war and for personal ease in killing, it helps to dehumanize the enemy.

After violent conflict, how will the enemy be rehumanized, if at all? The question is central for the repair of a civic culture or for building one from scratch. Paul Arthur states grimly that Northern Ireland is "a society without empathy," trapped in "the egoism of victimhood."[24] If that is true, democracy will tarry a long time in those six counties. Some analysts have said that a democratic order depends on the ability of citizens, when they step into the voting booth, to vote for someone else's interests in addition to their own.[25] In order to have reason to do that, one must bring into that voting booth a respect for fellow citizens that accords their interest a status akin to one's own. This is O'Neill's "prejudice of respect," the presumption that others have a right to our care for their existence and welfare. Egocentric self-interest does not a democratic order make; a lot depends on what sort of self one is interested in. Without the ascription of equal value to one's neighbors, a fissure opens into which an ideologue can pour the suspicion that, after all, it is no great matter to kill them.

But as common experience informs us, empathetic ascription of co-humanity to people who have harmed us or have been harmed by us has to be learned. In 1980, an Egyptian intellectual and journalist, meeting in a workshop organized by the American Psychiatric Assocation, said that "the newest and most important thing [I] learned in the meetings was that Israelis could be afraid."[26] This was akin to Anwar Sadat's testimony to the effect of his first visit to Israel in 1977: "I had always thought that [the Holocaust] was exaggerated for mere propaganda. . . . I saw with my own eyes how Israelis, and Jews the world over, must feel. They are victims not of war alone but also of politics and hatred."[27]

In South Africa, the Truth and Reconciliation Commission seeks to rehumanize both victims and perpetrators, the one by the respect of listening to the stories of their suffering, the other by the insistence that only through confession of crime can they return to the dignity of citizenship. Respect of victims begins with the very invitation to them to tell their stories publicly.[28] Respect for perpetrators begins with treating them as moral agents, not as automatons of a governmental system. (I am reminded of St. Augustine's comment in his *Confessions*: "There is something in humility that lifts up the head"; and of T. S. Eliot: "We must come to the point where humiliation is no longer humiliating.")[29]

Which form of empathy is the hardest to acquire will depend, of course, on which side of a conflict one sympathizes with. Empathy is not sympathy, but acquiring it toward one's enemies is a very hard discipline. The psychological threat that looms here is the suspicion that the more one comes to understand an evil antagonist, the more vulnerability to evildoing one may begin to perceive in oneself. Villa-Vicencio reports a conversation with a South African laborer who was proud of his son's advancement as a member of the South African police. He "asked in disbelief whether his son could possibly have been a willing member of the police riot squad sent into Mlungisi, the African township outside of Queenstown, to quell an anti-apartheid uprising." Villa-Vicencio goes on to refute the old aphorism "to understand all is to forgive all." Rather:

> Our task is to explain and understand, making every effort to enter the mind of even the worst perpetrators, without allowing those who violate the norms for social existence and social decency to escape the censure of society. Guilt rests not only with those who pull the trigger, but also with those who wink when the shot is fired. It does, however, rest decidedly more with those who kill. The one who plots and designs death may well be more guilty than the person who pulls the trigger.[30]

Here, of course, enters the perennial moral question that inheres in all collectively implemented evil: How shall we assess and how shall we punish various *degrees* of guilt? How shall we deal with "responsibility spread thin"?[31] Prior to this difficult strategic and tactical question, however, is the breaking of the image of a strict distinction between the guilty and the innocent. I cannot prove it, but three months in South Africa in 1992 left me with the strong impression that somehow in that country, while not so evidently in Rwanda, the Christian movement made some headway in convincing many of its members that Paul the Apostle was speaking down-to-earth truth when he said: "All have sinned and fall short of the glory of God."[32] On grounds of that sobering perception, one has a reason to tolerate the thought that, under some seductive circumstances, "I too might have done that." It is, I believe, an important ingredient of any political culture *if* it gets translated into due combinations of moral judgment, distinctions between degrees of evil, punishments that stop short of vengeance, and definitions of justice that lean in the restorative direction. Greatly to be avoided is the trap into which Daniel Goldhagen's book on "Hitler's willing executioners" seems sometimes to fall: wrapping a whole people in a seamless cultural robe legitimizing evil. For Goldhagen, says Fritz Stern, "Hitler was Germany."[33] No society deserves such sweeping, indiscriminate moral characterization.

Bridges of empathy take time and contiguity to build. They grow from determination to take that time and to take advantage of that contiguity. Ehud Barak, Israeli military hero and former foreign minister in Shimon Peres's Labor government, was quoted in December 1996 by Anthony Lewis as saying,

The prerequisite for a stable Middle East is that we recognize the needs
and sensitivities of our inevitable partners. They're going to be there forever. You don't choose your parents, and a people cannot choose their
neighbors. . . . The question is: are we going to settle [with the Palestini-
ans], or are we going to manipulate it to let us control them without appearing to?[34]

Duncan Morrow observes that the very fact that the Northern Irish "troubles" have lasted thirty years without the advent of partition is itself an
index to the determination of Protestants and Catholics to make it, somehow, together.[35]

When one thinks of long-standing neighborly proximities of Rwan-
dans, Bosnians, and some U.S. urban dwellers, one has to concede that living next door to one another does not guarantee a civil neighborhood. Paul
Arthur and Keith Jeffrey describe the other side of the Northern Ireland
conundrum in less hopeful terms than does Morrow. In this small country
of 1.5 million,

the proximity, both of the communities to each other and of politicians
to the people they represent, has enormously enhanced the primacy of
specifically local issues and tragically reduced the capability of politicians of one tradition to empathize with their colleagues of the other.[36]

Almost all studies of the repair of civil society agree that geographical
segregation may be a necessary temporary strategy to check the killing; but
the empathies of true citizenship will not emerge without what Steven L.
Burg calls "cross-cutting cleavages" on both interpersonal and institutional
levels.[37] Rothstein is rightly suspicious of Thomas Friedman's rule, "Coexistence begins with barbed wire, not block parties."[38] At best, barbed wires
are a temporary halt to war that give the combatants time to consider how to
organize the equivalents of block parties. People long accustomed to view
others stereotypically require the cognitive dissonance of meeting one another in schools, political associations, the mass media, and religious organizations that crosscut the previous alignments of war. The may even have
to learn to talk politics in one another's bars. All this hopeful learning requires collaborative, crosscutting leadership initiatives that seduce citizens,
so to speak, into new experiences of one another. Everett M. Rogers, professor of communications at the University of Southern California, for example, points out that mere mass media images are important, but they are
not enough to convince many citizens to change their minds about their antagonists. Joseph Montville summarizes Rogers's argument accordingly:

Change of attitude depends, instead, on interpersonal communications
networks in which respected opinion leaders and then near peers accept

the new information as valid and thus change their attitudes. He reports consistent empirical findings that once an innovative idea is accepted by 15 to 20 percent of the population, it takes on a diffusion rate that cannot be stopped.[39]

Doubtless it can be stopped; for, as Burg reminds us, "cross-cutting cleavages contribute to the moderation of conflict only when they become the basis for political identity, electoral competition, and participation in representative institutions and decisionmaking processes."[40] Educational and media institutions can be important in this process; but the final test of peacemaking after war is the ability of ethnically, geographically, and ideologically separated interest groups to enter into new competitive, collaborative, and institutionalized relationships that gradually build mutual trust. Essential to this trust is the growing security of minorities in these processes and security of all interests that participants regard as nonnegotiable. Language, religion, family customs, and certain human rights may be among the nonnegotiables at the beginning, but as both Burg and Chester Crocker point out, in the ongoing course of a political relation, people may change their minds about their nonnegotiables. Contact in shared institutions may demonstrate that civic culture does not require the assimilation of all ethnic cultures but is a mode of respectful relation among them. Winner-take-all election rules may yield to power sharing that guarantees minorities a place at the table; politics then becomes no longer a zero-sum game, but an invitation to participate in the game; and gradually, participants learn that there are beneficial "compromises and deals that would have been unthinkable *before* the settlement."[41]

As a dimension of real politics, the empathy here described consists not only of a new complex of feelings, but also of a growing commonality of interests based on true perceptions of the "other." In that perception, possibilities for forgiveness grow, as former antagonists learn that they can and must live together. The learning can begin anywhere, inside or outside of official governmental stuctures. Indeed, in countries like Nigeria and Bosnia, crosscutting cleavages in nongovernmental organizational contexts may be the only promising start to preparing for the day when government is no longer factional, authoritarian, and military-dependent. In a classic chicken-and-egg dilemma, this promise may be weak or nonexistent in states that systematically suppress all "free spaces" for political discussion among citizens. Without the prior availability of such spaces in Eastern Europe in 1989 and in South Africa before 1990, the nonviolent changes there would have been very unlikely. By the same token, the shortage of such spaces in Bosnia poses great problems for the development of democracy there. As Crocker observes, the current Implementation Force presence will merely strengthen the power of authoritarian leaders if it does not manage to nourish the beginnings of civil society. But can an army do so? Military forces are hardly strong candidates for the task, which leaves open the question of who will construct the political parties, educational institutions, and interreligious dialogues that were precursors to the recent changes in South Africa. Bosnia, Burundi, Haiti, and many another "troubled land," says Crocker, possess few of the civil institutions or leadership skills that helped effect the remarkable recent changes in the apartheid regime.[42] For forty years, in churches, labor unions, and business corporations, confrontations of antagonistic citizen "views and demands" intermingled with joint public expression of "hopes and wishes."[43] When citizens get free enough of their past resentments to express to one another their hopes and wishes for the future, they are likely to discover both the differences and the overlap in their values that are the stuff of genuine political compromise. They are the stuff of concrete political empathy too, and of the transition that Ma'oz yearns to see between the Israelis and the Palestinians: from "how we can fight each other" to "how we can benefit each other."

The Longer Road to Reconciliation: Reparation and Leadership

Among the chief first stepping-stones toward civic reconciliation of former antagonists, acts of public truth-telling, forbearance from revenge, and growing empathy would seem to be indispensable. They are principal ingredients of forgiveness. But forgiveness, like each of these ingredients, can be a long process in politics, never quite completed, and subject often to reprocessing. If the 1389 Battle of Kosovo is still there in the memory of Serbs for power-seeking political leaders to exploit, then the more recent sufferings of war are likely to remain as potential explosive charges in Balkan cultures of the coming century.

That they may be drained of their ability to poison a future political order would seem to depend on at least two further dimensions of collective forgiveness: one is the justice of reparations, the other is the significance of representative contrite leadership.

The cry for public truth about political atrocity is too universal among its victims worldwide for any of us to doubt that real justice requires real response to that cry. But the "speech acts" of the victim's story and the perpetrator's confession will lack credibility in the long run if unaccompanied by other acts of concrete restorative justice. The latter is likely to be complex and long term, especially if it means, in Villa-Vicencio's claim, "to address the need of reparation of the victim" and also "the rehabilitation of the perpetrator."[44] Tragically, there are many repairs to victims beyond the reach of human achievement; nobody can restore the life of a dead husband or the limbs of a crippled child. But homes can be rebuilt, and money compensations can be offered, however short of real restoration of lost assets these gestures may fall. It is a relatively new emphasis in criminal law around the world, but it seems both just to the victim and rehabilitative to the perpetrators that the latter should have a part in supplying the reparations, which may have to be supplemented by the resources of the state. The resources of both may be severely limited and productive of little more than symbolic help to the victim. But that symbol is better than nothing, for it too serves the dignity of the injured and the growth of a justice-prone public culture.

Perhaps the outstanding modern example of official reparation to victims has been the fifty-year effort of the Federal Republic of Germany to grant both symbolic and material payments to surviving victims of Nazism. In addition to the payment of some $70 billion to date to Israel, individual Jewish families, and other "survivors," that government in 1952 passed its remarkable "equalization of burdens law" (*Lastenausgleichsgesetz*), whereby citizens who suffered little damage to their assets in the war are required over a thirty-year period to cede half of those assets to fellow citizens who were not so lucky. One speculates whether the new South African government is likely to find this precedent worth some form of imitation. As one contemporary German church leader put it, after a 1996 visit to South Africa:

> [In South Africa] up to this point the costs of the process of transition have been borne by the majority of the people and by their stupendous capacity of forgiveness and forbearance. Should it turn out, however, that the beneficiaries of Apartheid wish to carry their advantages over to the new South Africa without being ready to let go some of their wealth, . . . then it can safely be expected that the patience will be exhausted and violence increase even further.[45]

For the making of such contributions to the creation of new political cultures after huge political traumas, courageous leaders are needed on all levels of the society. We know from the recent histories of all the countries mentioned here what damage leaders can do to any civic culture. But what leaders can greatly damage, leaders can greatly repair, especially in their public speech. Montville relates how a vociferous Palestinian said to a group of Israelis: "If you Israelis would only acknowledge that you have wronged us, that you have taken away our homes and our land—if you did that, we would be able to proceed without insisting, without needing to get them back." This was said "somewhat wistfully," Montville reports; but "no such acknowledgment was made. The Israelis were frightened of the consequences, of what it might imply to make such an acknowledgment."[46]

One of these days, we may hope, Israeli and Palestinian leaders will exchange some public contrition for how their peoples have harmed each other. If backed up by concrete changes in political structures and economic relationships, that contrition will have its own invaluable place in the new political culture. My guess is that in the future of Northern Ireland, people will remember that, in 1994, in connection with their cease-fire, militant loyalist leaders publicly expressed regret for all the deaths on both sides since 1969. Unfortunately, that contrition was not matched on the side of the IRA.

Confessions by politicians are a hard test of their ability to combine the humiliating as well as the proud truth about their peoples' past. To be sure, "the consummate collective apology is a diplomatic accomplishment of no mean order."[47] It takes time for them and their constituents to acquire courage for public utterance of such truth. But some leaders and some publics do acquire it, and in doing so, they rise above partisan ideologies to tell a "story that unites" the victims and the perpetrators of the past in new truth-filled civic bonds. In telling such a story to the German Bundestag on the fortieth anniversary of the end of World War II in Europe, German president Richard von Weizsacker ended with the words, "We older people do not owe youth the fulfllment of dreams, but rather integrity. . . . Let us look truth in the eye as well as we are able."

The possibility of forgiveness in politics rests on the possibility of contrition in politics. Whether they call it that or not, the makers of lasting peace will have to consider the utter practicality of that rule. "To be social is to be forgiving," said Robert Frost.[48] To be political may be the same.

Notes

1. Job 2:12–13, New Revised Standard Version (NRSV).

2. Hannah Arendt, "A Reply" (published in the *Review of Politics*), as quoted by William J. O'Neill, "Death's Other Kingdom: Human Rights and the Politics of Genocide in Rwanda," paper presented at the annual meeting of the Society of Christian Ethics, New York, N.Y., January 10, 1997.

3. Donald W. Shriver Jr., *An Ethic for Enemies: Forgiveness in Politics* (New York: Oxford University Press, 1995).

4. The line of poetry is from William Shakespeare, *Macbeth.*

5. I believe this was Kurt Lewin, but I do not have the precise source.

6. Nicholas Tavuchis, *Mea Culpa: A Sociology of Apology and Reconciliation* (Stanford, Calif.: Stanford University Press, 1991), p. 6.

7. Paz Rojas Baeza, "Breaking the Human Link: The Medico-Psychiatric View of Impunity," in Charles Harper, ed., *Impunity: An Ethical Perspective* (Geneva: World Council of Churches, 1996), p. 91.

8. Charles Villa-Vicencio, *A Different Kind of Justice: The South-African Truth and Reconciliation Commission* (Maryknoll, N.Y.: Orbis Books, 1988), p. 1. Villa-Vicencio is director of research for the commission.

9. O'Neill, "Death's Other Kingdom," p. 3.

10. Paulin J. Hountondji, "The Master's Voice: Remarks on the Problem of Human Rights in Africa," *Philosophical Foundations of Human Rights* (Paris:

United Nations Educational, Scientific, and Cultural Organization, 1986), p. 325, as quoted by O'Neill, "Death's Other Kingdom," pp. 20–21.

11. From Lapsley's *South Africa 1995,* as quoted by Villa-Vicencio, "The Burden of Moral Guilt" (p. 1), via personal communication, October 1996.

12. Ernst Renan, *History of the People of Israel* (Boston: Roberts Brothers, 1888), p. 417.

13. This phrase was used at a conference at the World Council of Churches in Geneva, of which Alan Falconer is an official.

14. Villa-Vicencio, "The Burden of Moral Guilt," p. 18. The quote from Niebuhr is from *The Meaning of Revelation* (New York: Macmillan, 1941), p. 115.

15. Cf. Jon Sobrino, "Theological Reflections on the Report of the Truth Commission," in Harper, ed., *Impunity,* p. 120.

16. Robert L. Rothstein, "After the Peace: The Political Economy of Reconciliation," Inaugural Rebecca Meyerhoff Memorial Lecture (Jerusalem: Harry S. Truman Institute, Hebrew University, 1996), p. 11. Cf. also p. 31.

17. Cf. Genesis 4:14–15, Deuteronomy 32:35, Romans 12:19, NRSV.

18. David Cortright and George A. Lopez, "Carrots, Sticks, and Cooperation: Economic Tools of Statecraft," paper prepared for a conference of the Center for Preventive Action of the Council on Foreign Relations, New York, N.Y., December 12, 1996, p. 15; used by permission.

19. See Moshe Ma'oz, Chapter 3 of this volume.

20. Cortright and Lopez, "Carrots, Sticks, and Cooperation," p. 16.

21. The history of vengeance is replete with illustrations not only of "just revenge," but of unjust, measureless revenge. In wars, vengeance escalates, eventually losing all mooring in ethical restraint. For a discussion of distinctions between just and unjust punitive responses to injustice, cf. Shriver, *An Ethic for Enemies,* pp. 30–32.

22. No less a trio than Richard Holbrooke, John Shattuck, and Richard Goldstone apparently agreed, in early February 1997, that unless the indicted war criminals in Bosnia are arrested and tried in The Hague's International Court of Justice, Bosnia and the Dayton Accords would fall apart. Goldstone was thus quoted by the two U.S. leaders in an on-the-record meeting of the Council on Foreign Relations, New York, N.Y., February 4, 1997.

23. John W. Dower, *War Without Mercy: Race and Power in the Pacific War* (New York: Pantheon Books, 1986), p. 72.

24. See Paul Arthur, Chapter 4 of this volume.

25. This is a standard argument in the literature on stable democracy.

26. Joseph V. Montville, "The Healing Function in Political Conflict Resolution," in Hugo van der Merwe, ed., *Conflict Resolution Theory and Practice: Integration and Application* (Manchester: Manchester University Press, 1993), p. 114.

27. As quoted by Trude B. Feldman, "History's Sadat," *New York Times,* November 20, 1982, two years after his assassination.

28. Paragraph 11 of the National Unity and Reconciliation Act, which authorized South Africa's TRC, speaks of the "compassion and respect" that the commission owes those victims who come forward to testify. Observers of the process speak of the gentleness and carefulness with which these witnesses are led from their seats to the front of the room.

29. T. S. Eliot, *Confessions/Augustine* (New York: Oxford University Press, 1992), p. 243; T. S. Eliot, *After Strange Gods: A Primer of Modern Heresy* (London: Faber and Faber, 1934), p. 75.

30. Villa-Vicencio, *A Different Kind of Justice,* pp. 7–8.

31. The phrase is Catholic theologian John Mahoney's, in his discussion of the individualistic focus of much Catholic and Protestant ethical theory and sacramental practice. Cf. Mahoney, *The Making of Moral Theology: A Study of the Roman Catholic Tradition* (Oxford: Clarendon, 1987), p. 34, and Shriver, *An Ethic for Enemies,* pp. 54–55 and 112–116.

32. Romans 3:23, NRSV.

33. Fritz Stern, Review of Goldhagen's *Hitler's Willing Executioners,* in *Foreign Affairs* (November–December 1996): 131.

34. In Anthony Lewis, "No Messianic Dreams," *New York Times,* December 19, 1996.

35. See Duncan Morrow, Chapter 5 of this volume.

36. Paul Arthur and Keith Jeffrey, *Northern Ireland Since 1968* (London: Blackwell, 1988), p. 21.

37. Steven L. Burg, "Some Observations on the Art of Preventive Action," paper prepared for the annual conference on preventive action of the Center for Preventive Action of the Council on Foreign Relations, New York, N.Y., December 12, 1996, pp. 3–4.

38. Quoted by Rothstein, "After the Peace," p. 20, from Thomas L. Friedman, "It's Time to Separate," *New York Times,* January 29, 1995, p. E15.

39. From E. M. Rogers, "Diffusion of the Idea of Beyond War," in A. Gromyko and M. Hellman, eds., *Breakthrough: Emerging New Thinking* (New York: Walker, 1988), as summarized by Montville, "The Healing Function in Political Conflict," p. 124.

40. Burg, "Some Observations," p. 3.

41. Chester A. Crocker and Fen Osler Hampson, "Making Peace Settlements Work," *Foreign Policy* (fall 1996): 57, 63.

42. Ibid., p. 56.

43. The phrase is from Burg, "Some Observations," p. 10.

44. Villa-Vicencio, *A Different Kind of Justice,* p. 13.

45. Geiko Muller-Fahrenholz, "Truth and Reconciliation in South Africa: A Case Study," an unpublished paper based on observations of the TRC's work in the fall of 1996. The author is a minister and leader of the Evangelical Church in Germany.

46. Montville, "The Healing Function in Political Conflict Resolution," p. 112.

47. Tavuchis, *Mea Culpa,* p. 100. The collective or political apology is one of four forms of that "speech act" described by Tavuchis. It is the most difficult of the four. See also Shriver, *An Ethic for Enemies*, pp. 220–224.

48. Robert Frost, "The Star Splitter," in Edward Connery Lathem, ed., *The Poetry of Robert Frost* (New York: Holt, Rinehart, and Winston, 1979), p. 178.

10

Fragile Peace and Its Aftermath

Robert L. Rothstein

A weak "peace" agreement rarely produces genuine peace, that is, a situation in which both sides accept the need for painful compromises of long-term goals, an end to violence and terrorism (or at least a sharp curtailment of such actions), and the beginning of an effort to transform the structural conditions that have sustained a bitter and protracted conflict. What we usually get, after a period of euphoria and dangerously rising expectations, are frustration, disillusionment, misunderstandings about what has and has not been agreed to, the exacerbation of underlying structural conditions (distrust, weakened leadership, psychological alienation, etc.), and perhaps a return to violence and terror.

None of this is especially surprising. There is very rarely a shared vision of a final outcome that is driving the peace process; consent to begin moving toward compromise is frequently forced by external powers or by the stronger side (thus guaranteeing minimal commitment to an apparently temporary truce agreement); peace itself means different things not only between the parties, but also within each party (thus guaranteeing prolonged negotiations and unstable concessions); and weak leaders whose stature has come from leading and symbolizing the conflict become even weaker as they are challenged by extremists, fail to produce substantial gains, and are able or willing to risk less and less. In these circumstances, although the attractions of a high-risk, high-gain strategy are apparent—note the at least relative success of the Camp David Agreement between Israel and Egypt and the Nelson Mandela–F. W. de Klerk negotiations in South Africa—weak and threatened leaders are more likely to see the high risks but not the high gains.[1] A low-risk, low-gain strategy may be suboptimal, but it may also reflect the limits of the possible. By the same token, these limitations may set the frame of reference for the period after a weak peace agreement has been negotiated: an agreement with a significant chance of making things worse—a bad peace—that can survive and become a good peace only if both sides and critical external actors understand the nature of the (partially) new game, its (partially) new risks, and its (partially) new needs.

Still, it is a mistake to be unrelentingly pessimistic about the prospects for long-term, stable peace. It is obvious that the latter can be established only after the underlying structural conditions of conflict have been transformed, a process that could take a generation or more.[2] At the same time, however, the establishment of a negotiating process and a tentative—perhaps even temporary—peace agreement may be useful and even essential steps along the way. They change the political calculuses, they may increase the availability of external resources, and they may even begin to alter cognitive maps in both communities. Moreover, more subterranean changes in socioeconomic trends, in "battle fatigue," and in political expectations (especially as new leaders emerge) may be working away, slowly and fitfully, to defrost the iceberg of unending conflict—making thinking about the unthinkable at least possible, if not yet popular. What has not yet been resolved and what may be changing enough to open up opportunities for progress thus coexist uneasily. The fluidity and complexity of the picture suggest a slow, erratic, ambivalent, and painful peace process, but one with more possibilities of progress than is apparent from the headlines: terrorist actions, accusations of deceitfulness and a failure to fulfill commitments, discordant voices in both communities, and episodic involvement by external actors.

The peace strategy—the strategy that seeks to deepen, widen, and sustain a weak peace agreement—that needs to be constructed to deal with these complexities must be multidimensional. It must begin with an awareness that the peace agreement has not created peace but, rather, only a new set of opportunities that can be grasped or thrown away; that persisting and still powerful elements of the ancient structure of conflict will remain powerful for decades to come and must be protected against and steadily diminished. The tentative negotiating process that has been established needs constant support, and small but consistent steps to increase mutual respect, to change the rhetoric of hatred and bitterness, and to reduce tensions, resentments, and disappointments by working to ensure an increasing degree of mutual prosperity (and not merely among the cronies of the ruling elite) and the acquisition of enough material assets to generate risk aversion in both communities. The creation of joint institutions to facilitate these tasks may also be necessary, not least because it may begin to establish and deepen useful channels of communication and mutual respect. This complex and nuanced strategy—difficult in the best of circumstances, and circumstances are hardly likely to be the best—may be easier to implement if there is some initial agreement on mutually bearable compromises of crucial issues, even if these are compromises that will be implemented gradually and only after prior performance standards are met. But this may not be possible because one or both sides may not yet have reached the point of willingness (or ability) to sacrifice the final practical and symbolic obstacles to agreement. Stumbling forward and muddling through may thus be the most for which we can hope. Even so, there are better or worse things that can be done in the present to increase the chances of a bearable future for both sides, though perhaps not the future that either considers most preferable.[3]

There is another factor that might make the implementation of a nuanced postagreement strategy even more problematic. Risk, pervasive and unavoidable, is an intrinsic component of the peacemaking process in protracted conflicts. The risk is frequently asymmetric because the status quo party must give up something tangible—land, resources, control—in exchange for promissory notes that may never be collected. There is thus an understandable bias toward prudence and incremental adjustments to the status quo by one party and demands for rapid and fundamental changes from the other party. One side feels the need to go slowly to increase support for a risky peace, but the other side feels it must go rapidly to achieve the same end. An asymmetrical response to high levels of risk inevitably generates misunderstandings and policies that work at cross-purposes.

There are two contextual problems that are particularly difficult to manage. The first is that the conventional techniques to manage risk, which seek to reduce vulnerability and increase the likelihood of compliance or the costs of noncompliance, may decrease short-run but increase long-run risks to the peace process. Measures such as phased implementation, close supervision of terms (or high initial performance standards), starting with small pilot projects, and clear and powerful sanctions for violations are perfectly sensible and may succeed in diminishing the risk of catastrophic, worst-case outcomes; but they may also delay the achievement of the kind of rapid, substantive benefits that are necessary to build support for an agreement and to avoid a rapid descent into disillusionment and bitterness. The second problem concerns the calculus of political costs and benefits by leaders. The latter may be very well aware that they do not have any risk-free choices, but they are also not likely to risk the most dangerous and controversial policy initiatives because they fear that the ensuing domestic conflict will be fierce and that the high-risk policy will not produce the anticipated high-value benefits. The result could be severe damage to a leader's reputation and career, not to mention severe damage to the peace process.

The central issue, a staple of risk analysis (or the analysis of complex, linked systems), is that the leader rarely controls the variables that will determine success or failure of any grand initiative.[4] Perhaps this problem can be diminished—it can never be entirely eliminated—by increasing the joint benefits of cooperation, by enhancing communications and contact between the parties to reduce mistrust and to generate more cross-group elite unity, by emphasizing confidence-building measures, and by third-party intervention via performance guarantees, resource transfers, and perhaps surveillance and peacekeeping forces. It might also help, as noted earlier, if joint institutions were to be created to analyze unresolved issues, to monitor compliance, and to provide early warning of trouble. Such institutions, if they work properly, provide a framework for continuing cooperation and a constituency to support that cooperation.

One final point is worth making in these preliminary comments. If one is seeking peace or seeking to deepen a peace agreement between two communities in a single state, there is a kind of obvious and dominant solution, no matter how difficult working out the details may be. This is some form of power sharing in (one hopes) an increasingly pluralist political culture, as has been suggested for Northern Ireland, South Africa, and Sri Lanka (and, at least notionally, for Bosnia). This effort, once under way, can be reinforced by establishing procedural mechanisms that increase political incentives to cooperate—for example, by making it necessary for politicians to seek votes and support across group lines. To a degree, this may diminish the top-down aspect of many peace processes because it gives leaders a strong incentive to pay attention to bottom-up demands. It may also gradually diminish the level of terrorism by reducing the isolation of groups from each other and compelling attention to the needs of all citizens.[5] The point is not that procedural devices by themselves will bring peace; rather, they are an important component of a broader peace strategy.

By contrast, power-sharing formulas do not work very well when the conflict is between two states or between a state and a community that wants to secede from it or take over territory it holds to create a state of its own. Some form of separation between the Israelis and the Palestinians will be a central component of the Middle East peace process, and it has also been advocated at various times in Northern Ireland, South Africa, Sri Lanka, Cyprus, Bosnia, and the Sudan. Complete separation may be impractical even after decades of conflict and profound patterns of segregation, and indeed it may become an increasingly "attractive" option only if terrorism makes both the status quo and the peace process unstable. In any case, the simple point here is that in discussing postpeace policies in the pages that follow, it may be necessary in some cases to make adjustments that reflect whether power sharing or separation, or some combination of the two, is the central (potentially) shared goal.

In this chapter, I cannot articulate fully a comprehensive set of strategies to deal with the policymaking environment after a flawed peace agreement has been negotiated. Rather, I hope only to be indicative and suggestive, sketching out some elements of a set of responses that take account of both the persisting structural conditions of conflict and the new context generated by an ongoing peace process.

Politics After Peace

Everybody wants peace, or at least a peace process that holds out the prospect of achieving valued ends, but everybody also wants other things just as much or even more. The task of the political process in the post-agreement period is to broaden the coalition supporting peace and to diminish and isolate extremists on both sides. The situation bears a rough resemblance to another "post" situation: the problems confronting new democratic regimes as they try to deal with inherited socioeconomic dysfunctions, an embittered but still powerful remnant of the old regime, and an international environment dominated by surprise, complexity, and an increased reluctance to transfer resources to antagonists who prefer posturing to peace. In these cases, as in the cases of peaceful settlement of ancient conflicts, bitter enemies must learn to live together—not in friendship, but in wary, peaceful coexistence—and must begin to think about new modes of behavior and new ways of thinking about problems. And it is the political process—between the antagonists, within each side, and with external allies—that must facilitate, manage, and nurture these extraordinarily difficult tasks.

Many analysts who have studied the transition to stable democracy have come to a common conclusion. They emphasize the necessity of a politics of accommodation between the new democracy and its supporters and the still powerful forces of the old regime. This may well be an unappetizing, perhaps even immoral, politics of strange bedfellows, but it is premised on the assumption that the new regime is too weak to survive without some cooperation with and from the old elite or that it is easier or less risky to co-opt the old leaders than destroy them, especially if doing the latter could become bloody and economically disastrous. The basic point here is not to retaliate indiscriminately against enemies (seek retribution only for the most heinous things) and not to destroy the basic power position of the old ruling class in one rapid and concerted effort, at least until the new regime is firmly entrenched. For the peace process, the lesson here may be especially appropriate when the two sides must share power in a single country, more so than when they are separating—although the general point about changing mind-sets is critically important even in the latter cases.

The deal worked out between Mandela and de Klerk of South Africa is illustrative. The two leaders, both strong and both with a vision of the future (visions only partially overlapping), focused on a political economy of conciliation not only between blacks and whites, but also between blacks and blacks.[6] The wisdom of not transforming a clear political victory by Mandela and the African National Congress into an assault on the remnants of white economic power and Zulu political power is perhaps best illustrated by what did *not* happen, despite many predictions to the contrary: black-white outbreaks of sustained violence and terrorism (black versus black is clearly more problematic), massive capital flight, and dangerously escalating expectations among the masses of poor blacks. This obviously may not last, especially if economic performance does not begin to improve, but then again it is surprising that it has lasted at all.[7] Note, by contrast, the disastrous failures of policy and insight by Yasir Arafat and Benjamin Netanyahu in the Middle East. Arafat created an administration marked by corruption, inefficiency, cronyism, and brutality, thus losing support among his own people, and he failed to understand that manipulating terrorism to seek political gains was bound to be a disastrous tactic in a very fragile postpeace period. Conversely, Netanyahu attempted to impose a victor's peace that satisfied no one, and he became hostage to an extremist fringe that never accepted the premise of the peace process—an exchange of territory for a secure peace.

A politics of accommodation may require compromise with some very unsavory characters and groups (thus raising the difficult issue of transitional justice), it may lose some support within one's own constituency, and it will certainly limit the resources available to the new regime to reward supporters and to buy off potential dissidents. But it may also buy a period of social peace, and it may keep the economy from quickly collapsing, preventing an effective transition to a (social) market economy. In the context of a fragile peace with high distrust, resources in short supply, expectations on the rise (if gradually, initially), and the need to generate and sustain momentum toward a deepening of the peace process, timing is of the essence. All good things do not go together, some things need to be done first even if they require some short-run sacrifice of important values (like full-scale retribution for past sins or economic efficiency), and the goal is to ensure that there *is* a long-run peace process.

What chance does the shift from a politics of total war to a politics of accommodation have of being implemented? An answer can probably be given only on a case-by-case basis. Nevertheless, there is one crucial variable that is likely to be critical. This concerns whether the elites within a community and between two communities are deeply divided or whether their views are converging and compatible. Sharp elite divisions within a community imply that policy proposals become political footballs and that compromise with external enemies becomes increasingly difficult because dissenting elites will threaten to undermine agreements and arouse domestic constituencies against any compromise, any "sell-out." The problem is compounded if the external enemy is equally divided and if communication across the lines is still minimal or largely limited to a few academics or peaceniks. The point here is that the way policy will be implemented in the postagreement period is likely to be fundamentally affected by the degree of internal and external elite consensus.[8] The Middle East again may represent the worst-case scenario: both communities sharply divided and high degrees of distrust and manipulation in back-channel efforts to communicate across the lines.[9]

Elite consensus is also important because there is usually a significant lag between (some) elite views about the need for peace and the views of the masses. The latter, less aware of the nature of external changes that may be making a compromise agreement more imperative, may still focus on ancient hatreds and the need for a "pure" solution to the conflict: complete victory. If the elite is not unified, and if political leadership is weak and indecisive, dissident elites can easily manipulate mass sentiments to undermine any agreement. Consequently, without elite unity on the need to seek new means to end the conflict (or perhaps sufficient elite power to suppress dissent), progress is bound to be minimal. Moreover, because the struggle is not really about winning support for a specific agreement but, rather, about gaining support for a change in the very nature of the conflict, elite consensus needs to be continually broadened and deepened. This may, upon occasion, be generated from a push from below—the masses demanding peace ahead of an elite consensus on the need for it—and this relatively rare event might compel the elites to accept what might seem a "premature" compromise; more frequently, the push will come from the top if the elites fear losing influence or leverage and consequently seek to generate a "maximum winning coalition" for peace.[10]

We take for granted that reciprocity, each side gaining something that seems of nearly equal value, will be a guiding principle of any agreement. But this criterion needs to be sharply adjusted in the case of a flawed and incomplete peace agreement. Reciprocity must be asymmetrical in both the timing and the extent of achieved benefits. The stronger and usually wealthier party must be willing to defer benefits to the future in order to give the masses of the poorer side quick and, if possible, relatively larger benefits. The stronger must understand the need to weigh generalized and uncertain long-term benefits (establishing the grounds for genuine peaceful coexistence) more significantly and must understand the need not to benefit disproportionately in the short run. (This also implies the need to choose an economic strategy in the immediate postagreement period that does not increase inequalities [within each side or between the two] or destroy the social welfare net of the poor, a point to which I will return.)

In short, the obvious lesson here is that the rules of the political game must change—must be perceived differently by elites on both sides—so that not only cooperation and reconciliation become the norm, but also strengthening of the ancient enemy becomes a potential benefit to oneself. A confrontational, zero-sum perspective must be replaced by an acceptance of the need for (initially asymmetric) shared gains and an awareness of linked fates—lest the outcome return to an even more rapidly deteriorating status quo ante. Arafat and Netanyahu show the difficulty of the task: weak leaders trapped by the limits of their own insight and vision. Perhaps progress in other aspects of the postagreement policy environment will generate a slow learning process even for such leaders, but the damage they do along the way may make this hope irrelevant.

I have said nothing thus far about the political benefits of the creation of, or movement toward, a genuine democracy (or two democracies). This is not because the point is unimportant. Over time, as democracy becomes rooted in what is usually (initially) alien and inhospitable soil, the existence of a stable democracy or joint democracies may facilitate cooperation and the peaceful resolution of conflict. In the short run, however, a newly created democracy, where many of the background conditions that sustain democracy are absent, where some of the potentially negative aspects of democracy may dominate the potentially positive aspects, and where the resort to violence is still taken for granted, might not behave as older democracies behave.[11] Put differently, postagreement regimes will have to deal with rising demands from multiple constituencies without sufficient resources or time.

In these circumstances, the first tasks will be to set priorities, to determine how to allocate costs and benefits, and presumably to make further concessions and gestures of reconciliation toward a partner that many, if not most, still perceive as an enemy. A democracy may perform these tasks relatively well in the long run, or better than the alternatives; but it may not perform these tasks well in the short run, and *some* authoritarian regimes might perform them better. In any case, one central task in these circumstances is to begin meeting the needs of citizens quickly and fairly, and it is far from clear that holding more elections, creating more political parties, and allowing choices (and appeals) to be affected by the electoral cycle will be of much use in this regard. Still, if the alternative is an inept, corrupt, and brutal authoritarian regime, even a weak democracy, warts and all, may begin to look like a better gamble.

The New Security Dilemma

The security issue is present in one way or another in every aspect of protracted conflict, affecting how other issues are perceived and, in turn, being affected by the other issues. In one sense, the dilemma is quite simple. Both sides have very good reasons for not trusting each other and for seeing ulterior, nefarious intentions in whatever the other offers or does. Good faith cannot be taken for granted, and the potential costs of being deceived are so great (in lives lost, resources expended, advantages dissipated, safety threatened) that risk aversion is very high.

Ultimately, the solution to the dilemma may be a learning process that generates the conviction that the other side can be trusted and that there are greater mutual benefits in acting in a trustworthy fashion than in seeking to deceive. But surviving the learning process to get to the ultimate is likely to be very painful, fraught with misconceptions and misunderstandings, and potentially self-destructive—as the post-Oslo peace process in the Middle East illustrates so vividly and so sadly. There is no single policy or perhaps even set of policies that will suffice here to eliminate pervasive mistrust and to isolate and contain the extremist fringes on both sides. But there may be some means available to diminish the scale of the problem and perhaps to diminish the emotional intensity of the reaction to inevitable failures and disappointments.

In the classic Prisoners' Dilemma game, one can try to avoid the double defection box—a loss for both—by collusion, which is not very likely in real-world cases (at least initially) between deeply distrustful players, or by very effective means of detecting violations of commitments and powerful and credible sanctions against violators. This too is unlikely to work when it most needs to work, given the risks and uncertainties, but some confidence-building measures and compliance mechanisms may still be useful. I shall discuss some of these very briefly. One needs also to look separately at the problem of terrorism and the control of extremism because terrorism, always painful but not usually very effective in achieving policy goals, may exert a disproportionately negative effect in the context of a weak peace agreement only reluctantly and tentatively accepted by both sides—and unlikely to produce hoped-for gains quickly. Another potentially critical factor, the role of third parties in providing security guarantees, troops, and resources to increase the willingness of adversaries to take risks, shall be left for discussion in other sections.

Confidence-building measures are largely a procedural response to a substantive problem. But if such a problem cannot be dealt with quickly, procedures can be helpful in a variety of ways. They can decrease risk by providing timely information, they can provide indications about future intentions, they can provide some insurance against the dangers of cheating, and they can gradually build trust about what the other side can, will, or wants to do.[12] Perhaps even more important, they can give a sense of movement, if not yet momentum, to a situation where major breakthroughs are as yet premature. Of course, if one or both sides are merely seeking to destroy the other (or even to use the peace agreement as a stepping-stone to further demands), and if there has been no movement away from a "your gain is my loss" perspective, then the process of building confidence is not likely to be successful and may indeed exacerbate distrust. However, if the parties have conflicting interests but also "share a common aversion to a particular outcome," or have moved toward some recognition of potentially overlapping interests in ending the conflict, confidence-building measures may help to "break the ice."[13] For example, confidence-building measures can help to avert the unintended use of weapons or the escalation of conflict through misperception, misinformation, or miscalculation.[14]

The trouble with such measures is not only that they do not resolve or deal with central issues in the conflict, but also that they are most relevant for interstate conflicts where substantial military forces are deployed directly against each other. They are less relevant in internal conflicts where the threat is more amorphous and indistinct and where the measures implemented may have to be less salient and less immediate in their impact. Still, weaving a new tapestry takes time, and small steps may become more important as negotiations intensify and a new postagreement environment needs to be created. Accordingly, joint cooperation between educational institutions on research projects, or on mutually beneficial economic projects (even if only to discuss and set out alternative perspectives), or—after the agreement—on intelligence and police cooperation may have some small impact on their own but may have an even greater impact in the long run by establishing channels of communication and diminishing demonization of an unfamiliar "other."

In any agreement between distrustful partners, the incentive to defect will be great because of fears about how the other will behave or because the agreement does not produce anticipated benefits. There is thus a strong need to develop credible enforcement strategies against violations; such strategies may indeed be a prerequisite for agreement itself. Presumably, the punishment against the violator must at least be as great as the potential benefits of cheating.[15] But there is one point worth making here. In the real world of conflict resolution, between asymmetrically powerful enemies, punishment or sanctions for noncompliance need to be adjusted to circumstances. There needs to be some awareness of the internal costs (especially to the weaker party) of full and rapid compliance with some agreements and a willingness to punish less than proportionately if continuation of the agreement is more important than demonstrating the *immediate* need for full compliance. In fact, asking for full compliance with the terms of a weak agreement by a weak (and weakened by compromise) leader is to misunderstand what has been achieved and what can be expected; it may be nothing more than a tactic to destroy the agreement by extremists on one or both sides. This hardly means that wholesale noncompliance should be condoned or ignored, since it obviously could destroy the agreement, but it does suggest a more nuanced, phased, or graded application of sanctions—and expectation of results. Sanctions may be theoretically justified but practically disastrous if they demand that a weak leader does more than is possible, thus destroying his credibility with *both* peace parties and giving the extremists the very outcome they seek: a return to violence and war in pursuit of total victory.

By their very nature, weak peace agreements between parties that are themselves deeply divided give extremists great influence and leverage. In virtually all efforts to end protracted conflicts, moderates on both sides have been threatened, constrained, and frequently outbid by small groups of dedicated terrorists, as willing to use violence against their own community as against the enemy. Violence against their own may seem necessary, especially if the community is beginning to tire of endless conflict, because terrorist groups cannot survive over a long period unless they have a safe haven among their own—the only means to avoid the kind of isolation that increases vulnerability to counterterrorist tactics.[16] Moreover, it is extremely difficult to seek compromises with men and women for whom "politics is a dirty word" not only because it is the willingness to use violence that gives the terrorist a role and a status that would obviously disappear with peace, but also because "compromise" may be a meaningless term to people driven by religious or ideological motives.[17] One needs also to remember that, while terrorism may reflect frustration over the failure to achieve gains by nonviolent means, the men (and women) of violence may also be reluctant to give up the one thing that gives them stature and respect: the willingness to kill and to be killed. The seeming absence of alternatives brings to mind an old Arab proverb: "When the only tool you have at hand is a hammer, every problem looks like a nail."

This suggests why the conventional police measures to deter violent actions, punish the guilty, and—sometimes—inflict painful retaliatory measures on the terrorists or their communities are likely to be only episodically successful. Indeed, in espousing such tactics and becoming as brutal and violent as the terrorists themselves—as in Algeria, Egypt, or Turkey—one may make the terrorist and the community he or she hides in pay a high price for their actions, but it may also be counterproductive in that it diminishes the prospects of future agreement and it undermines the rule of law in the retaliating community. Vile acts generate more vile acts, the cycle of extremism continues, and each side confirms that the other is evil. The "politics of the last atrocity" continues.

Terrorism, which is rarely successful in achieving central goals, is nonetheless a critically important issue in the context of stabilizing and deepening a weak and tentative peace agreement. This is because it deepens the skepticism of the doubters and undermines the support for the peace constituency on both sides. Distrust that needs to be ameliorated is instead hardened, especially on the government side, as it feels compelled to react disproportionately—to try to stem the dissipation of support—and to reject further compromises. It does not help very much in these circumstances to be told that support for terrorism would decline if the government or the most powerful side would seek to remove more grievances more rapidly: if it were in fact able to do that, we would be dealing with the aftermath of a strong peace.

Are there any means available other than police tactics to deal with this situation? Nothing looks very promising. For example, it clearly makes sense to try to split the extremist community by offering a deal to one or another subgroup, but a deal may not be possible or may be too costly. Still, Charles de Gaulle did succeed in turning the Organisation Armée Secrète (OAS) against itself by offering honorable terms to some of its "moderates," but de Gaulle's leverage was great and the OAS had very minimal public support. By contrast, Mandela has thus far managed to contain and limit black-on-black violence by not challenging the basic power position of the Zulu leadership in its own domain. But a politics of conciliation will probably work only as long as there are enough resources around to satisfy everyone's needs. When that is no longer true, and when Mandela passes from the political scene, a nasty conflict may break out that will undermine the conciliation process. The tactics in both of these cases are similar: make the extremists (or some of them) an attractive enough offer (jobs for the elite, a place in the electoral process, economic benefits, foreign aid) to tempt all but the truest of believers to "give peace a chance," as bumper-sticker slogans used to say. This might splinter the rejectionist front, diminish the amount of terrorism that occurs, and give both sides some breathing space to strengthen commitments to peace. One crucial problem, apart from the fact that many in the "community of violence" will not be tempted, is that a tempting offer to (some) terrorists may split one's own side or be used by the extremists merely as a platform for new demands or as a means of acquiring power via the electoral process and then establishing an extremist state.

In the last analysis, given the ease with which dedicated terrorists can strike, and given the (sometimes ambivalent) support of the community within which he or she resides, it seems likely that peace will have to be made and strengthened in spite of terrorism. Extremism cannot easily be stopped on its own terms, but, if the other aspects of the postpeace environment can be strengthened, terrorism may become increasingly marginalized. The broader community that provides the terrorist a safe haven will begin to turn against terror only as it achieves gains that it wants to protect, begins to feel that it can live with the other side in peace, and has some hopes for continued progress in the future. But, as the Middle East illustrates, achieving these goals when resources are scarce, when one's own leaders are inept and corrupt, when the other side will accept peace only on its own terms, and when the outside world is losing interest will be extraordinarily difficult. This suggests that terrorism may undermine the other elements of a postpeace strategy before the peace process can undermine the terrorists.

The Political Economy of Survival

The economic costs of protracted conflict are extraordinarily high: high levels of military expenditure, heavy debt burdens (especially if weaponry has to be imported), low levels of intraregional trade, a weak or nonexistent regional infrastructure, high levels of inefficiency, low levels of tourism—the list could go on and on.[18] For the most part, the potential gains from peace are simply the obverse of the costs. One should not, however, assume that the economic benefits of peace will be automatic, rapid, or equitable. Most of the benefits, at least in the long run, are likely to go to those who reform and liberalize their domestic economies, and it is far from certain that this will be attempted even if the security threat is diminished, which is unlikely in the short run. After all, authoritarian leaders or the leaders of rebellious groups usually arm to protect themselves as much as to fight the enemy. This set of calculations is unlikely to be affected by a weak peace agreement and may indeed generate even greater short-run fears and insecurities. In addition, since there is no guarantee that the peace will be durable, and since there are unlikely to be major economic (and political) reforms undertaken in response to a "cold" or fragile peace, the "peace dividend" may be a long time coming. If an internal threat does become more salient after peace, as protests against deteriorating standards of living and disappointed expectations are not constrained by the need to maintain unity against the common enemy, then the whole reform process might grind to a halt, and one or both sides might continue to use economic resources to pay off supporters and bribe opponents, not to create a new and more efficient economic structure. A weak peace may therefore generate internal instability and inappropriate economic choices.[19] One might also note that regional economic cooperation, a great hope (along with new "Marshall Plans") of most peacemakers, is unlikely to produce many near-term benefits because the size of most regional markets is small, infrastructure is inadequate, intraregional trade is very limited and likely to remain so for some time, and the economic fit between the two sides is sometimes not very complementary.[20]

Much of the economic literature on the peace process and its aftermath simply extrapolates from the more general arguments about the benefits of market-oriented reforms. But this perspective may very well be insufficiently contextual or political in the context of the need to devise prudent economic policies after a weak peace has been negotiated. Given that the peace agreement will not have resolved many central issues and that it will not (usually) reflect major improvements in many of the structural conditions of conflict (discussed in Chapter 1), significant economic inequalities will still be present, resentments and bitterness will still be profound, and expectations of some kind of *rapid* dividend from peace will surely be growing. These expectations are unlikely to be revolutionary, but they are certainly likely to be powerful enough to demand an effective response (evidence of benign intentions toward quality of life issues, a willingness to share both the benefits that may ensue and the deprivations that must be endured, and clear attempts to diminish corruption), without which the peace itself will be endangered, not to mention the incumbent political leadership.[21] This implies that the preeminent aim during the immediate postagreement period is not merely to establish the conditions for long-term prosperity—as crucial as that is—but to respond quickly and fairly to the desire of the masses for felt improvements in their standard of living. The best in economic terms may be the enemy of the necessary in political terms. In other words, to maintain and deepen the momentum for peace, the masses must be given a stake in that peace, something that they are averse to losing and that they hope will form the basis for further progress. This is what Arafat's Palestinian National Authority has failed utterly to do, thus losing support and legitimacy among the Palestinian people.

The problem with market-oriented reforms, especially in poor and deeply divided societies, is that they may redistribute costs and benefits inequitably, they may increase unemployment (particularly among the unskilled), they may reduce subsidies that are critical for the masses, and they may injure vested interests that have benefited from the old economic order but whose support is necessary in the new order. Sharp budget cuts may also damage the ability of the political leadership to provide vital services, and the attempt to increase taxes to pay for services may generate more resentment (and corruption) than revenues. Moreover, when aid donors and international financial institutions focus primarily on efficiency and accountability in aid disbursement, and not on the need for immediate poverty alleviation and job creation, they may be responding prudently in terms of their own rules and their own experience in the Third World (prudently in terms of reasonable fears of corruption and incompetence), but they may undermine the very stability and support that are crucial if long-run growth rates are to improve, if domestic and foreign investment are to be attracted, and if flight capital is to be induced to return. There is a clash of norms and rules here—between the accountability and efficiency demanded by the donors and the survival ethic of the peacemakers—but the conflict can be ameliorated by the awareness that it exists, that compromise between two conflicting goods is necessary, that timing is of the essence, and that there are some trade-offs that meet present political and psychological needs with relatively less damage to future economic prospects.

Still, for the moment, in the Middle East, increasingly in South Africa, and perhaps in Bosnia, the external donors *and* the internal recipients have achieved the worst outcome by promising much and delivering little—blaming each other for the miserable results.[22] The very difficult balancing act between ensuring that the peace agreement will survive and deepen and that the grounds for long-term economic viability are established reasonably quickly and firmly has not been effectively achieved. Instead, vacillation between the extremes, halfhearted and inconsistent implementation of one or another rhetorical "solution," and mutual recrimination have become the norm, especially in the Middle East. The simple point that economic aid needs to be used politically in the short run, or at least economic cost, in order to ensure that there will be something left in the long run to enjoy the benefits of economic reform has been lost from sight or treated in a simplistic either/or fashion. One might also note here that, in the "great debate" between shock treatment and gradualism as the most effective means of converting to a market orientation, there is a strong argument for gradualism in the postpeace environment: shock treatment is likely to generate inequitable short-run results, it may increase corruption, and it may undermine support for a fragile peace, even if—and this is a big if—it generates the promised and rapid benefits. The rationale for shock treatment is that rapid and comprehensive reforms will produce significant benefits at less long-run cost than gradual and piecemeal reforms. This may well be true in some cases (Poland in contrast to the Czech Republic), but in the context of fragile peace, the benefits are unlikely to be produced quickly enough, the costs will be severe and will diminish the likelihood of broadening the coalition for peace (especially when it most needs to be broadened), and external aid and investment are unlikely to be either rapid enough or generous enough.

Toward Reconciliation:
Psychological Aspects and Transitional Justice

Reconciliation is the long-term goal at the end of any process of conflict resolution. Since reconciliation requires subjective and objective changes by both parties to a conflict, and since this may never occur or may occur at different rates and to different degrees, it is important to emphasize the obvious point that peace can be negotiated—and perhaps even deepened—without reconciliation or with very limited reconciliation if interests overlap sufficiently, if means are available to lower the risks of cheating, or if other pressures toward peace are strong enough. Still, even slow and in-consistent movement toward reconciliation may provide important support for the peace process (and for the aftermath of peace), and total failure at reconciliation will guarantee a very cold peace and perhaps a return to vi-olent conflict.

Are there steps that can be taken to accelerate or to facilitate the process of reconciliation during the postagreement period? It is during this period that the need for reconciliation is greatest, given the continuing presence of distrust, bitterness, and demonization of the other, but its like-lihood is smallest. The psychological traumas of the past are still powerful because the past is neither forgotten nor forgiven, whatever the nature of the peace agreement.[23] The collective turning from the past, which must underlay the process of reconciliation, is not likely to have begun and may indeed begin only after other aspects of the peace produce results that seem to indicate that peace is worthwhile and here to stay.

In these circumstances, it is of course naive to expect rapid rap-prochement, a mistake the Israelis made after the Camp David negotia-tions. Illusions about how much has changed or can change after a tenta-tive peace agreement may undermine the agreement itself by generating prematurely disappointed expectations, continued distrust of the other's in-tentions, and a quick return to the zero-sum, nothing-has-changed views of the past. And if fears about the other persist, the tendency to define group identity in terms of hatred for the other side will also persist.[24] Neverthe-less, although developing realistic expectations and altering the image of the enemy will take time, there are some things that can be done in the short run to accelerate the transition and to deepen what Herbert Kelman calls "working trust" between ancient enemies.

Let us begin by noting the contrasting behavior of Germany and Japan after World War II. Germany officially and repeatedly apologized for its behavior, made clear that the government and most citizens—with some notable neo-Nazi exceptions—were aware that they had profoundly vio-lated the norms of the international community, offered reparations for some of its crimes, and sought some degree of forgiveness for its actions, at least for subsequent generations. This repentance was *one* important fac-tor facilitating Germany's full reentrance into the community of nations. Conversely, Japan has behaved completely differently. Its apologies have been reluctant and ambiguous, it has given little convincing evidence that it feels the need to be forgiven, and its tentative statements of sorrow have elicited more resentment at home than applause abroad. As a result, the shadow of World War II still hangs over Japan, it is despised and feared by many of its former Asian victims, and its successes are resented. And there have been other cases in Eastern Europe, Asia Minor, and the Middle East where the unwillingness to apologize for violating acceptable standards of behavior has allowed conflicts to fester and reignite with extraordinary bitterness.

For hard-nosed realists or for analysts content to rely on an interest-based approach to peacemaking, the psychological aspects of reconciliation and the potential benefits of apologizing for past sins may appear irrelevant or naive. But, since there is obviously an important psychological or emotional component of protracted conflicts, there is surely likely to be an equally important psychological or emotional component to their resolution. This is not to argue, of course, that an emphasis on such factors is superior to, or should supplant, an interest-based approach; rather, they need each other. I cannot here deal with these issues in detailed fashion, not only because of their complexity, but also because of the wide variety of psychological or psychocultural theories that might provide useful insights and guidance. I shall instead, in an illustrative fashion, discuss very briefly some arguments that relate to collective expressions of guilt, apology, and reconciliation.

Thomas Scheff has argued that, in any prolonged conflict, a cycle of insult, humiliation, and revenge destroys human bonds and that shame—one of the key bonds—causes the escalation of conflict and thus a renewed cycle of anger, insults, and aggression.[25] The cycle entraps both sides in a conflict that can easily end in catastrophe. Scheff suggests that reconciliation may be hastened by an acknowledgment of interdependence—of the need to live together—and a willingness to apologize for previous transgressions.[26] Donald Shriver also argues that forgiveness is crucial in terms of ending cycles of violence and retaliation, a forgiveness in which both see that a wrong has been done, that the transgressor must apologize for his and her actions and offer appropriate compensation, and that the victim will therefore abandon vengeance and revenge to reestablish a relationship of coexistence, "a civil relationship between strangers."[27] Scheff and Shriver thus focus on the notion of apology, of expressing sorrow for a wrongful act and seeking forgiveness for it, which permits the sinners—bar the ones convicted of crimes against humanity—to be reintegrated into a community of states or individuals.[28] Needless to say, if the sorrow that drives an apology is not felt, or if it seems cynical and contrived, the apology itself will fail and the conflict will continue and perhaps even deepen.

One needs to be careful not to overstate the value of apology. Other factors, including fear, anger, and hard conflicts of interest, may be as or even more important in sustaining a conflict, and apology itself can fail in an atmosphere of profound distrust and hatred. Yet it is also important to recognize how alienated and conflictual a relationship can become when one or both sides deny the legitimacy of the other's grievances and/or refuse to acknowledge guilt or the need to apologize. In such circumstances, apparently trivial sins of omission—failing to denounce terrorist actions, failing to acknowledge responsibility for officially sanctioned normative violations, and so forth—can assume a life of their own, reappearing as justifications for further sins. If one seeks to establish a new relationship between ancient enemies, it helps to begin by clarifying the record, compensating for past sins, and setting off with not a completely new relationship—the evils of the past may be forgiven but not forgotten—but at least a relationship that has been cleared of its worst grievances. Small steps toward reconciliation may be a useful way of supporting large steps toward political accommodation.[29]

* * *

Linked to, but separate from, the psychological aspects of reconciliation is the issue of transitional justice. What should be done about individuals who have committed crimes against humanity before a peace agreement has been negotiated? In the literature on transitions to democracy, where a similar problem has arisen, effective punishment has been rare and, as Samuel Huntington notes, "justice was a function of political power."[30] The dilemmas are acute in both cases because there is a sharp clash between the need to pursue a politics of accommodation to end the conflict and widen the constituency for peace (and democracy) and the need to punish the guilty to accelerate the process of psychological healing. As a kind of compromise, various truth commissions have been established in South Africa and elsewhere, presumably in the hope that revelation of the truth, combined with amnesty, will be a partially effective substitute for the quest for justice and the ensuing dangers of instability. It is far from clear that this has resolved or will resolve either the political or psychological dilemmas implicit in being forced to choose between prosecution of, or amnesty for, the guilty.

Pragmatists tend to favor accommodation over justice on the apparently sensible notion that without accommodation neither peace nor democracy will survive—and, in turn, any institution to seek or ensure justice. There are, however, several reasons to believe that short-run pragmatism may generate long-run instability—that is, the resumption of a conflict that has continued to fester. In the first place, as many have argued, if there is no retribution for the guilty, the victims and their friends will go on blaming the demonized enemy group—not merely the individual victimizers—thus ensuring continued bitterness and an endless cycle of generalized retaliation.[31] In the second place, psychologically, the victimized individual and the victimized group need to have their losses recognized by the enemy so that their "grief is validated" and their self-esteem is raised.[32] Finally, for both new democracies and new peace agreements, there is a clear political need to show citizens that things have indeed changed and that something more than new labels on old practices is in store.[33]

These comments do not resolve the dilemma, nor are they meant to imply that accommodation is less important than justice. Rather, the simple point is that short-run accommodation may be bought at too high a cost if it rationalizes policies that allow resentments to fester and grow and if it promotes policies that make long-run reconciliation more difficult. In the end, decisions or trade-offs between different values will have to be made on a case-by-case basis, but two rough rules of thumb may be useful guides: (1) there can be no amnesty for leaders who are complicit in crimes against humanity, or the rule of law will become a farce; and (2) establishing the truth may help individuals to begin mourning their losses, but they will not be able to forgive, and thus begin the process of reconciliation, if the other side does not seem willing or able to apologize for inflicting wrongs, no matter how difficult or painful that apology may be.

In Fear of Peace

The costs of protracted conflicts are devastating: among other things, the brutal and unending violence; the tensions and traumas of living in fear in a neighborhood of hatred; the perversion of civil values, as unsavory tactics generate more unsavory tactics and thus the gradual destruction of the rule of law; the economic losses attendant on high levels of military expenditures and low levels of foreign investment and regional cooperation; the shame of pariah status; and the inability to be accepted as an "ordinary" state. Why, then, with people so desperate to find a way out or even to see a glimmer of hope, has it been so difficult to negotiate a compromise more bearable than an ugly status quo?

One critical explanatory factor has been the ability of both sides to adapt to an ugly status quo that still seems preferable to relinquishing the deeply held and sometimes theologically ordained maximalist goals of the past. The limited offers that weak leaders can make to each other and the uncertainty that such offers will produce enough benefits (especially quickly) or become the building blocks for further progress imply that the structural conditions that have sustained the conflict persist or change too slowly to generate a breakthrough. Consequently, a weak peace, frequently generated by external pressures on weak leaders, rarely engenders a basic shift in the calculus of conflict, and each side continues to fear that compromises will lead only to new demands or to an appearance of weakness. For both sides, what can be offered and what can be gotten seem insufficient, and it seems less dangerous to complain bitterly about the status quo but to risk little to change it. These doubts and fears are buttressed by the negotiating failures of the past and by the fear that promises of external aid to decrease the risks of compromise will not arrive quickly enough or in sufficient depth to protect leaders against the disappointed expectations of their followers. "After the peace" thus has many continuities with "before the peace," but it entails some differences also—consequential differences that are, however, only if all the key actors adjust and adapt their behavior to a situation that mixes together old constraints and some new opportunities.

Another implication of this argument is that there is bound to be a large gap between what the peace negotiations are about (the issues on the top of the current political agenda between both sides) and what the conflict has been and continues to be about (the deep-seated structural conditions discussed in Chapter 1). The pace at which this gap can be diminished will determine whether and how quickly genuine peace can be established. This will obviously be an extraordinarily difficult task not only because of the inherited problems of the past, but also because external powers may rapidly lose interest and patience after the peace agreement has been negotiated and because internal splits within each coalition may compel one or both sides to increase demands too quickly or to slow implementation of agreed terms.

The argument here is *not* that efforts to reach flawed and tentative peace agreements should be abandoned until that halcyon day when all or most of the structural conditions that have sustained the conflict have been diminished in force. That would set a utopian standard for peace; it would fail to recognize that structural conditions can be improved only after a peace process has begun; and it would ignore the small, but potentially important, gains from any break in the cycle of violence, retaliation, and hatred. Still, by the same token, it should not be automatically assumed that any agreement, no matter how flawed, is better than the status quo because some agreements may make things worse if they increase expectations unrealistically (which increases support for extremist violence as expectations are disappointed) or if the agreement creates a moral hazard in that all think they can now relax and that the momentum toward peace is inexorable. In fact, all concerned need to be aware of the fragile nature of peace, they need to be careful not to promise too much too soon (and maybe avoid premature celebrations on the White House lawn, which serve U.S. interests more than they serve peace), and they need to recognize and to make clear to followers that dreams of rapid normalization of relations are dangerous because they are bound to be disappointed (as after Camp David or the more recent Israeli-Jordanian peace talks). A weak peace agreement and an unstable peace process may begin movement in a new direction and may begin to chip away at the encrustations of the past, but they cannot produce instant miracles of reconciliation.

A weak peace agreement obviously needs to be consolidated. A kind of staged deepening is imperative. In the first stage, emphasis has to be on the survival of the agreement itself (and whatever institutions it has created), which means a focus on satisfying the most salient expectations of the masses (jobs, education, health, etc.), on carefully implementing and monitoring compliance with existing agreements, on diminishing and controlling terrorist actions, and on changing mind-sets (at least among the elites) toward cooperation and the notion of hanging together or hanging separately. In the second stage, the onset of which will depend on progress in the first stage, attention needs to turn to the effort to establish the long-term basis for stability by moving more rapidly toward democracy and the market, revising educational texts and practices to avoid mutual demonization, and creating joint institutions in areas such as security, education, and economic cooperation. In the third stage, the spread of prosperity and the development of some elements of a democratic culture—among other things—will help to establish the grounds for normalization, mutually beneficial cooperation, effective procedures for dispute settlement, and psychological reinforcement of more positive images of the other.

In the earlier stages, the stronger party needs to be willing to make short-term sacrifices to increase the possibility of joint long-term benefits. One might even suggest that if both parties, initially mostly the stronger party, are not willing to accept outcomes that strengthen the other side, even at some *bearable* cost to oneself, they have not yet made the crucial psychological adjustment necessary to deepen the peace process and to move slowly toward peaceful coexistence. The problem, of course, is that a weak peace agreement can make only a minimal contribution to these efforts. A deeper peace will require making the peace agreement itself only one part of a wider effort to alter how both sides think about each other—what they take for granted, what seems to "stand to reason."

The existential question in most peace processes that attempt to end protracted conflicts is whether it is worth the risk to give up more than one really wants to give in order to reach an agreement that might fail, that might even make matters worse, but that also might begin the long process of reconciliation. There can never be a clear or simple answer to this question because one is never "getting to yes" in such circumstances but, rather, only "getting to maybe." And yet battle fatigue, awareness of what is going on elsewhere, an immense desire to begin living normal lives, a growing sense that the status quo is becoming unsustainable, and growing external political and economic pressures all suggest that the iceberg is finally beginning to crack in many apparently insoluble conflicts—that growing numbers are beginning to think about the unthinkable. Extremists will resist melting the iceberg further and faster, but extremists may not be as powerful as they seem, and they will not receive support from the masses if the latter are given something they want to preserve.

In short, some efforts at peace may fail—as with the badly designed and foolishly negotiated Oslo Agreements between Israel and the Palestinians—but the peace process itself is here to stay, and the next round or the round after that is likely to be more successful if the negotiators do not forget how deep the roots of conflict run and that the agenda of the moment is only the surface manifestation of a more profound struggle, one that may be diminished with some speed but not resolved.

* * *

In the first chapter of this volume, I suggested that the period after a weak peace agreement has been signed is sufficiently distinct to warrant independent analysis. That argument, at best, has only been very tentatively elucidated here, in part because it is still necessary to focus on getting to peace in all too many cases and in part because we do not as yet have a consensus on what needs to be done "after the peace." However, let me restate some of the changes in perceptions, attitudes, and behavior that seem appropriate for the postpeace period, even if these are as yet incomplete and tentative: elites on both sides must abandon the mentalities of the past and recognize that they must hang together or separately; different rhetorics for different audiences must be abandoned because they generate continued mistrust; the stronger must be willing to make short-run sacrifices out of self-interest, not altruism, and the weaker side needs to make genuine efforts to control extremists, corruption, and brutality—to opt for open accountability and not the closed tactics of a revolutionary group; economic policy must balance efficiency and equity but especially be willing to sacrifice some of the former to ensure that expectations can be managed in the short run and that the peace agreement survives; a start needs to be made on creating joint institutions to generate cross-group cooperation and familiarity, and each group needs to begin revising partisan histories and educational processes; some of the new offices and new opportunities should be reserved for, or offered to, individuals or groups who are willing to abandon violence; apologies for past sins and mistakes are crucial; and the vexing issue of punishment—which has no completely satisfactory solution—must be dealt with in a way that at least begins to dissipate bitterness and hatred and that does not allow them to fester and grow. In sum, one seeks to refashion a vision of the conflict, so that peace can be strengthened and reconciliation can begin.

Notes

1. For an argument in favor of a high-risk, high-gain strategy in the Middle East, see Ian S. Lustick, "Necessary Risks: Lessons for the Israeli-Palestinian Peace Process from Ireland and Algeria," *Middle East Policy* 3, no. 3 (1994): 42ff. I disagree with Lustick's argument because it seems to me that the very context of peacemaking in protracted conflicts implies that a low-risk, low-gain strategy will be chosen—unless much stronger leaders and much stronger external pressures make a different choice or risk seem necessary.

2. The need for time is also implicit in Edward Moxon-Browne's comment on Northern Ireland: "To seek a solution to *the* Northern Ireland problem is to pursue a mirage in the desert: a better ploy would be to irrigate the desert until the landscape looks more inviting" (quoted in John Whyte, *Interpreting Northern Ireland* [Oxford: Clarendon, 1990], p. 237). My argument, which follows below, is somewhat different: we certainly need to "irrigate the desert," but we need also to work on strengthening and deepening the peace process while the irrigation goes on.

3. For a different version of this argument in reference to Northern Ireland, see Whyte, *Interpreting Northern Ireland*, pp. 235ff.

4. There is a vast literature on risk, but I have benefited from reading Alan C. Lamborn, "Risk and Foreign Policy Choice," *International Studies Quarterly* 29, no. 4 (December 1985): 385–410, and Kenneth R. MacCrimmon and Donald A. Wehrung, with W. T. Stanbury, *Taking Risks: The Management of Uncertainty* (New York: Free Press, 1986).

5. On various procedural mechanisms to increase incentives to cooperate, see Donald Horowitz, "Conflict and the Incentives to Political Accommodation," in Dermot Keogh and Michael H. Haltzel, eds., *Northern Ireland and the Politics of Reconciliation* (Cambridge: Cambridge University Press, 1993), pp. 173–188.

6. See Martin J. Murray, "Humanizing or Modernizing Capitalism? The 'New' South Africa at the Crossroads," unpublished manuscript, n.d., p. 10. I thank Professor Murray for letting me see his paper.

7. On the South African peace process, see Patti Waldmeir, *Anatomy of a Miracle: The End of Apartheid and the Birth of the New South Africa* (New York: W. W. Norton and Co., 1997).

8. Note that I am *not* arguing that elite unity is the only factor affecting implementation or that agreements unbolstered by such unity are doomed to failure. Rather, the point is that it is an important but frequently ignored factor. Other factors that may be of equal importance include the nature of the policy (for example, redistributive policies are inherently conflictual) and the availability of resources.

9. Elite "pacts"—useful in some contexts—may be futile in such circumstances. In any case, the more important point, frequently ignored in the literature on pacts, is what the pact is about. If we have an elite pact that registers a commitment to a politics of accommodation, but if the "accommodation" is merely to split the spoils between the old and the new ruling elite, then the pact will be a disaster, a facade for a return to the past with new labels.

10. Fear of losing support among the masses, tired of a bloody stalemate and declining standards of living, may have had some "bottom-up" effects in both Northern Ireland and the Middle East—but it is unclear how effective reluctant or ambivalent elites will be as peacemakers.

11. For my own comments on the strengths and weaknesses of democracy in such circumstances, see my two essays in Edy Kaufman, Shukri Abed, and Robert L. Rothstein, eds., *Democracy, Peace, and the Israeli-Palestinian Conflict* (Boulder, Colo.: Lynne Rienner, 1993), and "Democracy in the Third World: Definitional Dilemmas," in David Garnham and Mark Tessler, eds., *Democracy, War, and Peace in the Middle East* (Bloomington: University of Indiana Press, 1995).

12. See especially Janice Gross Stein, "Confidence Building and Dilemmas of Cooperation: The Egyptian-Israeli Experiment," in Gabriel Ben-Dor and David B. Dewitt, eds., *Confidence Building Measures in the Middle East* (Boulder, Colo.: Westview, 1994), pp. 199–217.

13. Ibid., p. 200.

14. Howard Adelman, "Towards a Confidence Transformational Dynamic," in Ben-Dor and Dewitt, eds., *Confidence Building Measures,* p. 311.

15. See George W. Downs, David M. Rocke, and Peter N. Barsoom, "Is the 'No-Fault' Theory of Compliance Too Good to Be True? The Role of Enforcement in Regulatory Regimes," paper prepared for the annual meeting of the International Studies Association, Chicago, February 1994. Note the difficulty of measuring proportionality in conflict circumstances. Even the General Agreement on Tariffs and Trade and the World Trade Organization, where proportionality can sometimes be measured in quantitative terms, have had difficulties when compelled to measure compensation across different issues or sectors.

16. For an excellent analysis of the Irish Republican Army's use of violence, see M. L. R. Smith, *Fighting for Ireland? The Military Strategy of the Irish Republican Movement* (London: Routledge, 1995).

17. For the quoted phrase, see Kevin Toolis, "Why the IRA Stopped Talking," *New York Times*, February 21, 1996, p. A19.

18. For the Middle East, see the various essays in Stanley Fischer, Dani Rodrik, and Elias Tuma, eds., *The Economics of Middle East Peace: Views from the Region* (Cambridge, Mass.: MIT Press, 1994). See also part 3 of Krishna Kumar, ed., *Rebuilding Societies After Civil War* (Boulder, Colo.: Lynne Rienner, 1997); and Nicole Ball, with Tammy Halevy, *Making Peace Work: The Role of the International Development Community* (Washington, D.C.: Overseas Development Council, 1996).

19. Fischer et al., eds., *The Economics of Middle East Peace*, pp. 1–16.

20. Note the limited economic benefits that have ensued for either Egypt or Israel from the "cold peace" that has followed Camp David—although the increases in foreign aid may have been relatively more beneficial to Egypt.

21. If expectations were truly revolutionary, there would be no way of meeting them. However, if South Africa is a guide, expectations may remain moderate because people understand that reform will take time and that the government is now on their side—a crucial point for people who have distrusted politicians and the political process. See Bill Keller, "After Apartheid, Change Lags Behind Expectations," *New York Times*, April 27, 1995, pp. A1 and A10.

22. For a similar point in regard to the Middle East, see Patrick Clawson, "Mideast Economies After the Israel-PLO Handshake," *Journal of International Affairs* 48, no. 1 (summer 1994): 163.

23. See Donald W. Shriver Jr., *An Ethic for Enemies: Forgiveness in Politics* (New York: Oxford University Press, 1995), pp. 4–8.

24. Interesting on this is Vamik D. Volkan, *The Need to Have Enemies and Allies: From Clinical Practice to International Relations* (Northvale, N.J.: Jason Aronson, 1988).

25. Thomas J. Scheff, *Bloody Revenge: Emotions, Nationalism, and War* (Boulder, Colo.: Westview, 1994), pp. 3–6.

26. *Ibid.*, pp. 131–132.

27. Shriver, *An Ethic for Enemies*, p. 8. See also Volkan, *The Need to Have Enemies and Allies*, p. 173.

28. Much of their work on apology draws on Nicholas Tavuchis, *Mea Culpa: A Sociology of Apology and Reconciliation* (Stanford, Calif.: Stanford University Press, 1991).

29. Progress may also be facilitated if leaders watch their rhetoric closely. The tendency of some—Arafat is an especially bad example—to say one thing in public and another in ostensibly private circumstances only generates distrust and cynicism, whatever the short-run political benefits for the leader. Other efforts to

clarify intentions, create joint projects, and develop new and shared norms may also help.

30. Samuel P. Huntington, *The Third Wave* (Norman: University of Oklahoma Press, 1991), p. 228.

31. See, for example, Aryeh Neier, "What Should Be Done About the Guilty?" *New York Review of Books*, February 1, 1990, pp. 34ff.

32. See Volkan, *The Need to Have Enemies and Allies*, pp. 172ff. The point here is important because absence of respect is one of the most deeply felt charges or indictments of the "other"—especially a stronger other—in these conflicts.

33. A similar point is made by Neal J. Kritz, "The Dilemmas of Transitional Justice," in his edited collection *Transitional Justice: Review Sampler* (Washington, D.C.: United States Institute of Peace Press, 1995), p. xiii. The point here is essentially educational. Citizens who have developed a visceral distrust of politics and who are unfamiliar with, or skeptical about, the theory and practice of democracy may benefit from and learn from a clear illustration of the rule of law at work. This effort will obviously be imperfect in that some criminals and criminal activities are bound to go unpunished, but if the major violators are punished, it may suffice.

Selected Bibliography

Adams, Gerry, *The Politics of Irish Freedom* (Dingle: Brandon Books, 1986).

Aggestam, K., *Two-Track Diplomacy: Negotiations Between Israel and the PLO Through Open and Secret Channels* (Jerusalem: Hebrew University Press, 1996).

Akenson, Donald Harman, *God's Peoples: Covenant and Land in South Africa, Israel, and Northern Ireland* (Ithaca, N.Y.: Cornell University Press, 1992).

Alpher, Y., *The Netanyahu Government and the Israeli-Arab Peace Process: The First Half Year,* no. 4 (London: Institute for Jewish Policy Research, 1997).

Apter, David, *Democracy, Violence, and Emancipatory Movements: Notes for a Theory of Inversionary Discourse* (Geneva: United Nations Research Institute for Social Development, 1997).

———, ed., *The Legitimization of Violence* (London: Macmillan, 1997).

Arthur, Paul, and Keith Jeffrey, *Northern Ireland Since 1968* (London: Blackwell, 1988).

Asmal, Kader, *Victims, Survivors, and Citizens: Human Rights, Reparations, and Reconciliation* (Cape Town, South Africa: University of Western Cape, 1992).

Aughey, Arthur, *Under Siege* (London: Hurst, 1989).

Aughey, Arthur, and Duncan Morrow, eds., *Northern Ireland Politics* (New York: Longman, 1996).

Awartani, Hisham, "Palestinian-Israeli Economic Relations: Is Cooperation Possible?" in Stanley Fischer, Dani Rodrik, and Elias Tuma, eds., *The Economics of Middle East Peace: Views from the Region* (Cambridge, Mass.: MIT Press, 1994).

Ball, Nicole, *Pressing for Peace: Can Aid Induce Reform?* (Washington, D.C.: Overseas Development Council, 1992).

Ball, Nicole, with Tammy Halevy, *Making Peace Work: The Role of the International Development Community* (Washington, D.C.: Overseas Development Council, 1996).

Barzilai, Gad, *Wars, Internal Conflicts, and Political Order* (Albany: State University of New York Press, 1996).

Ben-Dor, Gabriel, and David B. Dewitt, eds., *Confidence Building Measures in the Middle East* (Boulder, Colo.: Westview, 1994).

249

Berdal, Mats R., *Disarmament and Demobilisation After Civil Wars: Arms, Soldiers, and the Termination of Armed Conflicts,* Adelphi Paper No. 303 (London: Oxford University Press, August 1996).

Bew, Paul, Peter Gibbon, and Henry Patterson, *The State of Northern Ireland, 1921–72: Political Forces and Social Classes* (Manchester: Manchester University Press, 1979).

Bland, Byron, *Marching and Rising: The Rituals of Small Differences and Great Violence in Northern Ireland* (Stanford, Calif.: Center for International Security and Arms Control, Stanford University: 1996).

Brown, Michael E., Owen R. Cote Jr., Sean M. Lynn-Jones, and Steven E. Miller, eds., *Nationalism and Ethnic Conflict* (Cambridge, Mass.: MIT Press, 1997).

Bryant, Ralph, *International Coordination of National Stabilization Policies* (Washington, D.C.: Brookings Institution, 1992).

Budge, Ian, and Cornelius O'Leary, *Belfast: Approach to Crisis. A Study of Belfast Politics, 1613–1970* (London: Macmillan, 1973).

Clarity, James F., "As More Catholics Turn Against IRA the Number of Police Informers Rises," *New York Times,* January 14, 1997, p. 7.

Clawson, Patrick, "Mideast Economies After the Israel-PLO Handshake," *Journal of International Affairs* 48, no. 1 (summer 1994).

Cobban, H., The *Palestinian Liberation Organization* (New York: Cambridge University Press, 1984).

Coogan, Tim Pat, *The Troubles: Ireland's Ordeal, 1966–1995, and the Search for Peace* (London: Hutchinson, 1996).

Crocker, Chester A., and Fen Osler Hampson, eds., *Managing Global Chaos: Sources of and Responses to International Conflict* (Washington, D.C.: United States Institute of Peace Press, 1996).

Darby, John, *Intimidation and the Control of Conflict in Northern Ireland* (Dublin: Gill and Macmillan, 1986).

Deng, Frances M., and I. William Zartman, eds., *Conflict Resolution in Africa* (Washington, D.C.: Brookings Institution, 1991).

De Tocqueville, Alexis, *Democracy in America* (New York: Vintage Books, 1990).

Diamond, Larry, and Marc E. Plattner, eds., *Nationalism, Ethnic Conflict, and Democracy* (Baltimore: Johns Hopkins University Press, 1994).

Donoghue, Denis, *Warrenpoint* (London: Jonathan Cape, 1991).

Dower, John W., *War Without Mercy: Race and Power in the Pacific War* (New York: Pantheon Books, 1986).

Dunlop, John, *A Precarious Belonging: Presbyterians and the Conflict in Ireland* (Belfast: Blackstaff, 1995).

Edwards, Owen Dudley, *The Sins of Our Fathers: Roots of Conflict in Northern Ireland* (Dublin: Gill and Macmillan, 1970).

Elliott, Marianne, *Wolfe Tone: Prophet of Irish Independence* (New Haven, Conn.: Yale University Press, 1989).

Enloe, Cynthia, *Ethnic Conflict and Political Development* (Boston: Little, Brown, and Co., 1973).

Eybin, Karen, Duncan Morrow, and Derick Wilson, *A Worthwhile Venture? Equity, Diversity, and Interdependence in Northern Ireland* (Belfast: University of Ulster Press, 1997).

Gastrow, Peter, *Bargaining for Peace: South Africa and the National Peace Accord* (Washington, D.C.: United States Institute of Peace Press, 1995).

Goodall, David, "Terrorists on the Spot," *Spectator,* January 1, 1994.

Guelke, Adrian, *Northern Ireland: An International Perspective* (London: Gill and Macmillan, 1988).

————, *Improving the Political Process: Peace by Analogy* (London: British Irish Association, 1994).

Gurr, Ted Robert, *Minorities at Risk: A Global View of Ethnopolitical Conflicts* (Washington, D.C.: United States Institute of Peace Press, 1993).

Haass, Richard N., *Conflicts Unending: The United States and Regional Disputes* (New Haven, Conn.: Yale University Press, 1990).

Hampson, Fen Osler, *Nurturing Peace: Why Peace Settlements Succeed or Fail* (Washington, D.C.: United States Institute of Peace Press, 1996).

Hopmann, P. Terrence, *The Negotiation Process and the Resolution of International Conflicts* (Columbia: University of South Carolina Press, 1996).

Hume, Cameron, *Ending Mozambique's War: The Role of Mediation and Good Offices* (Washington, D.C.: United States Institute of Peace Press, 1994).

Huntington, Samuel P., *The Third Wave* (Norman: University of Oklahoma Press, 1991).

Hurewitz, J. C., *The Struggle for Palestine* (New York: W. W. Norton and Co., 1950).

Johnson, R. W., and Lawrence Schlemmer, eds., *Launching Democracy in South Africa* (New Haven, Conn.: Yale University Press, 1996).

Johnston, Douglas, and Cynthia Sampson, eds., *Religion: The Missing Dimension of Statecraft* (New York: Oxford University Press, 1994).

Kaufman, Edy, Shukri Abed, and Robert L. Rothstein, eds., *Democracy, Peace, and the Israeli-Palestinian Conflict* (Boulder, Colo.: Lynne Rienner, 1993).

Kearney, Richard, *Narratives* (Manchester: Manchester University Press, 1988).

————, *Postmodern Ireland* (London: Faber and Faber, 1996).

Lake, David, and Donald Rothchild, eds., *The International Spread and Management of Ethnic Conflict* (Princeton, N.J.: Princeton University Press, 1997).

Lapidoth, Ruth, *Autonomy: Flexible Solutions to Ethnic Conflicts* (Washington, D.C.: United States Institute of Peace Press, 1996).

Lederach, John Paul, *Building Peace: Sustainable Reconciliation in Divided Societies* (Washington, D.C.: United States Institute of Peace Press, 1997).

Little, David, *Sri Lanka: The Invention of Enmity* (Washington, D.C.: United States Institute of Peace Press, 1994).

Lund, Michael S., *Preventing Violent Conflicts: A Strategy for Preventive Diplomacy* (Washington, D.C.: United States Institute of Peace Press, 1996).

MacCrimmon, Kenneth R., and Donald A. Wehrung, with W. T. Stanbury, *Taking Risks: The Management of Uncertainty* (New York: Free Press, 1986).

MacDonagh, Oliver, *States of Mind: A Study of Anglo-Irish Conflict, 1780–1980* (London: Allen and Unwin, 1983).

Mack, John, "The Psychodynamics of Victimization Among National Groups in Conflict," in Vamik D. Volkan, Demetrios A. Julius, and Joseph V. Montville, eds., *The Psychodynamics of International Relationships*, vol. 1, *Concepts and Theories* (Lexington, Mass.: Lexington Books, 1990).

Makovsky, David, *Making Peace with the PLO: The Rabin Government's Road to the Oslo Accord* (Boulder, Colo.: Westview, 1996).

Mandel, N. J., *The Arabs and Zionism Before World War I* (Berkeley: University of California Press, 1976).

Ma'oz, Mosha, *Palestinian Leadership in the West Bank* (London: Frank Cass, 1984).

Mattar, Philip, *The Mufti of Jerusalem Al-Hajj Amin Al-Husayni and the Palestinian National Movement* (New York: Columbia University Press, 1988).

McGarry, John, and Brendan O'Leary, *Explaining Northern Ireland: Broken Images* (Oxford: Blackwell, 1995).

Miller, David, *Queen's Rebels* (London: Macmillan, 1985).

Mishal, S., *The PLO Under Arafat* (New Haven, Conn.: Yale University Press, 1986).

Murray, Martin J., *Revolution Deferred: The Painful Birth of Post-Apartheid South Africa* (London: Verso, 1994).

Murtagh, Brendan, *Life on a Rural Interface* (Belfast: Community Relations Council, 1997).

Nelson, Sarah, *Ulster's Uncertain Defenders: Protestant Political Paramilitary and Community Groups and the Northern Ireland Conflict* (Belfast: Appletree, 1984).

Nisan, Mordechai, *Israel and the Territories: A Study in Control, 1967–1977* (Ramat Gan, Israel: AMS Press, 1978).

O'Brien, Brendan, *The Long War: The IRA and Sinn Fein, 1985 to Today* (Syracuse, N.Y.: Syracuse University Press, 1995).

O'Brien, Conor Cruise, and William Dean Vanech, eds., *Power and Consciousness* (New York: New York University Press, 1969).

O'Connor, Fionnuala, *In Search of a State: Catholics in Northern Ireland* (Belfast: Blackstaff, 1995).

O'Leary, Brendan, and John McGarry, *The Politics of Antagonism: Understanding Northern Ireland* (London: Athlone, 1993).

O'Malley, Padraig, *Biting at the Grave: The Irish Hunger Strikes and the Politics of Despair* (Belfast: Blackstaff, 1990).

Ottaway, Marina, *Democratization and Ethnic Nationalism: African and Eastern European Experiences* (Washington, D.C.: Overseas Development Council, 1994).

Oz, Amos, *Under This Blazing Light: Essays* (Cambridge: Cambridge University Press, 1995).

Pappe, Ilan, *The Making of the Arab-Israeli Conflict: 1947–1951* (London: Tauris, 1992).

Quandt, W. B., *Camp David, Peacemaking, and Politics* (Washington, D.C.: Brookings Institution, 1986).

Rose, Richard, *Governing Without Consensus: An Irish Perspective* (London: Faber and Faber, 1971).

Ross, Marc Howard, *The Culture of Conflict: Interpretations and Interests in Comparative Perspective* (New Haven, Conn.: Yale University Press, 1993).

Rothstein, Robert L., "After the Peace: The Political Economy of Reconciliation," Inaugural Rebecca Meyerhoff Memorial Lecture (Jerusalem: Harry S. Truman Institute, Hebrew University, 1996).

Rudolph, Susanne Hoeber, and James Piscatori, eds., *Transnational Religion and Fading States* (Boulder, Colo.: Westview, 1997).

Sahliye, Emile, *West Bank Politics Since 1967* (Washington, D.C.: Brookings Institution, 1988).

Sartori, Giovanni, *The Theory of Democracy Revisited* (London: Chatham House, 1987).

Scheff, Thomas J., *Bloody Revenge: Emotions, Nationalism, and War* (Boulder, Colo.: Westview, 1994).

Schumpeter, Joseph, *Capitalism, Socialism, and Democracy* (London: Allen and Unwin, 1942).

Shriver, Donald W., Jr., *An Ethic for Enemies: Forgiveness in Politics* (New York: Oxford University Press, 1995).

Sinn Fein, *Toward a New Ireland* (Dublin: Sinn Fein, 1992).

———, *Setting the Record Straight* (Dublin: Sinn Fein, 1994).

Smith, M. L. R., *Fighting for Ireland? The Military Strategy of the Irish Republican Movement* (London: Routledge, 1995).

Sparks, Allister, *Tomorrow Is Another Country: The Inside Story of South Africa's Road to Change* (New York: Hill and Wang, 1995).

Stedman, Stephen J., *The New Is Not Yet Born: Conflict Resolution in Southern Africa* (Washington, D.C.: Brookings Institution, 1994).

———, ed., *South Africa: The Political Economy of Transformation* (Boulder, Colo.: Lynne Rienner, 1994).

Tambiah, S. J., *Sri Lanka: Ethnic Fratricide and the Dismantling of Democracy* (Chicago: University of Chicago Press, 1986).

Tavuchis, Nicholas, *Mea Culpa: A Sociology of Apology and Reconciliation* (Stanford, Calif.: Stanford University Press, 1991).

Todd, Jennifer, "Two Traditions in Unionist Political Culture," in *Irish Political Studies* (Galway: PSAI Press, 1987).

Van der Merwe, Hugo, ed., *Conflict Resolution Theory and Practice: Integration and Application* (Manchester: Manchester University Press, 1993).

Villa-Vicencio, Charles, *A Different Kind of Justice: The South-African Truth and Reconciliation Commission* (Maryknoll, N.Y.: Orbis Books, 1988).

Volkan, Vamik D., *The Need to Have Enemies and Allies: From Clinical Practice to International Relations* (Northvale, N.J.: Jason Aronson, 1988).

Waldmeir, Patti, *Anatomy of a Miracle: The End of Apartheid and the Birth of the New South Africa* (New York: W. W. Norton and Co., 1997).

Walter, Barbara, "The Resolution of Civil Wars: Why Negotiations Fail," Ph.D. diss., University of Chicago, December 1994.

Weschler, Laurence, *A Miracle, a Universe: Settling Accounts with Torturers* (New York: Penguin, 1990).

Whyte, John, *Interpreting Northern Ireland* (Oxford: Clarendon, 1990).

———, "Dynamics of Social and Political Change in Northern Ireland," in Dermot Keogh and Michael H. Haltzel, eds., *Northern Ireland and the Politics of Reconciliation* (Cambridge: Cambridge University Press, 1993).

Woodward, Susan L., *Balkan Tragedy: Chaos and Dissolution After the Cold War* (Washington, D.C.: Brookings Institution, 1995).

Wright, Frank, *Northern Ireland: A Comparative Analysis* (Dublin: Gill and Macmillan, 1987).

———, *Two Lands on One Soil* (Dublin: Macmillan, 1996).

Zartman, I. William, *Ripe for Resolution: Conflict and Intervention in Africa* (New York: Oxford University Press, 1989).

———, ed., *Elusive Peace: Negotiating an End to Civil Wars* (Washington, D.C.: Brookings Institution, 1995).

Zartman, I. William, and J. Lewis Rasmussen, eds., *Peacemaking in International Conflict: Methods and Techniques* (Washington, D.C.: United States Institute of Peace Press, 1997).

The Contributors

Paul Arthur, School of History, Philosophy, and Politics, University of Ulster; author of numerous books and articles on the conflict in Northern Ireland, including *Northern Ireland Since 1968* (with Keith Jeffrey).

Dusko Doder, a fellow at the United States Institute of Peace; former correspondent for the *Washington Post;* author of a highly regarded book on the Kremlin from L. I. Brezhnev to Mikhail Gorbachev; and currently writing a book about reconstructing the Balkans after the civil war.

Herbert C. Kelman, Richard Clarke Cabot Professor of Social Ethics and director of the Program on International Conflict Analysis and Resolution, Harvard University; and author of many works, including *Crimes of Obedience: Toward a Social Psychology of Authority and Obedience* (with Lee Hamilton).

Moshe Ma'oz, director of the Harry S. Truman Research Institute and professor of Middle East studies at Hebrew University, Jerusalem; and author of six books and many articles on the Middle East, including *Syria and Israel: From War to Peacemaking.*

Duncan Morrow, lecturer in politics at the School of History, Philosophy, and Politics, University of Ulster; and author of books and articles on the conflict in Northern Ireland, including *Northern Ireland Politics* (with A. Aughey) and *On the Way of Freedom* (with R. Kaptein).

Robert L. Rothstein, Harvey Picker Professor of International Relations, Colgate University; former fellow of the United States Institute of Peace;

and author or editor of eight books and many articles, including "After the Peace: The Political Economy of Reconciliation" (the Inaugural Rebecca Meyerhoff Lecture at the Harry S. Truman Institute, Hebrew University).

Khalil Shikaki, professor at Al-Najah University and director of the Center for Palestine Research and Studies; and author of a number of books and articles on the Arab-Israeli conflict, including *The Gaza Strip and the West Bank* and "The Peace Process, National Reconstruction and Transition to Democracy in Palestine," *Journal of Palestine Studies.*

Donald W. Shriver Jr., President Emeritus and William E. Dodge Professor of Applied Christianity, Union Theological Seminary; and author of many works, including *An Ethic for Enemies: Forgiveness in Politics.*

Susan L. Woodward, senior fellow in the Foreign Policy Studies Program at the Brookings Institution; and author of *Balkan Tragedy: Chaos and Dissolution After the Cold War* and *Socialist Unemployment: The Political Economy of Yugoslavia, 1945–1990.*

Index

About the Book

The fragile peace agreements of the post–Cold War years that have sought to resolve protracted conflicts fall well short of being genuine, stable settlements. This volume is concerned with how those agreements might be strengthened and, especially, how best to conceptualize the period after a tentative peace has been negotiated.

Six case studies explore three major conflicts from differing perspectives: Northern Ireland is discussed by Catholic and Protestant scholars, and Palestinian and Israeli researchers examine the Arab-Israeli relationship. Bosnia and the Dayton Accords are addressed in the third set of cases.

The concluding section of the book focuses on more general aspects of peacemaking and peace building, incorporating psychological, moral, and political approaches. In the final chapter, Rothstein suggests that attention to the ways in which the pre- and postpeace periods are different might inform a carefully constructed strategy with the potential to transform a tentative settlement into the reconciliation of ancient enemies.

Robert L. Rothstein is Harvey Picker Professor of International Relations, Colgate University. He is author of *The Third World and U.S. Foreign Policy: Cooperation and Conflict in the 1980s* and editor of *The Evolution of Theory in International Relations*.